C000145319

KIPLING AND WAR

Praise for *Kipling Abroad*

'[Kipling] was one of the great travel writers [...] This excellent selection shows us once again, if we were in any doubt, that this man really could write.'

Jad Adams, *Guardian*

'This perfect bedside book collects the most descriptive and revealing of Kipling's travel writing, never before published in a single volume. Kipling comes across as an engaging travel companion – thoughtful, curious, acute – and a writer perfectly able to evoke and crystallise the sights, sounds and spirit of a place.'

Clover Stroud, *The Telegraph*

'There is scarcely a single piece that isn't worth reading. Kipling's keen observation and gift for illuminating phrase are everywhere apparent.'

Allan Massie, *Literary Review*

RUDYARD KIPLING

KIPLING
AND WAR

From 'Tommy'
to 'My Boy Jack'

INTRODUCED AND EDITED BY
ANDREW LYCETT

I.B. TAURIS
LONDON · NEW YORK

First published in 2015 by
I.B.Tauris & Co. Ltd
London • New York
www.ibtauris.com

Copyright © 2015 Andrew Lycett

ISBN: 978 1 78453 333 5
eISBN: 978 0 85773 965 0

A full CIP record for this book is available from the British Library
A full CIP record is available from the Library of Congress

Library of Congress Catalog Card Number: available

Typeset by JCS Publishing Services Ltd., www.jcs-publishing.co.uk

Printed and bound in Sweden by ScandBook AB

CONTENTS

The First World War and After

Reflections on the Military Life

I would like to thank Lieutenant Colonel Roger Ayers, President of the Kipling Society, who kindly read through and commented on my original manuscript.

INTRODUCTION

By Victorian standards Rudyard Kipling's background was remarkably un-military. He was born in 1865 in Bombay, where his father Lockwood was an architectural sculptor in the service of the Raj. Although he was sent to England to be educated at the martial-sounding United Services College, a secondary school in Devon which specialised in turning out soldiers and administrators for service in the Empire, he only went there because the headmaster, Cormell Price, was a friend of his mother's from her time on the fringes of the Pre-Raphaelite artists' circle (her sister Georgiana married the painter Edward Burne-Jones).

Since his parents could not afford to send him to university, Kipling was forced to return to India when he was 17 to take up a job as a journalist on the *Civil and Military Gazette* in Lahore. The name of this newspaper had army connotations since Lahore was the capital of the Punjab, one of the more recent territorial additions to Britain's empire in India, having been annexed in 1849 after the defeat of the Sikhs at the Battle of Chilianwala. Thereafter it had been run on efficient, often militaristic, lines by a succession of evangelically minded chief commissioners, such as John Lawrence (later viceroy of India). One reason for this military tendency was that the Punjab provided an important buffer between the heartland of India and areas of continuing unrest beyond its north-west frontier. Although the internal tensions that followed the Indian Mutiny of 1857 had largely abated, there were still concerns about the threat of Russian incursions through the generally unstable neighbouring country of Afghanistan. As a result, the Punjab had an important role to play in British India's 'forward' foreign policy, and, along with its Mughal walled city and its modern European 'civil lines', Lahore boasted a large military cantonment at Mian Mir, five miles east of the town, where an infantry battalion and two artillery batteries – all British units – were permanently stationed.

Kipling soon discarded the Gladstonian liberalism of his teenage years and adopted the attitudes of the frontier society he was living in. He developed an intense respect for the British administrators, engineers, doctors, lawyers and soldiers who, he felt, were devoting their lives to bringing order, justice and the rudiments of health to the Punjab.

One of his favourite trips out of Lahore took him to Mian Mir, where he liked to mix with young subalterns not many years his senior in the officers' mess. After some of them invited him to dine when they were on guard duty at Fort Lahore, he penned a poem, 'On Fort Duty', which contrasted the boredom of their existence in the fort with the excitements of active service on the north-west frontier .

Kipling's journalistic assignments often required him to work closely with the military, as when he travelled to Peshawar in March 1885 to cover the visit of the Afghan Amir Abdurrahman and to Rawalpindi for the subsequent Durbar involving Viceroy Lord Dufferin. In one of his pieces for the paper he reported enthusiastically about the spectacle of the military parade put on for the Amir. He later recalled this event when he wrote his story 'Servants of the Queen', with its accompanying poem 'Parade Song of the Camp Animals', for his first *Jungle Book*.

In 1886 he volunteered to report for the *Civil and Military Gazette* on the military expedition that was sent to quell a rebellion in upper Burma. The news that a United Services College contemporary, Lieutenant Robert Dury, had been killed in this campaign encouraged Kipling to write 'Arithmetic on the Frontier', which was published in June that year as one of his *Departmental Ditties*. It gives an idea of his individual and often ironic approach to military subjects:

> A scrimmage in a Border Station –
> A canter down some dark defile –
> Two thousand pounds of education
> Drops to a ten rupee jezail –

By this time he had extended his contacts at Mian Mir to the other ranks. Whereas he was happy to poke gentle fun at naive young subalterns (notably in *Plain Tales from the Hills,* his stories which focused mainly on the political and emotional machinations of the ruling elite in Simla, the imperial summer capital), his admiration for the ordinary British soldier was rather deeper. He appreciated their humour and resolution, despite the hardships of living and fighting in India on behalf of 'Missis Victorier', 'the Widow at Windsor'. He lobbied on their behalf on issues such as improved facilities for sufferers from venereal disease. This was necessary because, although Lahore had a 'Lock' hospital specialising in these ailments, Kipling realised that the authorities turned a blind eye, particularly towards the health of native prostitutes, with the result that 9,000 'expensive white men a year [were] always laid up from venereal disease'.

This did not mean that he was po-faced about these ordinary soldiers. Drawing on his encounters, in March 1887 he wrote 'The Three Musketeers', the first of 18 stories about a mischievous but always engaging trio of privates in 'B' Company of the Ould Regiment – an Irishman, Terence Mulvaney, Cockney Stanley Ortheris and Yorkshire-born Jock Learoyd.

These 'Mulvaney stories' can be an acquired taste, with their casual racism and their widespread use of slang. But as no one since Shakespeare had written sympathetically, let alone humorously, about the realities of being a soldier, they became an instant hit, encouraging Kipling, from 1888, to gather them in a series of books which were published as part of the Indian Railway Library by the Calcutta firm Thacker and Spink.

The best of these stories mixed intimate detail about the indignities of regimental life in India with rollicking accounts of feats of courage and comradeship. In 'With the Main Guard', Mulvaney tries to enthuse fellow members of the guard at Lahore Fort with a stirring account of hand-to-hand fighting at 'Silver's Theatre', a fictional battlefield very similar to that at Maiwand, near Kandahar, where a British column was forced to retreat towards the end of the Second Afghan War in July 1880. The main unit involved on that occasion was the 66th (Berkshire) Regiment, for whom Kipling later wrote the ballad 'That Day', after he met up with them as the 2nd Battalion the Royal Berkshire Regiment while on a visit to Bermuda in 1894.

This same Afghan conflict (and specifically the return of the northern column to Peshawar at the end of the war in August 1880) also provides the background for 'Love o' Women', in which

Mulvaney describes in graphic details the tribulations of the gentleman-ranker soldier called Tighe who is dying of syphilis.

The three soldiers also participated in other imperial wars, such as the campaign in Burma in the mid-1880s, as featured in the comical tale 'The Taking of Lungtungpen', which had Mulvaney and friends subduing a Burmese village which they arrived at stark naked, after having had to swim a river. On their return from this conflict, Otheris (in the story 'The Madness of Private Otheris') is plunged into despair about his profession:

> I'm a Tommy – a bloomin', eight-anna, dog-stealin' Tommy, with a number instead of a decent name. Wot's the good o' me? If I 'ad a stayed of 'Ome, I might a married that gal and a kep' a little shorp in the 'Ammersmith 'Igh.– 'S. Orth'ris, Prac-ti-cal Taxi-dermist.' With a stuff' fox, like they 'as in the Haylesbury Dairies, in the winder, an' a little case of blue and yaller glass-heyes, an' a little wife to call 'shorp!' 'shorp!' when the door-bell rung. As it his, I'm on'y a Tommy – a Bloomin', Gawdforsaken, Beer-swillin' Tommy.

This tale is not based on any particular action, but is in keeping with another Kipling speciality – his stories about the harsh realities of life as a private soldier (the 'New Readers' Guide' on the Kipling Society website lists 25 such stories). In this case Otheris makes arrangements to desert and return to London. Luckily his depression lifts and he is soon eager to return to his pals and the military life he knows.

While in India, Kipling also wrote about the military life outside what are generally regarded as the 'Mulvaney stories'. For example, 'The Drums of the Fore and Aft' (first published in *Wee Willie Winkie and Other Child Stories*, No. 6 in the Indian Railway Library, in 1888) drew on a mix of the battles of Ahmed Khel in April 1880 and Maiwand in July that same year to depict two drummer boys, Jakin and Lew, who rouse their demoralised fellow troops by marching up and down the front, playing 'The British Grenadiers'.

Sub-continental conflicts provided the background for several other poems, such as 'Ford o' Kabul River' which recalled the incident when an officer and 46 troopers from the 10th Hussars were drowned trying to cross the Kabul River in March 1879. Additional stories and poems looked back to episodes in South Asian history

– including 'Gunga Din', based on an incident during the Mutiny, 'Snarleyow' about the Sikh wars, and 'The Ballad of East and West', a snapshot of two great warrior traditions ranged against each another, apparently referring to the Guides at Peshawar in the 1850s.

Kipling's journalistic sense of detail has sparked interest in the real-life models for the 'Ould Regiment' in the Mulvaney stories. While he was in Lahore the two main regiments at Mian Mir were the East Lancashires, followed by the 5th (Northumberland Fusiliers) Regiment of Foot. In his book *Sixty Years in Uniform*, John Fraser, a former colour sergeant with the 5th (the Tyneside Tail Twisters, Kipling called them), remembered being asked by a young officer to take Kipling to the canteen and to introduce him to some of the men. He was told that his visitor was a writer who, for professional reasons, wanted to get 'into direct touch with Tommy Atkins'. The sergeant took Kipling to meet the musketry fatigue party led by Corporal MacNamara who, he claimed, was the spitting image of Mulvaney in Kipling's later stories.

When Kipling moved to *The Pioneer* newspaper in Allahabad in late 1887, he fell in with another regiment, the 1st Battalion the East Surrey, 31st Foot, which added colour to his portrayal of the Ould Regiment as 'a London recruited confederacy of skilful dog-stealers, some of them my good and loyal friends'.

But the opportunities for Kipling's type of writing were limited in India, so in 1889 he made his way to London, where initially he lodged in the teaming heart of the city in Villiers Street, off the Strand, where his favourite form of relaxation was his evening visits to Gatti's Music Hall, underneath the arches at Charing Cross Station. There he met a new kind of soldier – garrisoned in London, often rowdy and eager to sing popular songs of any description. As Kipling wrote in his autobiography, *Something of Myself*, 'The Private Soldier in India I thought I knew fairly well. His English brother (in the Guards mostly) sat and sang at my elbow any night I chose.'

He recalled something of this atmosphere in his story 'My Great and Only' which he despatched to the *Civil and Military Gazette* from London in early 1890:

> I glanced at the gallery – the Red-coats were there. The fiddle-bows creaked, and, with a jingle of brazen spurs, a forage-cap

over his left eye, my Great and Only began to 'chuck it off his chest'. Thus –

'At the back of Knightsbridge Barracks,
When the fog was gatherin' dim,
The Life Guard talked to the Under-cook,
An' the girl she talked to him.'

'You may make a mistake when you're mashing a tart,
But you'll learn to be wise when you're older,
And don't try for things that are out o' your reach,
And that's what the Girl told the Soldier,
Soldier! Soldier!
An' that's what the Girl told the Soldier.'

I thought the gallery would never let go of the long-drawn howl on 'Soldier'. They clung to it as ringers to the kicking bell-rope. Then I envied no one – not even Shakespeare. I had my house hooked – gaffed under the gills, netted, speared, shot behind the shoulder – anything you please! With each verse the chorus grew louder, and when my Great and Only had bellowed his way to the fall of the Life Guard and the happy lot of the Under-cook, the Gallery rocked again, the reserved stalls shouted, and the pewters twinkled like the legs of demented ballet-girls. The conductor waved the now frenzied orchestra to softer Lydian strains. My Great and Only warbled, piano –

'At the back o' the Knightsbridge Barricks,
When the fog's a gatherin' dim,
The Life Guard waits for the Under-cook,
But she don't wait for 'im.'

The British literary world at the time was split between conservative romantics, who looked back to the adventure stories of Robert Louis Stevenson, and progressives inspired by the intimations of realism, aestheticism and even decadence making inroads from Europe. Kipling tended naturally to the former school, whose heartier elements – the proto-imperialists, known as the Henley Regatta, who congregated around W.E. Henley, editor of the *Scots* (later *National*) *Observer* – looked to him as a 'star from the east' to take up the mantle of manly storytelling.

Kipling's response was to bring together his knowledge of soldiers in India with his newfound enthusiasm for the lusty ballads of the music hall. He presented his synthesis in his Barrack-Room Ballads, which were printed initially in the *Scots Observer*. Starting with 'Danny Deever', a searing ballad about the execution of a British soldier in the heat of the sub-continent, these ranged widely over military themes – from details of artillery in 'Screw-Guns', through the realities of official and unofficial plundering in the field in 'Loot', to the phenomenon of well-bred men slumming it in the ranks in 'Gentleman-Rankers' (later taken up and parodied as a drinking song by students at Yale University). Kipling also nodded his respect for soldiers from other lands, including the eponymous water-bearer in 'Gunga Din' and even erstwhile enemies, such as the Sudanese in 'Fuzzy Wuzzy': 'You're a pore benighted 'eathen but a first-class fightin' man.'

One poem, 'Tommy', stands for all the others in its sympathetic portrayal of the plight of the ordinary soldier who generally found himself at the bottom of the social pile but who, at times of national crisis, when he expected to fight for Queen and Country, was widely feted. It ends:

You talk o' better food for us, an' schools, an' fires, an' all:
We'll wait for extry rations if you treat us rational.
Don't mess about them cook-room slops, but prove it to our face
The Widow's Uniform is not the soldier-man's disgrace.
    For it's Tommy this, an' Tommy that, an' 'Chuck him out, the
      brute!'
    But it's 'Saviour of 'is country' when the guns begin to shoot;
    An' it's Tommy this, an' Tommy that, an' anything you
      please;
    An' Tommy ain't no bleedin' fool – you bet that Tommy sees.

Kipling returned to the conflict in the Sudan in his first novel *The Light that Failed* in 1891. This featured the story of Dick Heldar, originally a war artist in the 1884–5 campaign against the Mahdi to avenge the death of General Gordon in Khartoum. When his illustrations prove popular, Heldar tries (amid the tribulations of a doomed love affair) to develop a career as a 'proper' artist. But his eyesight fails and he is reduced, somewhat despairingly, to return to his former career as a war artist in Sudan, in which capacity he is shot and killed. Although Kipling at this stage had still not witnessed any battle himself, he wrote some startlingly realistic scenes of fighting in *The Light that Failed*, notably early on when the British 'square' withstands a frenzied assault by the Mahdi's force.

Kipling's continuing interest in military subjects seemed to reflect his unease about the relaxed nature of the civilian society he found in London. As his poem 'In Partibus' suggested, he missed the regimented way of life in India. After decrying the laxness of British society, he writes,

> It's Oh to meet an Army man,
> Set up, and trimmed and taut,
> Who does not spout hashed libraries
> Or think the next man's thought
> And walks as though he owned himself,
> And hogs his bristles short.

Because of Kipling's coolness towards England, he was not dismayed to cross the Atlantic and live in the United States in 1892. The reason for the move was his marriage to Caroline Balestier, the sister of an American publisher friend who had died of typhoid. Kipling and his new wife built a house, Naulakha, in her hometown of Brattleboro, Vermont.

There, stimulated to an extent by his observations on the United States coming to terms with its emerging regional and indeed global power, Kipling began to think seriously about Britain's history and its place in the world. While living in Brattleboro, he wrote several poems about Britain's nautical tradition, which were collected in *The Seven Seas* in 1896, along with a second batch of Barrack-Room Ballads. At the same time he was trying to bring some order to his Indian experiences in the two Jungle Books and in *Kim* (though the latter was not published until 1901).

By the time Kipling was again back and living in England in 1896, his view of the world had become more political. Indeed, he had become something of an ideologue, arguing in favour of the importance and morality of extending Britain's empire, while drawing attention to the responsibilities which went with this (the stuff of his famous poem 'Recessional' in 1898). He was drawn to politicians who espoused expansionist views, including Joseph

Chamberlain, and to day-to-day practitioners of imperialism such as the South African businessman and financier Cecil Rhodes. This view of the world required a strong army and navy. So he met with leading soldiers, went out on naval reviews and lobbied for the extension of Britain's sea power abroad. At the same time (as recorded in his poem 'The White Man's Burden') he supported American interventions in Cuba and the Philippines.

In early 1898 Kipling accepted Rhodes's invitation to visit South Africa, an experience which intensified his sense of the value and potential of the Empire. Inevitably he became involved the following year in supporting the British cause in the Boer War. One of his propaganda pieces was the poem 'The Absent-Minded Beggar' (originally published in the *Daily Mail* in October 1899). When Kipling allowed the lyrics to be printed more widely and without charge, they proved highly popular, generating substantial royalties which he donated to a fund to support the families of fighting soldiers.

In 1900 he visited South Africa at the height of the Boer War. Initially he was there, as the author of 'Tommy' and 'The Absent -Minded Beggar', to boost morale. He lent his support to the British propaganda effort in Blomfontein, where he helped produce a field newspaper called *The Friend*. He had his first experience of actual fighting, when, in the company of the military correspondent Bennet Burleigh, he ventured 20 miles or so out of the city and was caught up in an exchange of fire at Karee Siding. He recalled how a detachment of Light Horse had passed close by, and suddenly, as the Mausers, pompoms (or Maxim heavy machine guns) and Krupp cannon loosed off around him, he found himself in the thick of the battle. This experience of being under attack left sharp impressions: 'Then to the left, almost under us, a small piece of hanging woodland filled and fumed with our shrapnel much as a man's moustache fills with cigarette smoke.' He would recall the setting, with the trees 'withered by fire', in his story 'A Sahib's War' later in the year.

In a letter dated 24 July 1900 he explained the conflict to an American medical friend, Dr James Conland:

War is a rummy job – it's a cross between poker and Sunday School. Sometimes poker comes out on top and sometimes Sunday School – but most often poker. The Boers hit us just as hard and as often as they knew how; and we advanced against 'em as if they were street-rioters that we didn't want to hurt. They spied on us at their leisure, and when they wanted a rest they handed up any old gun and said they'd be loyal subjects. Then they went to their homes and rested for a week or two; and then they went on the war path again with a new coat and a full stomach. They are an elegant people: and we are the biggest fools, in the way that we wage war, that this country has produced.

Over the course of the Boer War Kipling composed several new stories, such as 'Folly Bridge' and 'The Captive' and many more poems, including 'Bridge Guard in the Karroo', 'Stellenbosch' and 'M.I. (Mounted Infantry of the Line)', one of a sequence of 16 'service songs' which concluded his 1903 book *The Five Nations*. For Kipling a bonus was the commitment he found in the soldiers from British colonies such as Australia. He resurrected Tommy to applaud this comradeship in his poem 'The Parting of the Columns'.

There isn't much we 'aven't shared, since Kruger cut and run,
The same old work, the same old skoff, the same old dust and
    sun;
The same old chance that laid us out, and winked an' let us
    through;
The same old Life, the same old Death. Good-bye – good luck to
    you!

He also wrote 'Lichtenberg', in which a soldier from New South Wales is reminded of home by the smells of the South African wattle. Poems such as 'Piet' again showed that he could appreciate fighting qualities in Britain's enemies as well as in its own troops. And there was a nod to old Tommy again in 'Chant-Pagan', in which an ordinary soldier wonders how he will be able to return to the banalities of civilian life in Britain after all the experiences he has had in the southern hemisphere.

Kipling's involvement in South Africa caused him to think more deeply about Britain's defences. In poems such as 'The Islanders' he railed against the 'flannelled fools at the wicket' who were a symptom of the country's unpreparedness for military conflict.

More broadly, he was convinced of his country's need to learn from its South African failures. As he wrote in the poem, 'The Lesson', published in *The Times* in July 1901:

It was our fault, and our very great fault, and *not* the judgement of Heaven.
We made an Army in our own image, on an island nine by seven,
Which faithfully mirrored its makers' ideals, equipment, and mental attitude –
And so we got our lesson: and we ought to accept it with gratitude.

and he ended:

We have had an Imperial lesson. It may make us an Empire yet!

Back home, he threw himself into projects, such as building a rifle range at Rottingdean (where he then lived) and supporting the National Service League, set up by Field Marshal Lord Roberts, his old friend from India and South Africa, and other organisations which stressed alertness and vigilance, including the Boy Scouts. A fictional version of his ideas for Britain's military future could be found in his story 'The Army of a Dream'. Meanwhile he continued to go out on military manoeuvres, which he wrote about for *The Times* and the *Daily Telegraph*.

His message to his countrymen now was simple and unyielding – that the greatest threat to Britain's empire came from Germany. With his interest in history, he continued to take a long view in verses such as 'Dane-Geld', which counselled against any kind of appeasement or paying of tributes, and 'A Roman Centurion's Song', in which a centurion who has served in Britain for 40 years pleads to remain there, in the country which has become his home, rather than return to the unknown imperial city of Rome.

When war with 'the Hun' finally came in August 1914, Kipling poured out his invective in poems such as 'For All We Have and Are' and 'The Outlaws', as well as 'The Beginnings' with its chilling line, 'When the English began to hate'. At the same time, as a member of the Foreign Office's Propaganda Bureau at Wellington House, he promoted the war effort in several articles, including those collected in 'A New Army in Training'.

From his house, Bateman's, in Sussex, he could hear the pounding of the guns in Flanders. As he was nearly 50, and had poor eyesight, he was never likely to be called up. However, he pulled strings to obtain a commission for his son John in the Irish Guards. John's experience of the war proved brief, for he was killed at the Battle of Loos in September 1915. His body was never found, which meant that Kipling and his wife Carrie spent months trying to find out what had happened to him. Although they enlisted the help of the International Red Cross and others, in the hope that John might have been taken prisoner, their quest proved fruitless.

The closest he came to active service was when, to boost morale, he was asked to write about some lesser-known theatres of war. His articles on 'the auxiliaries', the sailors who served in submarines, minesweepers and forgotten east-coast patrols, appeared in the *Daily Telegraph*, and then were collected in *The Fringes of the Fleet* and *Sea Warfare*, along with several evocative poems, often in sea-shanty style, such as 'The Lowestoft Boat', a trawler 'out a-rovin' with a hastily mounted, quick-firing gun. He visited the Western Front in France, and the Dolomites, where, as a gesture of solidarity with Britain's Italian allies in their struggle with the Austrians, he wrote six vivid articles for the *Daily Telegraph*.

Changing his usual tune, he lambasted incompetent leaders (both military and political) in poems such as 'Mesopotamia', which was damning about the incompetence surrounding General Townshend's capitulation to Turkish forces at Kut el-Amara in 1915. He lamented the losses, largely of Indian troops – 'They shall not return to us, the resolute, the young' – while indicting those responsible:

How softly but how swiftly they have sidled back to power
By the favour and contrivance of their kind?

With his sense of fairness, he was determined that the thousands of Indian troops who had served with the British should not be forgotten. *The Eyes of Asia*, his confection of stories culled from letters of Indian combatants, was not his greatest work, but he insisted that fallen Indian soldiers should have their own memorial at Neuve-Chapelle and gave a speech at its inauguration in 1927. Although not known for his Irish sympathies, his son's position as an officer in the Irish Guards led him to write a respectful two-volume history of that regiment.

Kipling's short stories portrayed another aspect of warfare that had long fascinated him – the camaraderie experienced by those in situations of great danger. In 'The Janeites', Kipling adopted a light touch to convey how casual references to Jane Austen, a favourite author, created a sense of a secret society that gave the ordinary soldier a feeling of belonging. This companionship proved useful in dealing with shell-shock and trauma, afflictions that featured in postwar stories such as 'In the Interests of the Brethren'.

John Kipling's death inspired David Haig's 1997 play *My Boy Jack* (later a television film), which suggested that Kipling's bellicosity was responsible for the loss of his son at Loos. The work took its title from Kipling's 1916 poem of the same name, assuming that it was a father's expression of his pain over his son. But this was only part of the story. John Kipling was never known as Jack; the poem was a more all-embracing lament for those killed at Jutland. In typical Kipling style, 'Jack' was a more generic Jack Tar, or perhaps 'Jack' Cornwell, a young sailor awarded a posthumous Victoria Cross for his bravery in that sea battle.

As the war drew to a close, Kipling strongly opposed any talk of a negotiated peace with the Germans – the burden of his poem 'Justice'. However, he felt a newfound compassion for (rather than a brash journalistic understanding of) the victims of war. This was evident in 'The Children', written in the thick of war in 1917, which ended with the memorable refrain, both angry and restrained, 'But who shall return us our children?' In his 'Epitaphs of the War', verses such as 'The Coward', 'Hindu Sepoy in France' or 'Unknown Female Corpse' all attacked unnecessary bloodshed. Probably the most poignant had the all-embracing title 'Common Form':

> If any question why we died
> Tell them, because our fathers lied.

The death of Kipling's son made him more aware than ever of the importance of commemorating the war, and particularly the sacrifice of those who had given their lives in the conflict. As an adviser to the Imperial War Graves Commission, he helped compose or choose most of its memorial inscriptions, including the words on the Stone of Remembrance in every large war cemetery – 'Their name liveth for evermore'.

Over the years Kipling had moved from youthful bravado about the military to a mature understanding of the hardships and horrors of war – the brutal consequences of having an army, if you like. He had been pilloried (and still often is) for his militarism, which some have likened to a form of fascism (his love of regimental life was really a deep yearning for order, it is said). He was not a lover of unrestricted freedom, it is true, but he was never a fascist. His enthusiasm for the military came from his journalistic precociousness, his desire to see and understand everything. This was then overlaid with his imperialistic politics, which means that his writings on soldiers are mixed with propaganda. But his observations on what it was like to be a member of the British armed services remain unparalleled, while his more polemical output makes for a fascinating historical document.

KIPLING AND WAR

EARLY MATERIAL

In this youthful work, Kipling was commememorating the Battle of Assaye of September 1803, when the East India Company's army, led by Major General Arthur Wellesley, younger brother of Richard, the first Marquess Wellesley, governor-general in India, defeated the combined Mahratta armies. Kipling wrote it as a prize poem in 1882, towards the end of his career at the United Services College. It was published in the school magazine four years later.

THE BATTLE OF ASSAYE

SAVE WHERE OUR HUGE sea-castles from afar
Beat down, in scorn, some weak Egyptian wall,
We are too slothful to give heed to war.

As a gorged Lion will not stir at all,
Although the hunter mock him openly,
So we are moveless when the trumpets call.

A soldier's letter, written long ago
(The ink lies yellow on the tattered page),
Telling of war, with rugged overflow
Of epithet, and burst of uncouth rage;
And as I find the letter – so I write
My record of brave deeds in a dead age.

[…]

'On the left the Kaitua hemmed us in,
On the right a rushing watercourse;
In front their masses of infantry,
Their surging waves of Mahratta horse,
Came down on us like a winter sea;
And we fought as they fight who fight for life –
Each one as though the army's fate
Hung on the strength of his own right wrist
When he warded away the cold curved knife,
And the wiry devil that wielded it
Recoiled from the bayonet – just too late –
And the steel came out with a wrench and a twist,
So we fought and slew in the midst of the din
Till their line was broken – till man and horse
Fled over the rushing watercourse,
And the greatest fight of the world was our own!
And now my face is scarred to the bone,
And I am lame maybe from a musket-ball –
Yet I thank God (and ever shall)
That I fought in a fight the world will applaud;
For the new generations by and by
Shall be proud of that long September day,
When ten men fled from the face of one,
And the river ran red on its seaward way,
As it flowed through the village of Bokerdun –
Red with the blood that was spilt at Assaye!'

[First published in the *United Services College Chronicle* 28, 2 July 1886.]

INDIA

A young soldier, serving time in monotonous barracks, dreams of the excitements of active service, particularly on the Khyber Pass. Kipling hadn't visited the Khyber at this stage, but he was beginning to find out about the military life through his conversations with army personnel at Mian Mir Fort, just outside Lahore.

ON FORT DUTY

THERE'S A TUMULT IN the Khyber,
There's feud at Ali Kheyl,
For the *Maliks* of the Khyber
Are at it tooth and nail –
With the stolen British carbie
And the long Kohat *jezail*.

And I look across the ramparts
To the northward and the snow –
To the far Cherat cantonments;
But alas I cannot go
From the dusty, dreary rampart
Where the cannons grin arrow!

There's fighting in the Khyber,
But it isn't meant for me,

Who am sent upon 'Fort-duty'
By this pestilent Ravi,
With just one other subaltern,
And not a soul to see.

Oh! it's everlasting gun-drill
And eight-o'clock parades,
It's cleaning-up of mortars
(Likewise of carronades),
While the passes ring with rifles
And the noise of Afghan raids.

And I look across the ramparts
To the river broad and grey,
And I think of merry England
Where the festive Horse Guards play.
Oh! take the senior grades for this
And spare the young R.A.!

[First published in the *United Services College Chronicle* 18, 28 March 1884.]

In April 1885 Kipling was sent to the north-west frontier by his newspaper, the *Civil and Military Gazette* in Lahore, to report on the Durbar given for Abdur Rahman, the ruler of Afghanistan, by Lord Dufferin, the newly appointed viceroy of India. Kipling visited the Khyber Pass, where he claimed he was fired on, as well as Peshawar and Rawalpindi, where the Durbar (and this procession) took place.

To Meet the Ameer

From our special correspondent
Rawalpindi April 6

AT LAST WE SEEM to have started work in earnest and the gloomy forecasts of yesterday have been but partially fulfilled. To be sure the sky is as black as in all round the horizon, but the clear patch of blue in the centre, and the restless winds, promise April showers at the utmost, and not the steady wet to which we dwellers in tents have become so painfully accustomed. In an hour or so, the grand Review of troops in camp will begin. Meantime, carriages and riders are already beginning to assemble by the three huge sheep pens which mark the spots whence the Viceroy, the Punjab Chiefs, are to view the ceremony. Of decoration, beyond of the naked pole of the saluting base, there is no sign – the Army here gathered together is to march by with no scenic accessories, beyond those of gloomy skies, wind-shaken woods in the background and the shrill whistle of the iron horse in front. The King's Dragoon Guards' parade ground lies to the right of the Jhelum Road and to the left of the Rawal Pindi Fort, but looking in the same direction. [...]

The Review is to be merely a March Past, without manoeuvrings of any kind, and Abdur Rahman is to sit still by the Viceroy's side, and watch the living tide roll by. He should be weary of watching before the work is over. Pindi Fort is the better part of a mile away from here, and already the slope below the bastions is sown with little red specks, which shuffle and agglomerate themselves, until they finally assume the shape of two red bars, and moving on, are lost to view behind the trees on the Jhelum Road. This is the first Regiment getting ready for the March Past, and at least half a score of field glasses proclaim that it was the 33rd. The company, in every sort of vehicle, from the lordly 'fitton' to rattling ticca gharri, is assembling as fast as may be; and whenever there is a lull in the rolling of wheels, the air becomes alive with the music of unseen bands of regiments moving into position along Jhelum Road. Already half a dozen worthy gentlemen of mature years, mounted on fiery untamed steeds, and thickly covered with gold lace and red cloth, are caracoling from one end of the ground to another, and shouting multitudinous directions, apparently about nothing at all. Certainly, the police who have been told to keep the crowd in order, pay not the least attention to their blandishments; certainly the regimental bands, which have taken up their position in front of the saluting base, are beyond their jurisdiction, and as yet no regiments have appeared. But their exercise appears to afford the wandering knights errant considerable satisfaction, and they are riding as if for life. First a hasty gallop from left to right of the parade ground, and a peremptory mandate, so it seems, to the rolling clouds in that direction. Then a tug at the curb, a flourish of horse tail and human spurs, and a fourteen anna burst in the opposite direction. [...]

11 o'clock or there abouts. The guns are fired, the horses have protested and his Excellency, Earl Dufferin, Viceroy and Governor General of India, and His Highness, Abdur Rahman Khan, ruler of Afghanistan and its dependencies, are riding side-by-side to the saluting point. The Viceroy is in plain clothes, with a star on his breast. The Ameer, like Alice Fell, is clad in duffel grey, with a gold embroidered black belt, long boots, and the Tartar cap of grey Astrakhan fur. He is riding a small bay pony, and looks burlier and more thickset, than ever. With these two, ride a miscellaneous escort of English and Afghan officers, all well-mounted, and ablaze with gold and silver trappings. They take up position to the right and left of the saluting point, and the show begins.

First the Commander-in-Chief and his staff, and Sir Michael Biddulph and his staff, ride past to their post, opposite the Viceroy's, and draw up in line with the bands. Then, without a word or warning, the railway bridge to the left becomes alive with the glitter of steel, and the bevy of redcoats, as the 33rd, the head of the first division, debouches into the open, at the double. And here I may point out the one disadvantage of the ground chosen. To get down from the Jhelum Road to the open ground below, the troops have to walk down an embankment – which naturally threw them out of their step – dress and close up as best they can, and go on straight on past the Viceroy. They have about 300 yards wherein to recover themselves, and except to some ultra military eye, seemed to go past perfectly. After the 33rd, come the Royal Irish – a strong regiment in every respect, and now we are fairly settled down to business. The bands in front of the saluting point, play the men through as they go. The unattached officers have ceased from galloping, and there is a great quiet over us all.

The 14th Sikhs, the 21st Punjab Native Infantry, the Rifle Brigade, the 4th and 5th Goorkhas, little men taking long strides, the Royal Irish, the 1st Goorkhas and the Volunteers, have passed by. Red, khaki, green, buff, maroon, coats and facings – an infinity of booted feet coming down and taking up, with the exactness of a machine – thousands of pipe-clayed pouches swinging all in the same direction, and all with the same impetus, dazzle the eyes, and produce on the mind the impression of some interminable nightmare. Finally, one loses all idea that the living waves in front are composed of men. It has no will, no individuality – nothing, it seems, save the power of moving forward in a mathematically straight line to the end of time. It was a positive relief to cast one's eyes to the end of the parade ground, and watch the columns, ragged and extended, in their scramble down the side of the road. The procession still continues, and the Scotch regiments are appearing on the scene. The Highland Light Infantry, the 78th, followed by the Guides, the 19th Punjab Native Infantry, the Cheshire, with their riddled colours and the wreath atop, the 1st Punjab Native Infantry, the 3rd Sikhs, the 2nd Manchester, the 24th and 25th Punjab Native Infantry, and then, thank goodness, a pause for the cavalry. The Jhelum Road, as far as the horizon, is covered with returning troops, outlining the curves of the road, in red and dun colour. Abdur Rahman Khan is not to be likely spoken to, so that it is impossible to say for certain what he thinks; but his hands are dropped on his ponie's withers, and with head slightly bent forward, he is watching the incoming and outgoing line. Even an Englishman, accustomed as he is to talk of the degeneracy of our Armed Forces in these days, has, for once, to let such idle cavilling be, and content himself with wonder, pure and simple, and the harvest of the dragon's teeth, which we garner within our borders. Dublin and the Deccan, Paisley and the Punjab, Nepal and Lancashire, one might continue the antitheses indefinitely, have all contributed to the crop of armed men ready for war, and it may be that the grey clad figure in the fur, is reading, marking and inwardly digesting the lesson. But no muscle on his face shows any signs of emotion, and the arrival of the Cavalry bands forces me to relinquish gush, in order to gaze on the next scene of the pageant. This has at least more life and movement than the former, saying that no regulations on earth will keep horses heads from nodding up and down in a regular time, and there was something terrible in the utter immobility of the foot soldiers. The 9th Lancers open the ball, and of these can only be said, as of all the others, but they are fine men on fine horses – albeit the latter look a trifle drawn and tuckered up, from marching and exposure to the rain. After the 9th come the 14th and 19th Bengal Lancers, the 3rd Bengal Cavalry, the 15th Bengal Cavalry, the Carabiniers, the Guides and the 15th Bengal Cavalry [sic], in Squadrons, shaking the earth as they pass. Are there any words to describe adequately the appearance of well-mounted, well-drilled cavalry? The military world here contents itself with saying, that such and such a regiment went by better than such another; but one squadron kept its distance, whereas another did not, and so on; but the absolute symmetry of the whole; the wonder of it all, are taken as matters of course, grown familiar by long usage.

Abdur Rahman Khan made no sign throughout this last revelation – for this it must be to him. But when the artillery makes its appearance there is certainly something very like surprise visible on his countenance. Three batteries of Royal Horse Artillery, four field batteries, the European screw gun batteries, and three native mountain batteries filed by, all as neat as new pins. The Field and Horse batteries go past as one gun. A little thickened and blurred in the outlines, as if seen through a mist, but nevertheless one gun. How it's done, the civilian's mind cannot tell. To all appearance, the driver of the near wheeler lays the stock of his whip likely on the withers of the off wheeler – and there you are, with about six inches between axle and axle, as level as though all six guns had been planed across the muzzles, jammed into a gauge and left there. This too, after guns and limber had to plunge down the embankment, recover themselves, and reform in about 300 yards. It may be said: 'But this is only what we pay for, and all you have described, but the incidents of an ordinary march past.' When twenty thousand men march past in a straight line for two hours, in the presence of the men who will have to make the history of the next four years, the occasion isn't anything but ordinary importance; and it is only fair, therefore, to record how superbly the whole function went off. The one touch of the ludicrous, to relieve the almost oppressive gravity of the proceedings, comes in appropriately enough at the end, in the shape of the elephant battery. Left to himself, my Lord, the elephant, is an imposing beast; but there is something very comic in his appearance when he is harnessed, 'random' fashion, to a siege gun. The weighty piece of ordnance bundles after him like a child's toy. And all the ropes and chains and pads, wherewith his massive form is begirt, look like so many pieces of pack-thread. The Campbellpore behemoths bring up the rear of the Indian Army, at a sober and dignified pace; while behind them come the battery bullocks, and our old friend the Punjabi *bylewalla*, thinly disguised in a uniform, prodding them with a stick. So we drop from all the pomp and circumstance of glorious war, from patriotic enthusiasm and a much gush, to the things of everyday life again. But for a little while only. The Ameer has yet to see what manner of troops our feudatories could bring into the field, should occasion arise. Pattiala, Nabha, Jhind, Faridkot, Kapurthalla, Bahawalpore, have all contingents to show – and to the side must shock the Ameer exceedingly. [...] Truly the native contingents are magnificent troops to look at. A little ragged in their dressing here and there, and below comparison with English batteries, as regards their artillery, but still magnificent men. [...]

They were all good, and would have been better as regards the cavalry, if so many of the horses had not been the pink nosed, mottled squealer that one is accustomed to associate with circuses, all the world over. About three thousand in all have gone by, and the guns are making ready to salute. Viceroy, Ameer and escort have swept round to the road, and are making haste to be gone, as a sharp thunderstorm is doing its worst among us now. [...] Abdur Rahman has seen for himself the harvest of dragons' teeth as we grow it in this country, and doubtless has drawn his own conclusions. The sword is mightier than the pen by far to an Afghan; and each bayonet and field piece will carry more weight with our guest, than the courteous preambles of the Conference proper.

[First published in the *Civil and Military Gazette*, 8 April 1885.]

※ ※ ※

These often-quoted verses refer to the precariousness of serving in the British army, where the life of an expensively educated young soldier could be ended by a 'ten-rupee jezail', an elementary but highly efficient musket, often manufactured in the marketplace and much used by Afghan soldiers. The jezail is known elsewhere in fiction as the weapon which wounded Dr Watson, the companion of Sherlock Holmes, at the Battle of Maiwand.

ARITHMETIC ON THE FRONTIER

A GREAT AND GLORIOUS thing it is
To learn, for seven years or so,
The Lord knows what of that and this,
Ere reckoned fit to face the foe –

The flying bullet down the Pass,
That whistles clear: 'All flesh is grass.'

Three hundred pounds per annum spent
On making brain and body meeter
For all the murderous intent
Comprised in 'villanous saltpetre!'
And after – ask the Yusufzaies
What comes of all our 'ologies.

A scrimmage in a Border Station –
A canter down some dark defile –
Two thousand pounds of education
Drops to a ten-rupee jezail –
The Crammer's boast, the Squadron's pride,
Shot like a rabbit in a ride!

No proposition Euclid wrote,
No formulae the text-books know,
Will turn the bullet from your coat,
Or ward the tulwar's downward blow
Strike hard who cares – shoot straight who can –
The odds are on the cheaper man.

One sword-knot stolen from the camp
Will pay for all the school expenses
Of any Kurrum Valley scamp
Who knows no word of moods and tenses,
But, being blessed with perfect sight,
Picks off our messmates left and right.

With home-bred hordes the hillsides teem,
The troop-ships bring us one by one,
At vast expense of time and steam,
To slay Afridis where they run.
The 'captives of our bow and spear'
Are cheap – alas! as we are dear.

[First published in *Departmental Ditties and Other Verses* (Calcutta: Thacker, Spink and Co., 1886).]

✠ ✠ ✠

This poem recalls an incident on 31 March 1879 during the 1878–80 Afghan War, when 19 cavalrymen from the 10th Hussars died trying to cross the Kabul River at Kalai Sak near Jallalabad.

FORD O' KABUL RIVER

KABUL TOWN'S BY KABUL river –
Blow the bugle, draw the sword –
There I lef' my mate for ever,
Wet an' drippin' by the ford.
Ford, ford, ford o' Kabul river,
Ford o' Kabul river in the dark!
There's the river up and brimmin', an' there's 'arf a squadron swimmin'
'Cross the ford o' Kabul river in the dark.

Kabul town's a blasted place –
Blow the bugle, draw the sword –
'Strewth I sha'n't forget 'is face
Wet an' drippin' by the ford!
Ford, ford, ford o' Kabul river,
Ford o' Kabul river in the dark!
Keep the crossing-stakes beside you, an' they will surely guide you
'Cross the ford o' Kabul river in the dark.

Kabul town is sun and dust –
Blow the bugle, draw the sword –
I'd ha' sooner drownded fust
'Stead of 'im beside the ford.
Ford, ford, ford o' Kabul river,
Ford o' Kabul river in the dark!
You can 'ear the 'orses threshin', you can 'ear the men a-splashin',
'Cross the ford o' Kabul river in the dark.

Kabul town was ours to take –
Blow the bugle, draw the sword –

I'd ha' left it for 'is sake –
'Im that left me by the ford.
Ford, ford, ford o' Kabul river,
Ford o' Kabul river in the dark!
It's none so bloomin' dry there; ain't you never comin' nigh there,
'Cross the ford o' Kabul river in the dark?

Kabul town'll go to hell –
Blow the bugle, draw the sword –
'Fore I see him 'live an' well –
'Im the best beside the ford.
Ford, ford, ford o' Kabul river,
Ford o' Kabul river in the dark!
Gawd 'elp 'em if they blunder, for their boots'll pull 'em under,
By the ford o' Kabul river in the dark.

Turn your 'orse from Kabul town –
Blow the bugle, draw the sword –
'Im an' 'arf my troop is down,
Down an' drownded by the ford.
Ford, ford, ford o' Kabul river,
Ford o' Kabul river in the dark!
There's the river low an' fallin', but it ain't no use o' callin'
'Cross the ford o' Kabul river in the dark.

[First published in the *National Observer*, 22 November 1890, and then
collected in *Ballads and Barrack-Room Ballads* (New York: Macmillan, 1892).
The British edition of this book, entitled *Barrack-Room Ballads and Other
Verses* (London: Methuen, 1892) was published a week after the American
one.]

In this story Kipling first introduces his 'Soldiers Three' – the Irishman Terence Mulvaney, the Yorkshireman John Learoyd and the London Cockney, Stanley Ortheris – who would feature in 18 stories about army life.

THE THREE MUSKETEERS

An' when the war began, we chased the bold Afghan,
An' we made the bloomin' Ghazi for to flee, boys O!
An' we marched into Kabul, an' we tuk the Balar 'Issar,
An' we taught 'em to respec' the British Soldier.

Barrack Room Ballad

MULVANEY, ORTHERIS, AND LEAROYD are Privates in B Company of a Line Regiment, and personal friends of mine. Collectively, I think, but am not certain, they are the worst men in the regiment so far as genial blackguardism goes.

They told me this story in the Umballa Refreshment Room while we were waiting for an up-train. I supplied the beer. The tale was cheap at a gallon and a half.

All men know Lord Benira Trig. He is a Duke, or an Earl, or something unofficial; also a Peer; also a Globe-trotter. On all three counts, as Ortheris says, ''e didn't deserve no consideration.' He was out in India for three months collecting materials for a book on 'Our Eastern Impedimenta,' and quartering himself upon everybody, like a Cossack in evening-dress.

His particular vice – because he was a Radical, men said – was having garrisons turned out for his inspection. He would then dine with the Officer Commanding, and insult him, across the Mess table, about the appearance of the troops. That was Benira's way.

He turned out troops once too often. He came to Helanthami Cantonment on a Tuesday. He wished to go shopping in the bazars on Wednesday, and he 'desired' the troops to be turned out on a Thursday. *On-a-Thursday.* The Officer Commanding could not well refuse; for Benira was a Lord. There was an indignation meeting of subalterns in the Mess Room, to call the Colonel pet names.

'But the rale dimonstrashin,' said Mulvaney, 'was in B Comp'ny barrick; we three headin' it.'

Mulvaney climbed on to the refreshment-bar, settled himself comfortably by the beer, and went on, 'Whin the row was at ut's foinest an' B Comp'ny was fur goin' out to murther this man Thrigg on the p'rade-groun', Learoyd here takes up his helmut an' sez – fwhat was ut ye said?'

'Ah said,' said Learoyd, 'gie us t' brass. Tak oop a subscripshun, lads, for to put off t' p'rade, an' if t' p'rade's not put off, ah'll gie t' brass back agean. Thot's wot ah said. All B Coomp'ny knawed me. Ah took oop a big subscripshun – fower rupees eight annas 'twas – an' ah went oot to turn t' job over. Mulvaney an' Orth'ris coom with me.'

'We three raises the Divil in couples gin'rally,' explained Mulvaney.

Here Ortheris interrupted. "Ave you read the papers?' said he.

'Sometimes,' I said.

'We 'ad read the papers, an' we put hup a faked decoity, a – a sedukshun.'

'Abdukshin, ye cockney,' said Mulvaney.

'Abdukshun or sedukshun – no great odds. Any 'ow, we arranged to taik an' put Mister Benhira out o' the way till Thursday was hover, or 'e too busy to rux 'isself about p'raids. Hi was the man wot said, "We'll make a few rupees off o' the business."'

'We hild a Council av War,' continued Mulvaney, 'walkin' roun' by the Artill'ry Lines. I was Prisidint, Learoyd was Minister av Finance, an' little Orth'ris here was—'

'A bloomin' Bismarck! Hi made the 'ole show pay.'

'This interferin' bit av a Benira man,' said Mulvaney, 'did the thrick for us himself; for, on me sowl, we hadn't a notion av what was to come afther the next minut. He was shoppin' in the bazar on fut. 'Twas dhrawin' dusk thin, an' we stud watchin' the little man hoppin' in an' out av the shops, thryin' to injuce the naygurs to *mallum* his *bat*. Prisintly, he sthrols up, his arrums full av thruck, an' he sez in a consiquinshal way, shticking out his little belly, "Me good men," sez he, "have ye seen the Kernel's b'roosh?" – "B'roosh?" says Learoyd. "There's no b'roosh here – nobbut a *hekka*." "Fwhat's that?" sez Thrigg. Learoyd shows him wan down the sthreet, an' he sez, "How thruly Orientil! I will ride on a *hekka*." I saw thin that our Rigimintal Saint was for givin' Thrigg over to us neck an' brisket. I purshued a *hekka*, an' I sez to the dhriver-divil, I sez, "Ye black limb, there's a *Sahib* comin' for this *hekka*. He wants to go *jildi* to the Padsahi Jhil" – 'twas about two moiles away – "to shoot snipe

– *chirria*. You dhrive *Jehannum ke marfik, mallum* – like Hell? 'Tis no manner av use *bukkin'* to the *Sahib*, bekaze he doesn't *samjao* your talk. Av he *bolos* anything, just you *choop* and *chel*. *Dekker?* Go *arsty* for the first *arder* mile from cantonmints. Thin *chel, Shaitan ke marfik,* an' the *chooper* you *choops* an' the *jildier* you *chels* the better *kooshy* will that *Sahib* be; an' here's a rupee for ye?"

'The *hekka*-man knew there was somethin' out av the common in the air. He grinned an' sez, "*Bote achee*! I goin' damn fast." I prayed that the Kernel's b'roosh wudn't arrive till me darlin' Benira by the grace av God was undher weigh. The little man puts his thruck into the *hekka* an' scuttles in like a fat guinea-pig; niver offerin' us the price av a dhrink for our services in helpin' him home. "He's off to the Padsahi *jhil*," sez I to the others.'

Ortheris took up the tale –

'Jist then, little Buldoo kim up, 'oo was the son of one of the Artillery grooms – 'e would 'av made a 'evinly newspaper-boy in London, bein' sharp an' fly to all manner o' games. 'E 'ad bin watchin' us puttin' Mister Benhira into 'is temporary baroush, an' 'e sez, "What *'ave* you been a doin' of, *Sahibs*?" sez 'e. Learoyd 'e caught 'im by the ear an 'e sez—'

'Ah says,' went on Learoyd, '"Young mon, that mon's gooin' to have t' goons out o' Thursday – to-morrow – an' thot's more work for you, young mon. Now, sitha, tak' a *tat* an' a *lookri*, an' ride tha domdest to t' Padsahi Jhil. Cotch thot there *hekka*, and tell t' driver iv your lingo thot you've coom to tak' his place. T' *Sahib* doesn't speak t' *bat*, an' he's a little mon. Drive t' *hekka* into t' Padsahi Jhil into t' watter. Leave t' *Sahib* theer an' roon hoam; an' here's a rupee for tha."'

Then Mulvaney and Ortheris spoke together in alternate fragments: Mulvaney leading [You must pick out the two speakers as best you can] – 'He was a knowin' little divil was Bhuldoo, – 'e sez *bote achee* an' cuts – wid a wink in his oi – but *Hi* sez there's money to be made – an' I wanted to see the ind av the campaign – so *Hi* says we'll double hout to the Padsahi Jhil – an' save the little man from bein' dacoited by the murtherin' Bhuldoo – an' turn hup like reskooers in a Vic'oria Melodrama – so we doubled for the *jhil*, an' prisintly there was the divil av a hurroosh behind us an' three bhoys on grasscuts' ponies come by, poundin' along for the dear life – s'elp me Bob, hif Buldoo 'adn't raised a rig'lar *harmy* of decoits – to do the job in shtile. An' we ran, an' they ran, shplittin' with laughin', till we gets near the *jhil* – and 'ears sounds of distress floatin' molloncolly on the hevenin' hair.' [Ortheris was growing poetical under the influence of the beer. The duet recommenced: Mulvaney leading again.]

'Thin we heard Bhuldoo, the dacoit, shoutin' to the *hekka* man, an' wan of the young divils brought his stick down on the top av the *hekka*-cover, an' Benira Thrigg inside howled "Murther an' Death." Buldoo takes the reins and dhrives like mad for the *jhil*, havin' dishpersed the *hekka*-dhriver – 'oo cum up to us an' 'e sez, sez 'e, "That *Sahib*'s nigh mad with funk! Wot devil's work 'ave you led me into?" – "Hall right," sez we, "you catch that there pony an' come along. This *Sahib*'s been decoited, an' we're going to resky 'im!" Says the driver, "Decoits! Wot decoits? That's Buldoo the *budmash*" – "Bhuldoo be shot!" sez we. "'Tis a woild dissolute Pathan frum the hills. There's about eight av thim coercin' the *Sahib*. You remimber that an you'll get another rupee!" Thin we heard the *whop-whop-whop* av the *hekka* turnin' over, an' a splash av water an' the voice av Benira Thrigg callin' upon God to forgive his sins – an' Buldoo an' 'is friends squatterin' in the water like boys in the Serpentine.'

Here the Three Musketeers retired simultaneously into the beer.

'Well? What came next?' said I.

'Fwhat nex'?' answered Mulvaney, wiping his mouth. 'Wud ye let three bould sodger-bhoys lave the ornamint av the House av Lords to be dhrowned an' dacoited in a *jhil*? We formed line av quarther-column an' we discinded upon the inimy. For the better part av tin minutes you could not hear yerself spake. The *tattoo* was screamin' in chune wid Benira Thrigg an' Bhuldoo's army, an' the shticks was whistlin' roun' the *hekka*, an' Orth'ris was beatin' the *hekka*-cover wid his fistes, an' Learoyd yellin', "Look out for their knives!" an' me cuttin' into the dark, right an' lef', dishpersin' arrmy corps av Pathans. Holy Mother av Moses! 'Twas more disp'rit than Ahmid Kheyl wid Maiwand thrown in. Afther a while Bhuldoo an' his bhoys flees. Have ye iver seen a rale live Lord thryin' to hide his nobility undher a fut an' a half av brown swamp-wather? 'Tis the livin' image av a water-carrier's goatskin wid the shivers. It tuk toime to pershuade me frind Benira he was not disimbowilled: an' more toime to get out the *hekka*. The dhriver come up afther the battle, swearin' he tuk a hand in repulsin' the inimy. Benira was sick wid the fear. We escorted him back, very slow, to cantonmints, for that an' the chill to soak into him. It suk! Glory be to the Rigimintil Saint, but it suk to the marrow av Lord Benira Thrigg!'

Here Ortheris, slowly, with immense pride – "'E sez, "You har my noble preservers," sez 'e. "You har a *honour* to the British Harmy," sez 'e. With that 'e describes the hawful band of dacoits wot set on 'im. There was about forty of 'em an' 'e was hoverpowered by numbers, so 'e was; but 'e never lorst 'is presence of mind, so 'e didn't. 'E guv the *hekka*-driver five rupees for 'is noble assistance, an' 'e said 'e would see to us after 'e 'ad spoken to the Kernul. For we was a *honour* to the Regiment, we was.'

'An' we three,' said Mulvaney, with a seraphic smile, 'have dhrawn the par-ti-cu-lar attinshin av Bobs Bahadur more than wanst. But he's a rale good little man is Bobs. Go on, Orth'ris, my son.'

'Then we leaves 'im at the Kernul's 'ouse, werry sick, an' we cuts hover to B Comp'ny barrick an' we sez we 'ave saved Benira from a bloody doom, an' the chances was agin there bein' p'raid on Thursday. About ten minutes later come three envelicks, one for each of us. S'elp me Bob, if the old bloke 'adn't guv us a fiver apiece – sixty-four rupees in the bazar! On Thursday 'e was in 'orspital recoverin' from 'is sanguinary encounter with a gang of Pathans, an' B Comp'ny was drinkin' 'emselves into Clink by squads. So there never was no Thursday p'raid. But the Kernul, when 'e 'eard of our galliant conduct, 'e sez, "Hi know there's been some devilry somewheres," sez 'e, "but I can't bring it 'ome to you three."'

'An' my privit imprisshin is,' said Mulvaney, getting off the bar and turning his glass upside down, 'that, av they had known they wudn't have brought ut home. 'Tis flyin' in the face, firstly av Nature, secon' av the Rig'lations, an' third the will av Terence Mulvaney, to hold p'rades av Thursdays.'

'Good, ma son!' said Learoyd; 'but, young mon, what's t' notebook for?'

'Let be,' said Mulvaney; 'this time next month we're in the *Sherapis*. 'Tis immortial fame the gentleman's goin' to give us. But kape it dhark till we're out av the range av me little frind Bobs Bahadur.'

And I have obeyed Mulvaney's order.

[First published in the *Civil and Military Gazette*, 11 March 1887, and then collected in *Plain Tales from the Hills* (Calcutta: Thacker, Spink and Co., 1888).]

In this, another story in the Soldiers Three series. Mulvaney helps his colleagues get through the stifling conditions of 'Fort Amara' in Lahore by telling them a rousing story of the 'Ould Regiment' fighting the Pathans on the north-west frontier. The 'Ould Regiment' was based on the 59th, in which Ortheris also served. This was later amalgamated with the 30th to form the East Lancashire Regiment, a battalion of which was stationed at Mian Mir from 1880 to 1885.

WITH THE MAIN GUARD

Der jungere Uhlanen
Sit round mit open mouth
While Breitmann tell dem sdories
Of fightin' in the South;
Und gif dem moral lessons,
How before der battle pops,
Take a little prayer to Himmel
Und a goot long drink of Schnapps.

C.G. Leland

'MARY, MOTHER AV MERCY, fwhat the divil possist us to take an' kape this melancolious counthry? Answer me that, sorr.'

It was Mulvaney who was speaking. The time was one o'clock of a stifling June night, and the place was the main gate of Fort Amara, most desolate and least desirable of all fortresses in India. What I was doing there at that hour is a question which only concerns M'Grath the Sergeant of the Guard, and the men on the gate.

'Slape,' said Mulvaney, 'is a shuparfluous necessity. This Gyard'll shtay lively till relieved.' He himself was stripped to the waist; Learoyd on the next bedstead was dripping from the skinful of water which Ortheris, clad only in white trousers, had just sluiced over his shoulders; and a fourth private was muttering uneasily as he dozed open-mouthed in the glare of the great guard-lantern. The heat under the bricked archway was terrifying.

'The worrst night that iver I remimber. Eyah! Is all Hell loose this tide?' said Mulvaney. A puff of burning wind lashed through the wicket-gate like a wave of the sea, and Ortheris swore.

'Are ye more heasy, Jock?' he said to Learoyd. 'Put yer 'ead between your legs. It'll go orf in a minute.'

'Ah doan't care. Ah would not care, but ma heart is plaayin' tivvy-tivvy on ma ribs. Let ma die! Oh, leave ma die!' groaned the huge Yorkshireman, who was feeling the heat acutely, being of fleshy build.

The sleeper under the lantern roused for a moment and raised himself on his elbow. 'Die and be damned then!' he said. '*I'm* damned and I can't die!'

'Who's that?' I whispered, for the voice was new to me.

'Gentleman born,' said Mulvaney; 'Corp'ril wan year, Sargint nex'. Red-hot on his C'mission, but dhrinks like a fish. He'll be gone before the cowld weather's here. So!'

He slipped his boot, and with the naked toe just touched the trigger of his Martini. Ortheris misunderstood the movement, and the next instant the Irishman's rifle was dashed aside, while Ortheris stood before him, his eyes blazing with reproof.

'You!' said Ortheris. 'My Gawd, *you*! If it was you, wot would *we* do?'

'Kape quiet, little man,' said Mulvaney, putting him aside, but very gently; ''Tis not me, nor will ut be me whoile Dinah Shadd's here. I was but showin' somethin'.'

Learoyd, bowed on his bedstead, groaned, and the gentleman-ranker sighed in his sleep. Ortheris took Mulvaney's tendered pouch, and we three smoked gravely for a space while the dust-devils danced on the glacis and scoured the red-hot plain.

'Pop?' said Ortheris, wiping his forehead.

'Don't tantalise wid talkin' av dhrink, or I'll shtuff you into your own breech-block an' – fire you off!' grunted Mulvaney.

Ortheris chuckled, and from a niche in the veranda produced six bottles of gingerade.

'Where did ye get ut, ye Machiavel?' said Mulvaney. ''Tis no bazar pop.'

''Ow do *I* know wot the orf'cers drink?' answered Ortheris. 'Arst the mess-man.'

'Ye'll have a Disthrict Coort-Martial settin' on ye yet, me son,' said Mulvaney, 'but' – he opened a bottle – 'I will not report ye this time. Fwhat's in the mess-kid is mint for the belly, as they say, 'specially whin that mate is dhrink. Here's luck! A bloody war or a – no, we've got the sickly season. War, thin!' – he waved the innocent 'pop' to the four quarters of heaven. 'Bloody war! North, East, South, an' West Jock, ye quakin' hayrick, come an' dhrink.'

But Learoyd, half mad with the fear of death presaged in the swelling veins of his neck, was begging his Maker to strike him dead, and fighting for more air between his prayers. A second time Ortheris drenched the quivering body with water, and the giant revived.

'An' Ah divn't see thot a mon is i' fettle for gooin' on to live; an' Ah divn't see thot there is owt for t' livin' for. Hear now, lads! Ah'm tired – tired. There's nobbut watter i' ma bones. Leave ma die!'

The hollow of the arch gave back Learoyd's broken whisper in a bass boom. Mulvaney looked at me hopelessly, but I remembered how the madness of despair had once fallen upon Ortheris, that weary, weary afternoon on the banks of the Khemi River, and how it had been exorcised by the skilful magician Mulvaney.

'Talk, Terence!' I said, 'or we shall have Learoyd slinging loose, and he'll be worse than Ortheris was. Talk! He'll answer to your voice.'

Almost before Ortheris had deftly thrown all the rifles of the guard on Mulvaney's bedstead, the Irishman's voice was uplifted as that of one in the middle of a story, and, turning to me, he said:–

'In barricks or out av it, as *you* say, sorr, an Irish rig'mint is the divil an' more. 'Tis only fit for a young man wid eddicated fisteses. Oh, the crame av disrupshin is an Irish rig'mint, an' rippin', tearin', ragin' scattherers in the field av war! My first rig'mint was Irish – Faynians an' rebils to the heart av their marrow was they, an' so they fought for the Widdy betther than most, bein' contrairy – Irish. They was the Black Tyrone. You've heard av thim, sorr?'

Heard of them! I knew the Black Tyrone for the choicest collection of unmitigated blackguards, dog-stealers, robbers of hen-roosts, assaulters of innocent citizens, and recklessly daring heroes in the Army List. Half Europe and half Asia has had cause to know the Black Tyrone – good luck be with their tattered Colours as Glory has ever been.

'They *was* hot pickils an' ginger! I cut a man's head too deep wid me belt in the days av me youth, an', afther some circumstances which I will obliterate, I came to the Ould Rig'mint, bearin' the character av a man wid hands an' feet. But, as I was goin' to tell you, I fell acrost the Black Tyrone agin wan day whin we wanted thim powerful bad. Orth'ris, me son, fwhat was the name av that place where they sint wan comp'ny av us an' wan av the Tyrone roun' a hill an' down agin, all for to tache the Paythans something they'd niver learned before? Afther Ghuzni 'twas.'

'Don't know what the bloomin' Paythans called it. We called it Silver's Theayter. You know that, sure!'

'Silver's Theatre – so 'twas. A gut betwix' two hills, as black as a bucket, an' as thin as a gurl's waist. There was over-many Paythans for our convaynience in the gut, an' begad they called thimsilves a Reserve – bein' impident by natur'! Our Scotchies an' lashin's av Gurkys was poundin' into some Paythan rig'mints, I think 'twas. Scotchies an' Gurkys are twins bekaze they're so onlike, an' they get dhrunk together whin God plazes. As I was sayin', they sint wan comp'ny av the Ould an' wan av the Tyrone to double up the hill an' clane out the Paythan Reserve. Orf'cers was scarce in thim days, fwhat wid dysint'ry an' not takin' care av thimsilves, an' we was sint out wid only wan orf'cer for the comp'ny; but he was a Man that had his feet beneath him an' all his teeth in their sockuts.'

'Who was he?' I asked.

'Captain O'Neil – Old Crook – Cruik-na-bul-leen – him that I tould ye that tale av whin he was in Burma. Hah! He was a Man. The Tyrone tuk a little orf'cer bhoy, but divil a bit was he in command, as I'll dimonsthrate prisintly. We an' they came over the brow av the hill, wan on each side av the gut, an' there was that ondacint Reserve waitin' down below like rats in a pit.

'"Howld on, men," sez Crook, who tuk a mother's care av us always. "Rowl some rocks on thim by way av visitin'-kyards." We hadn't rowled more than twinty bowlders, an' the Paythans was beginnin' to swear tremenjus, whin the little orf'cer bhoy av the Tyrone shqueaks out acrost the valley: "Fwhat the divil an' all are you doin', shpoilin' the fun for my men? Do ye not see they'll stand?"

'"Faith, that's a rare pluckt wan!" sez Crook. "Niver mind the rocks, men. Come along down an' take tay wid thim!"

'"There's damned little sugar in ut!" sez my rear-rank man; but Crook heard.

'"Have ye not all got spoons?" he sez, laughin', an' down we wint as fast as we cud. Learoyd bein' sick at the Base, he, av coorse, was not there.'

'Thot's a lie!' said Learoyd, dragging his bedstead nearer. 'Ah gotten *thot* theer, an' you knaw it, Mulvaaney.' He threw up his arms, and from the right armpit ran, diagonally through the fell of his chest, a thin white line terminating near the fourth left rib.

'My mind's goin',' said Mulvaney, the unabashed. 'Ye were there. Fwhat was I thinkin' av? 'Twas another man, av coorse. Well, you'll remimber thin, Jock, how we an' the Tyrone met wid a bang at the bottom an' got jammed past all movin' among the Paythans?'

'Ow! It *was* a tight 'ole. I was squeezed till I thought I'd bloomin' well bust,' said Ortheris, rubbing his stomach meditatively.

''Twas no place for a little man, but wan little man' – Mulvaney put his hand on Ortheris's shoulder – 'saved the life av me. There we shtuck, for divil a bit did the Paythans flinch, an' divil a bit dare we; our business bein' to clear 'em out. An' the most exthryordinar' thing av all was that we an' they just rushed into each other's arrums, an' there was no firin' for a long time. Nothin' but knife an' bay'nit when we cud get our hands free: an' that was not often. We was breast-on to thim, an' the Tyrone was yelpin' behind av us in a way I didn't see the lean av at first. But I knew later, an' so did the Paythans.

'"Knee to knee!" sings out Crook, wid a laugh whin the rush av our comin' into the gut shtopped, an' he was huggin' a hairy great Paythan, neither bein' able to do anything to the other, tho' both was wishful.

'"Breast to breast!" he sez, as the Tyrone was pushin' us forward closer an' closer.

'"An' hand over back!" sez a Sargint that was behin'. I saw a sword lick out past Crook's ear, an' the Paythan was tuk in the apple av his throat like a pig at Dromeen Fair.

'"Thank ye, Brother Inner Guard," sez Crook, cool as a cucumber widout salt. "I wanted that room." An' he went forward by the thickness av a man's body, havin' turned the Paythan undher him. The man bit the heel off Crook's boot in his death-bite.

'"Push, men!" sez Crook. "Push, ye paper-backed beggars!" he sez. "Am I to pull ye through?" So we pushed, an' we kicked, an' we swung, an' we swore, an' the grass bein' slippery, our heels wudn't bite, an' God help the front-rank man that wint down that day!'

''Ave you ever bin in the Pit hentrance o' the Vic. on a thick night?' interrupted Ortheris. 'It was worse nor that, for they was goin' one way, an' we wouldn't 'ave it. Leastaways, I 'adn't much to say.'

'Faith, me son, ye said ut, thin. I kep' this little man betune my knees as long as I cud, but he was pokin' roun' wid his bay'nit, blindin' an' stiffen' feroshus. The divil of a man is Orth'ris in a ruction – aren't ye?' said Mulvaney.

'Don't make game!' said the Cockney. 'I knowed I wasn't no good then, but I guv 'em compot from the lef' flank when we opened out. No!' he said, bringing down his hand with a thump on the bedstead, 'a bay'nit ain't no good to a little man – might as well 'ave a bloomin' fishin'-rod! I 'ate a clawin', maulin' mess, but gimme a breech that's wore out a bit an' hamminition one year in store, to let the powder kiss the bullet, an' put me somewheres where I ain't trod on by 'ulking swine like you, an' s'elp me Gawd, I could bowl you over five times outer seven at height 'undred. Would yer try, you lumberin' Hirishman?'

'No, ye wasp. I've seen ye do ut. I say there's nothin' better than the bay'nit, wid a long reach, a double twist av ye can, an' a slow recover.'

'Dom the bay'nit,' said Learoyd, who had been listening intently. 'Look a-here!' He picked up a rifle an inch below the fore-sight with an underhanded action, and used it exactly as a man would use a dagger.

'Sitha,' said he softly, 'thot's better than owt, for a mon can bash t' faace wi' thot, an', if he divn't, he can breeak t' forearm o' t' guaard. 'Tis nut i' t' books, though. Gie me t' butt.'

'Each does ut his own way, like makin' love,' said Mulvaney quietly; 'the butt or the bay'nit or the bullet accordin' to the natur' av the man. Well, as I was sayin', we shtuck there breathin' in each other's faces an' swearin' powerful; Orth'ris cursin' the mother that bore him bekaze he was not three inches taller.

'Prisintly he sez: "Duck, ye lump, an' I can get at a man over your shoulther!"

'"You'll blow me head off," I sez, throwin' my arrum clear; "go through under my arrumpit, ye bloodthirsty little scutt," sez I, "but don't shtick me or I'll wring your ears round."'

'Fwhat was ut ye gave the Paythan man forninst me, him that cut at me whin I cudn't move hand or foot? Hot or cowld was ut?'

'Cold,' said Ortheris, 'up an' under the rib-jints. 'E come down flat. Best for you 'e did.'

'Thrue, me son! This jam thing that I'm talkin' about lasted for five minut's good, an' thin we got our arrums clear an' wint in. I misremimber exactly fwhat I did, but I didn't want Dinah to be a widdy at the depot. Thin, afther some promishcuous hackin' we shtuck agin, an' the Tyrone behin' was callin' us dogs an' cowards an' all manner av names; we barrin' their way.

'"Fwhat ails the Tyrone?" thinks I. "They've the makin's av a most convanient fight here."

'A man behind me sez beseechful an' in a whisper: "Let me get at thim! For the love av Mary, give me room beside ye, ye tall man!"

'"An' who are you that's so anxious to be kilt?" sez I, widout turnin' my head, for the long knives was dancin' in front like the sun on Donegal Bay whin ut's rough.

'"We've seen our dead," he sez, squeezin' into me; "our dead that was men two days gone! An' me that was his cousin by blood cud not bring Tim Coulan off! Let me get on," he sez, "let me get to thim or I'll run ye through the back!"

'"My troth," thinks I, "if the Tyrone have seen their dead, God help the Paythans this day!" An' thin I knew why the Tyrone was ragin' behind us as they was.

'I gave room to the man, an' he ran forward wid the Haymakers' Lift on his bay'nit an' swung a Paythan clear off his feet by the belly-band av the brute, an' the iron bruk at the lockin'-ring.

'"Tim Coulan'll slape aisy to-night," sez he wid a grin; an' the next minut' his head was in two halves and he wint down grinnin' by sections.

'The Tyrone was pushin' an' pushin' in, an' our men was swearin' at thim, an' Crook was workin' away in front av us all, his sword-arrum swingin' like a pump-handle an' his revolver spittin' like a cat. But the strange thing av ut was the quiet that lay upon. 'Twas like a fight in a drame – excipt for thim that was dead.

'Whin I gave room to the Irishman I was expinded an' forlorn in my inside. 'Tis a way I have, savin' your presince, sorr, in action. "Let me out, bhoys," sez I, backin' in among thim. "I'm goin' to be onwell!" Faith, they gave me room at the wurrud, though they wud not ha' given room for all Hell wid the chill off. When I got clear, I was, savin' your presince, sorr, outrajis sick bekaze I had dhrunk heavy that day.

'Well an' far out av harm was a Sargint av the Tyrone sittin' on the little orf'cer bhoy who had stopped Crook from rowlin' the rocks. Oh, he was a beautiful bhoy, an' the long black curses was slidin' out av his innocint mouth like mornin' jew from a rose!

'"Fwhat have you got there?" sez I to the Sargint.

'"Wan av Her Majesty's bantams wid his spurs up," sez he. "He's goin' to Coort-Martial me."

'"Let me go!" sez the little orf'cer bhoy. "Let me go and command me men!" manin' thereby the Black Tyrone which was beyond any command – even av they had made the Divil Field-Orf'cer.

'"His father howlds my mother's cow-feed in Clonmel," sez the man that was sittin' on him. "Will I go back to *his* mother an' tell her that I've let him throw himsilf away? Lie still, ye little pinch of dynamite, an' Coort-Martial me aftherwards."

'"Good," sez I; "'Tis the likes av him makes the likes av the Commandher-in-Chief, but we must presarve thim. Fwhat d'you want to do, sorr?" sez I, very politeful.

'"Kill the beggars – kill the beggars!" he shqueaks, his big blue eyes brimmin' wid tears.

'"An' how'll ye do that?" sez I. "You've shquibbed off your revolver like a child wid a cracker; you can make no play wid that fine large sword av yours; an' your hand's shakin' like an asp on a leaf. Lie still and grow," sez I.

'"Get back to your comp'ny," sez he; " you're insolint!"

'"All in good time," sez I, "but I'll have a dhrink first."

'Just thin Crook comes up, blue an' white all over where he wasn't red.

'"Wather!" sez he; "I'm dead wid drouth! Oh, but it's a gran' day!"

'He dhrank half a skinful, and the rest he tilts into his chest, an' it fair hissed on the hairy hide av him. He sees the little orf'cer bhoy undher the Sargint.

'"Fwhat's yonder?" sez he.

'"Mutiny, sorr,' sez the Sargint, an' the orf'cer bhoy begins pleadin' pitiful to Crook to be let go; but divil a bit wud Crook budge.

'"Kape him there," he sez; "'Tis no child's work this day. By the same token," sez he, "I'll confishcate that iligant nickel-plated scent-sprinkler av yours, for my own has been vomitin' dishgraceful!"

'The fork av his hand was black wid the backspit av the machine. So he tuk the orf'cer bhoy's revolver. Ye may look, sorr, but, by my faith, *there's a dale more done in the field than iver gets into Field Ordhers!*

'"Come on, Mulvaney," sez Crook; "is this a Coort-Martial?" The two av us wint back together into the mess an' the Paythans was still standin' up. They was not *too* impart'nint though, for the Tyrone was callin' wan to another to remimber Tim Coulan.

'Crook holted outside av the strife an' looked anxious, his eyes rowlin' roun'.

'"Fwhat is ut, sorr?" sez I; "can I get ye anything?"

'"Where's a bugler?" sez he.

'I wint into the crowd – our men was dhrawin' breath behin' the Tyrone, who was fightin' like sowls in tormint – an' prisintly I came acrost little Frehan, our bugler bhoy, pokin' roun' among the best wid a rifle an' bay'nit.

'"Is amusin' yoursilf fwhat you're paid for, ye limb?" sez I, catchin' him by the scruff. "Come out av that an' attind to your jooty," I sez; but the bhoy was not plazed.

'"I've got wan," sez he, grinnin', "big as you, Mulvaney, an' fair half as ugly. Let me go get another."

'I was dishplazed at the personability av that remark, so I tucks him under my arrum an' carries him to Crook, who was watchin' how the fight wint. Crook cuffs him till the bhoy cries, an' thin sez nothin' for a whoile.

'The Paythans began to flicker onaisy, an' our men roared. "Opin ordher! Double!" sez Crook. "Blow, child, blow for the honour av the British Arrmy!"

'That bhoy blew like a typhoon, an' the Tyrone an' we opind out as the Paythans bruk, an' I saw that fwhat had gone before wud be kissin' an' huggin' to fwhat was to come. We'd dhruv thim into a broad part av the gut whin they gave, an' thin we opind out an' fair danced down the valley, dhrivin' thim before us. Oh, 'twas lovely, an' stiddy, too! There was the Sargints on the flanks av what was left av us, kapin' touch, an' the fire was runnin' from flank to flank, an' the Paythans was dhroppin'. We opind out wid the widenin' av the valley, an' whin the valley narrowed we closed agin like the shticks on a lady's fan, an' at the far ind av the gut where they thried to stand, we fair blew them off their feet, for we had expinded very little ammunition by reason av the knife-work.'

'I used thirty rounds goin' down that valley,' said Ortheris, 'an' it was gentleman's work. Might 'a' done it in a white 'andkerchief an' pink silk stockin's, that part. Hi was on in that piece.'

'You cud ha' heard the Tyrone yellin' a mile away,' said Mulvaney, 'an' 'twas all their Sargints cud do to get thim off. They was mad – mad – mad! Crook sits down in the quiet that fell whin we had gone down the valley, an' covers his face wid his hands. Prisintly we all came back agin accordin' to our natur's and disposishins, for they, mark you, show through the hide av a man in that hour.

'"Bhoys! bhoys!"sez Crook to himsilf. "I misdoubt we cud ha' engaged at long range an' saved betther men than me." He looked at our dead an' said no more.

'"Captain dear," sez a man av the Tyrone, comin' up wid his mouth bigger than iver his mother kissed ut, spittin' blood like a whale; "Captain dear," sez he, "if wan or two in the shtalls have been dishcommoded, the gallery have enjoyed the performinces av a Roshus."

'Thin I knew that man for the Dublin dockrat he was – wan av the bhoys that made the lessee av Silver's Theatre grey before his time wid tearin' out the bowils av the benches an' throwin' thim into the pit. So I passed the wurrud that I knew whin I was in the Tyrone an' we lay in Dublin. "I don't know who 'twas," I whishpers, "an' I don't care, but anyways I'll knock the face av you, Tim Kelly."

'"Eyah!" sez the man, "was you there too? We'll call ut Silver's Theatre." Half the Tyrone, knowin' the ould place, tuk ut up: so we called ut Silver's Theatre.

'The little orf'cer bhoy av the Tyrone was thremblin' an' cryin'. He had no heart for the Coort-Martials that he talked so big upon. "Ye'll do well later," sez Crook, very quiet, "for not bein' allowed to kill yoursilf for amusemint."

'"I'm a dishgraced man!" sez the little orf'cer bhoy.

'"Put me undher arrest, sorr, if you will, but, by my sowl, I'd do ut agin sooner than face your mother wid you dead," sez the Sargint that had sat on his head, standin' to attenshin an' salutin'. But the young wan only cried as tho' his little heart was breakin'.

'Thin another man av the Tyrone came up, wid the fog av fightin' on him.'

'The what, Mulvaney?'

'Fog av fightin'. You know, sorr, that, like makin' love, ut takes each man diff'rint. Now, I can't help bein' powerful sick whin I'm in action. Orth'ris, here, niver stops swearin' from ind to ind, an' the only time that Learoyd opins his mouth to sing is whin he is messin' wid other people's heads; for he's a dhirty fighter is jock. Recruities sometime cry, an' sometime they don't know fwhat they do, an' sometime they are all for cuttin' throats an' such-like dhirtiness; but some men get heavy-dead-dhrunk on the fightin'. This man was. He was staggerin', an' his eyes were half shut, an' we cud hear him dhraw breath twinty yards away. He sees the little orf'cer bhoy, an' comes up, talkin' thick an' drowsy to himsilf. "Blood the young whelp!" he sez; "Blood the young whelp"; an' wid that he threw up his arrums, shpun roun', an' dropped at our feet, dead as a Paythan, an' there was niver sign or scratch on him. They said 'twas his heart was rotten, but oh, 'twas a quare thing to see!

'Thin we wint to bury our dead, for we wud not lave thim to the Paythans, an' in movin' among the haythen we nearly lost that little orf'cer bhoy. He was for givin' wan divil wather and layin' him aisy against a rock. "Be careful, sorr," sez I; "a wounded Paythan's worse than a live wan." My troth, before the words was out av me mouth, the man on the ground fires at the orf'cer bhoy lanin' over him, an' I saw the helmit fly. I dropped the butt on the face av the man an' tuk his pistol. The little orf'cer bhoy turned very white, for the hair av half his head was singed away.

'"I tould you so, sorr!" sez I; an', afther that, whin he wanted to help a Paythan I stud wid the muzzle contagious to the ear. They dared not do anythin' but curse. The Tyrone was growlin' like dogs over a bone that has been taken away too soon, for they had seen their dead an' they wanted to kill ivry sowl on the ground. Crook tould thim that he'd blow the hide off any man that misconducted himsilf; but, seeing that ut was the first time the Tyrone had iver seen their dead, I do not wondher they was on the sharp. 'Tis a shameful sight! Whin I first saw ut I wud niver ha' given quarter to any man north of the Khyber – no, nor woman either, for the wimmen used to come out afther dhark – Auggrh!

'Well, evenshually we buried our dead an' tuk away our wounded, an' come over the brow av the hills to see the Scotchies an' the Gurkys takin' tay with the Paythans in bucketsfuls. We were a gang av dissolute ruffians, for the blood had caked the dust, an' the sweat had cut the cake, an' our bay'nits was hangin' like butchers' steels betune our legs, an' most av us was marked one way or another.

'A Staff Orf'cer man, clane as a new rifle, rides up an' sez: "What damned scarecrows are you?"

'"A comp'ny av Her Majesty's Black Tyrone an' wan av the Ould Rig'mint," sez Crook very quiet, givin' our visitors the flure as 'twas.

'"Oh!" sez the Staff Orf'cer. "Did you dislodge that Reserve?"

'"No!" sez Crook, an' the Tyrone laughed.

'"Thin fwhat the divil have ye done?"

'"Disthroyed ut," sez Crook, an' he took us on, but not before Toomey that was in the Tyrone sez aloud, his voice somewhere in his stummick, "Fwhat in the name av misfortune does this parrit widout a tail mane by shtoppin' the road av his betthers?"

The Staff Orf'cer wint blue, an' Toomey makes him pink by changin' to the voice av a minowdherin' woman an' sayin': "Come an' kiss me, Major dear, for me husband's at the wars an' I'm all alone at the depot."

'The Staff Orf'cer wint away, an' I cud see Crook's shoulthers shakin'.

'His Corp'ril checks Toomey. "Lave me alone," sez Toomey, widout a wink. "I was his batman before he was married an' he knows fwhat I mane, av you don't. There's nothin' like livin' in the hoight av society." D'you remimber that, Orth'ris?'

'Yuss. Toomey, 'e died in 'orspital, next week it was, 'cause I bought 'arf his kit; an' I remember after that—'

'GUARRD, TURN OUT!'

The Relief had come; it was four o'clock. 'I'll catch a kyart for you, sorr,' said Mulvaney, diving hastily into his accoutrements. 'Come up to the top av the Fort an' we'll pershue our invistigations into M'Grath's shtable.' The relieved guard strolled round the main bastion on its way to the swimming-bath, and Learoyd grew almost talkative. Ortheris looked into the Fort Ditch and across the plain. 'Ho! it's weary waitin' for Ma-ary!' he hummed; 'but I'd like to kill some more bloomin' Paythans before my time's up. War! Bloody war! North, East, South, and West.'

'Amen,' said Learoyd slowly.

'Fwhat's here?' said Mulvaney, checking at a blur of white by the foot of the old sentry-box. He stooped and touched it. 'It's Norah – Norah M'Taggart! Why, Nonie darlin', fwhat are ye doin' out av your mother's bed at this time?'

The two-year-old child of Sergeant M'Taggart must have wandered for a breath of cool air to the very verge of the parapet of the Fort Ditch. Her tiny nightshift was gathered into a wisp round her neck and she moaned in her sleep. 'See there!' said Mulvaney; 'poor lamb! Look at the heatrash on the innocint shkin av her. 'Tis hard – crool hard even for us. Fwhat must it be for these? Wake up, Nonie, your mother will be woild about you. Begad, the child might ha' fallen into the Ditch!'

He picked her up in the growing light, and set her on his shoulder, and her fair curls touched the grizzled stubble of his temples. Ortheris and Learoyd followed snapping their fingers, while Norah smiled at them a sleepy smile. Then carolled Mulvaney, clear as a lark, dancing the baby on his arm:–

'If any young man should marry you,
       Say nothin' about the joke;
   That aver ye slep' in a sinthry-box,
       Wrapped up in a soldier's cloak.'

'Though, on my sowl, Nonie,' he said gravely, 'there was not much cloak about you. Niver mind, you won't dhress like this ten years to come. Kiss your frinds an' run along to your mother.'

Nonie, set down close to the Married Quarters, nodded with the quiet obedience of the soldier's child, but, ere she pattered off over the flagged path, held up her lips to be kissed by the Three Musketeers. Ortheris wiped his mouth with the back of his hand and swore sentimentally! Learoyd turned pink; and the two walked away together. The Yorkshireman lifted up his voice and gave in thunder the chorus of *The Sentry-Box*, while Ortheris piped at his side.

'Bin to a bloomin' sing-song, you two?' said the Artilleryman, who was taking his cartridge down to the Morning Gun. 'You're over merry for these dashed days.'

'I bid ye take care o' the brat, said he
   For it comes of a noble race,'

Learoyd bellowed. The voices died out in the swimming-bath.

'Oh, Terence!' I said, dropping into Mulvaney's speech, when we were alone, 'it's you that have the Tongue!'

He looked at me wearily; his eyes were sunk in his head, and his face was drawn and white. 'Eyah!' said he; 'I've blandandhered thim through the night somehow, but can thim that helps others help thimsilves? Answer me that, sorr!'

And over the bastions of Fort Amara broke the pitiless day.

[First published in *The Week's News*, Allahabad, 4 August 1888, and then collected in *Soldiers Three*, Indian Railway Library No. 1 (Allahabad: A.H. Wheeler and Co., 1888).]

✠ ✠ ✠

In this poem Kipling was probably referring back to a story of a
similar incident involving a horse of this name which appeared
in the memoirs of retired Staff Sergeant Nathaniel W. Bancroft, of
the old Bengal Horse Artillery and later the Royal Horse Artillery.
Kipling reviewed this book, *From Recruit to Staff Sergeant*,
published in Calcutta in 1885, in the *Pioneer* on 5 February 1886.

SNARLEYOW

THIS 'APPENED IN A battle to a batt'ry of the corps
Which is first among the women an' amazin' first in war;
An' what the bloomin' battle was I don't remember now,
But Two's off-lead 'e answered to the name o' *Snarleyow*.
Down in the Infantry, nobody cares;
Down in the Cavalry, Colonel 'e swears;
But down in the lead with the wheel at the flog
Turns the bold Bombardier to a little whipped dog!

They was movin' into action, they was needed very sore,
To learn a little schoolin' to a native army corps,
They 'ad nipped against an uphill, they was tuckin' down the
    brow,
When a tricky, trundlin' roundshot give the knock to *Snarleyow*.

They cut 'im loose an' left 'im – 'e was almost tore in two –
But he tried to follow after as a well-trained 'orse should do;
'E went an' fouled the limber, an' the Driver's Brother squeals:
'Pull up, pull up for *Snarleyow* – 'is head's between 'is 'eels!'

The Driver 'umped 'is shoulder, for the wheels was goin' round,
An' there ain't no 'Stop, conductor!' when a batt'ry's changin'
    ground;
Sez 'e: 'I broke the beggar in, an' very sad I feels,
But I couldn't pull up, not for *you* – your 'ead between your 'eels!'

'E 'adn't 'ardly spoke the word, before a droppin' shell
A little right the batt'ry an' between the sections fell;
An' when the smoke 'ad cleared away, before the limber wheels,
There lay the Driver's Brother with 'is 'ead between 'is 'eels.

Then sez the Driver's Brother, an' 'is words was very plain,
'For Gawd's own sake get over me, an' put me out o' pain.'
They saw 'is wounds was mortial, an' they judged that it was best,
So they took an' drove the limber straight across 'is back an' chest.

The Driver 'e give nothin' 'cept a little coughin' grunt,
But 'e swung 'is 'orses 'andsome when it came to 'Action Front!'
An' if one wheel was juicy, you may lay your Monday head
'Twas juicier for the niggers when the case begun to spread.

The moril of this story, it is plainly to be seen:
You 'avn't got no families when servin' of the Queen –
You 'avn't got no brothers, fathers, sisters, wives, or sons –
If you want to win your battles take an' work your bloomin' guns!
Down in the Infantry, nobody cares;
Down in the Cavalry, Colonel 'e swears;
But down in the lead with the wheel at the flog
Turns the bold Bombardier to a little whipped dog!

[First published in the *National Observer*, 29 November 1890, and then
collected in *Ballads and Barrack-Room Ballads* (1892).]

🎖   🎖   🎖

This is another well-known Kipling verse about the nobility of
two different martial traditions ranged against one another. It
is written in the style of a Scottish border ballad. The first two
lines of its last stanza are often quoted as evidence of Kipling's
pessimistic view that East and West could never come together.
In fact, when read in conjunction with the final two lines, the
message is much more positive.

THE BALLAD OF EAST AND WEST

OH, EAST IS EAST, *and West is West, and never the twain shall meet,*
Till Earth and Sky stand presently at God's great Judgment Seat;
But there is neither East nor West, Border, nor Breed, nor Birth,
When two strong men stand face to face, tho' they come from the ends of
   the earth!

Kamal is out with twenty men to raise the Border side,
And he has lifted the Colonel's mare that is the Colonel's pride:
He has lifted her out of the stable-door between the dawn and the
  day,
And turned the calkins upon her feet, and ridden her far away.

Then up and spoke the Colonel's son that led a troop of the
  Guides:
'Is there never a man of all my men can say where Kamal hides?'
Then up and spoke Mahommed Khan, the son of the Ressaldar,
'If ye know the track of the morning-mist, ye know where his
  pickets are.
At dusk he harries the Abazai – at dawn he is into Bonair,
But he must go by Fort Bukloh to his own place to fare,
So if ye gallop to Fort Bukloh as fast as a bird can fly,
By the favor of God ye may cut him off ere he win to the Tongue
  of Jagai,
But if he be passed the Tongue of Jagai, right swiftly turn ye then,
For the length and the breadth of that grisly plain is sown with
  Kamal's men.
There is rock to the left, and rock to the right, and low lean thorn
  between,
And ye may hear a breech-bolt snick where never a man is seen.'

The Colonel's son has taken a horse, and a raw rough dun was he,
With the mouth of a bell and the heart of Hell, and the head of the
  gallows-tree.
The Colonel's son to the Fort has won, they bid him stay to eat –
Who rides at the tail of a Border thief, he sits not long at his meat.
He's up and away from Fort Bukloh as fast as he can fly,
Till he was aware of his father's mare in the gut of the Tongue of
  Jagai,
Till he was aware of his father's mare with Kamal upon her back,
And when he could spy the white of her eye, he made the pistol
  crack.
He has fired once, he has fired twice, but the whistling ball went
  wide.
'Ye shoot like a soldier,' Kamal said. 'Show now if ye can ride.'
It's up and over the Tongue of Jagai, as blown dust-devils go,
The dun he fled like a stag of ten, but the mare like a barren doe.

The dun he leaned against the bit and slugged his head above,
But the red mare played with the snaffle-bars, as a maiden plays
    with a glove.
There was rock to the left and rock to the right, and low lean thorn
    between,
And thrice he heard a breech-bolt snick tho' never a man was seen.

They have ridden the low moon out of the sky, their hoofs drum
    up the dawn,
The dun he went like a wounded bull, but the mare like a new-
    roused fawn.
The dun he fell at a water-course – in a woful heap fell he,
And Kamal has turned the red mare back, and pulled the rider free.
He has knocked the pistol out of his hand – small room was there
    to strive,
''Twas only by favor of mine,' quoth he, 'ye rode so long alive:
There was not a rock for twenty mile, there was not a clump of tree,
But covered a man of my own men with his rifle cocked on his knee.
If I had raised my bridle-hand, as I have held it low,
The little jackals that flee so fast, were feasting all in a row:
If I had bowed my head on my breast, as I have held it high,
The kite that whistles above us now were gorged till she could not
    fly.'
Lightly answered the Colonel's son:– 'Do good to bird and beast,
But count who come for the broken meats before thou makest a
    feast.
If there should follow a thousand swords to carry my bones away,
Belike the price of a jackal's meal were more than a thief could pay.
They will feed their horse on the standing crop, their men on the
    garnered grain,
The thatch of the byres will serve their fires when all the cattle are
    slain.
But if thou thinkest the price be fair – thy brethren wait to sup,
The hound is kin to the jackal-spawn – howl, dog, and call them up!
And if thou thinkest the price be high, in steer and gear and stack,
Give me my father's mare again, and I'll fight my own way back!'

Kamal has gripped him by the hand and set him upon his feet.
'No talk shall be of dogs,' said he, 'when wolf and gray wolf meet.
May I eat dirt if thou hast hurt of me in deed or breath;

What dam of lances brought thee forth to jest at the dawn with
    Death?'
Lightly answered the Colonel's son: 'I hold by the blood of my clan:
Take up the mare for my father's gift – by God, she has carried a
    man!'
The red mare ran to the Colonel's son, and nuzzled against his
    breast,
'We be two strong men,' said Kamal then, 'but she loveth the
    younger best.
So she shall go with a lifter's dower, my turquoise-studded rein,
My broidered saddle and saddle-cloth, and silver stirrups twain.'
The Colonel's son a pistol drew and held it muzzle-end,
'Ye have taken the one from a foe,' said he; 'will ye take the mate
    from a friend?'
'A gift for a gift,' said Kamal straight; 'a limb for the risk of a limb.
Thy father has sent his son to me, I'll send my son to him!'
With that he whistled his only son, that dropped from a
    mountain-crest –
He trod the ling like a buck in spring, and he looked like a lance in
    rest.
'Now here is thy master,' Kamal said, 'who leads a troop of the
    Guides,
And thou must ride at his left side as shield on shoulder rides.
Till Death or I cut loose the tie, at camp and board and bed,
Thy life is his – thy fate it is to guard him with thy head.
So thou must eat the White Queen's meat, and all her foes are thine,
And thou must harry thy father's hold for the peace of the
    border-line.
And thou must make a trooper tough and hack thy way to power –
Belike they will raise thee to Ressaldar when I am hanged in
    Peshawur.'

They have looked each other between the eyes, and there they
    found no fault,
They have taken the Oath of the Brother-in-Blood on leavened
    bread and salt:
They have taken the Oath of the Brother-in-Blood on fire and
    fresh-cut sod,
On the hilt and the haft of the Khyber knife, and the Wondrous
    Names of God.

The Colonel's son he rides the mare and Kamal's boy the dun,
And two have come back to Fort Bukloh where there went forth
  but one.
And when they drew to the Quarter-Guard, full twenty swords
  flew clear –
There was not a man but carried his feud with the blood of the
  mountaineer.
'Ha' done! ha' done!' said the Colonel's son. 'Put up the steel at
  your sides!
Last night ye had struck at a Border thief – to-night 'tis a man of
  the Guides!'

Oh, East is East, and West is West, and never the two shall meet,
Till Earth and Sky stand presently at God's great Judgment Seat;
But there is neither East nor West, Border, nor Breed, nor Birth,
When two strong men stand face to face, tho' they come from the ends of
  the earth.

[First published in *Macmillan's Magazine*, December 1889, and then
collected in *Ballads and Barrack-Room Ballads* (1892).]

✠ ✠ ✠

**This story of the two young drummer boys who inspire a
demoralised British invasion force is generally taken to draw on
two battles in the Second Afghan War (1878–80) – one a victory
at Ahmed Khel in April 1880 and the other a crushing defeat at
Maiwand in July later that year.**

THE DRUMS OF THE FORE AND AFT

IN THE ARMY LIST they still stand as 'The Fore and Fit Princess
Hohenzollern-Sigmaringen-Anspach's Merther-Tydfilshire Own
Royal Loyal Light Infantry, Regimental District 329A,' but the
Army through all its barracks and canteens knows them now as
the 'Fore and Aft.' They may in time do something that shall make
their new title honourable, but at present they are bitterly ashamed,
and the man who calls them 'Fore and Aft' does so at the risk of the
head which is on his shoulders.

Two words breathed into the stables of a certain Cavalry Regiment will bring the men out into the streets with belts and mops and bad language; but a whisper of 'Fore and Aft' will bring out this regiment with rifles.

Their one excuse is that they came again and did their best to finish the job in style. But for a time all their world knows that they were openly beaten, whipped, dumb-cowed, shaking and afraid. The men know it; their officers know it; the Horse Guards know it, and when the next war comes the enemy will know it also. There are two or three regiments of the Line that have a black mark against their names which they will then wipe out; and it will be excessively inconvenient for the troops upon whom they do their wiping.

The courage of the British soldier is officially supposed to be above proof, and, as a general rule, it is so. The exceptions are decently shovelled out of sight, only to be referred to in the freshest of unguarded talk that occasionally swamps a Mess-table at midnight. Then one hears strange and horrible stories of men not following their officers, of orders being given by those who had no right to give them, and of disgrace that, but for the standing luck of the British Army, might have ended in brilliant disaster. These are unpleasant stories to listen to, and the Messes tell them under their breath, sitting by the big wood fires, and the young officer bows his head and thinks to himself, please God, his men shall never behave unhandily.

The British soldier is not altogether to be blamed for occasional lapses; but this verdict he should not know. A moderately intelligent General will waste six months in mastering the craft of the particular war that he may be waging; a Colonel may utterly misunderstand the capacity of his regiment for three months after it has taken the field, and even a Company Commander may err and be deceived as to the temper and temperament of his own handful: wherefore the soldier, and the soldier of to-day more particularly, should not be blamed for falling back. He should be shot or hanged afterwards – to encourage the others; but he should not be vilified in newspapers, for that is want of tact and waste of space.

He has, let us say, been in the service of the Empress for, perhaps, four years. He will leave in another two years. He has no inherited morals, and four years are not sufficient to drive toughness into his fibre, or to teach him how holy a thing is his Regiment. He wants to drink, he wants to enjoy himself – in India he wants to save money – and he does not in the least like getting hurt. He has received just sufficient education to make him understand half the purport of the orders he receives, and to speculate on the nature of clean, incised, and shattering wounds. Thus, if he is told to deploy under fire preparatory to an attack, he knows that he runs a very great risk of being killed while he is deploying, and suspects that he is being thrown away to gain ten minutes' time. He may either deploy with desperate swiftness, or he may shuffle, or bunch, or break, according to the discipline under which he has lain for four years.

Armed with imperfect knowledge, cursed with the rudiments of an imagination, hampered by the intense selfishness of the lower classes, and unsupported by any regimental associations, this young man is suddenly introduced to an enemy who in eastern lands is always ugly, generally tall and hairy, and frequently noisy. If he looks to the right and the left and sees old soldiers – men of twelve years' service, who, he knows, know what they are about – taking a charge, rush, or demonstration without embarrassment, he is consoled and applies his shoulder to the butt of his rifle with a stout heart. His peace is the greater if he hears a senior, who has taught him his soldiering and broken his head on occasion, whispering: 'They'll shout and carry on like this for five minutes. Then they'll rush in, and then we've got 'em by the short hairs!'

But, on the other hand, if he sees only men of his own term of service, turning white and playing with their triggers and saying: 'What the Hell's up now?' while the Company Commanders are sweating into their sword-hilts and shouting: 'Front rank, fix bayonets. Steady there – steady! Sight for three hundred – no, for five! Lie down, all! Steady! Front rank kneel!' and so forth, he becomes unhappy, and grows acutely miserable when he hears a comrade turn over with the rattle of fire-irons falling into the fender, and the grunt of a pole-axed ox. If he can be moved about a little and allowed to watch the effect of his own fire on the enemy he feels merrier, and may be then worked up to the blind passion of fighting, which is, contrary to general belief, controlled by a chilly Devil and shakes men like ague. If he is not moved about, and begins to feel cold at the pit of the stomach, and in that crisis is badly mauled and hears orders that were never given, he will break, and he will break badly, and of all things under the light of the Sun there is nothing more terrible than a broken British regiment. When the worst comes to the worst and the panic is really epidemic, the men must be e'en let go, and the Company Commanders had better escape to the enemy and stay there for safety's sake. If they can be made to come again they are not pleasant men to meet; because they will not break twice.

About thirty years from this date, when we have succeeded in half-educating everything that wears trousers, our Army will be a beautifully unreliable machine. It will know too much and it will do too little. Later still, when all men are at the mental level of the officer of to-day, it will sweep the earth. Speaking roughly, you must employ either blackguards or gentlemen, or, best of all, blackguards commanded by gentlemen, to do butcher's work with efficiency and despatch. The ideal soldier should, of course, think for himself – the '*Pocket-book*' says so. Unfortunately, to attain this virtue, he has to pass through the phase of thinking *of* himself, and that is misdirected genius. A blackguard may be slow to think for himself, but he is genuinely anxious to kill, and a little punishment teaches him how to guard his own skin and perforate another's. A powerfully prayerful Highland Regiment, officered by rank Presbyterians, is, perhaps, one degree more terrible in action than a hard-bitten thousand of irresponsible Irish ruffians led by most improper young unbelievers. But these things prove the rule – which is that the midway men are not to be trusted alone. They have ideas about the value of life and an upbringing that has not taught them to go on and take the chances. They are carefully unprovided with a backing of comrades who have been shot over, and until that backing is re-introduced, as a great many Regimental Commanders intend it shall be, they are more liable to disgrace themselves than the size of the Empire or the dignity of the Army allows. Their officers are as good as good can be, because their training begins early, and God has arranged that a clean-run youth of the British middle classes shall, in the matter of backbone, brains, and bowels, surpass all other youths. For this reason a child of eighteen will stand up, doing nothing, with a tin sword in his hand and joy in his heart until he is dropped. If he dies, he dies like a gentleman. If he lives, he writes Home that he has been 'potted,' 'sniped,' 'chipped,' or 'cut over,' and sits down to besiege Government for a wound-gratuity until the next little war breaks out, when he perjures himself before a Medical Board, blarneys his Colonel, burns incense round his Adjutant, and is allowed to go to the Front once more.

Which homily brings me directly to a brace of the most finished little fiends that ever banged drum or tootled fife in the Band of

a British Regiment. They ended their sinful career by open and
flagrant mutiny and were shot for it. Their names were Jakin and
Lew – Piggy Lew – and they were bold, bad drummer-boys, both
of them frequently birched by the Drum-Major of the Fore and
Aft. – Jakin was a stunted child of fourteen, and Lew was about
the same age. When not looked after, they smoked and drank.
They swore habitually after the manner of the Barrack-room,
which is cold swearing and comes from between clenched teeth,
and they fought religiously once a week. Jakin had sprung from
some London gutter, and may or may not have passed through
Dr. Barnardo's hands ere he arrived at the dignity of drummer-
boy. Lew could remember nothing except the Regiment and the
delight of listening to the Band from his earliest years. He hid
somewhere in his grimy little soul a genuine love for music,
and was most mistakenly furnished with the head of a cherub:
insomuch that beautiful ladies who watched the Regiment in
church were wont to speak of him as a 'darling.' They never
heard his vitriolic comments on their manners and morals, as he
walked back to barracks with the Band and matured fresh causes
of offence against Jakin.

The other drummer-boys hated both lads on account of their
illogical conduct. Jakin might be pounding Lew, or Lew might
be rubbing Jakin's head in the dirt, but any attempt at aggression
on the part of an outsider was met by the combined forces of Lew
and Jakin; and the consequences were painful. The boys were the
Ishmaels of the corps, but wealthy Ishmaels, for they sold battles
in alternate weeks for the sport of the barracks when they were not
pitted against other boys; and thus amassed money.

On this particular day there was dissension in the camp. They
had just been convicted afresh of smoking, which is bad for little
boys who use plug-tobacco, and Lew's contention was that Jakin
had 'stunk so 'orrid bad from keepin' the pipe in pocket,' that
he and he alone was responsible for the birching they were both
tingling under.

'I tell you I 'id the pipe back o' barracks,' said Jakin pacifically.

'You're a bloomin' liar,' said Lew without heat.

'You're a bloomin' little barstard,' said Jakin, strong in the
knowledge that his own ancestry was unknown.

Now there is one word in the extended vocabulary of barrack-
room abuse that cannot pass without comment. You may call a

man a thief and risk nothing. You may even call him a coward without finding more than a boot whiz past your ear, but you must not call a man a bastard unless you are prepared to prove it on his front teeth.

'You might ha' kep' that till I wasn't so sore,' said Lew sorrowfully, dodging round Jakin's guard.

'I'll make you sorer,' said Jakin genially, and got home on Lew's alabaster forehead. All would have gone well and this story, as the books say, would never have been written, had not his evil fate prompted the Bazar-Sergeant's son, a long, employless man of five-and-twenty, to put in an appearance after the first round. He was eternally in need of money, and knew that the boys had silver.

'Fighting again,' said he. 'I'll report you to my father, and he'll report you to the Colour-Sergeant.'

'What's that to you?' said Jakin with an unpleasant dilation of the nostrils.

'Oh! nothing to *me*. You'll get into trouble, and you've been up too often to afford that.'

'What the Hell do you know about what we've done?' asked Lew the Seraph. '*You* aren't in the Army, you lousy, cadging civilian.'

He closed in on the man's left flank.

'Jes' 'cause you find two gentlemen settlin' their diff'rences with their fistes you stick in your ugly nose where you aren't wanted. Run 'ome to your 'arf-caste slut of a Ma – or we'll give you what-for,' said Jakin.

The man attempted reprisals by knocking the boys' heads together. The scheme would have succeeded had not Jakin punched him vehemently in the stomach, or had Lew refrained from kicking his shins. They fought together, bleeding and breathless, for half an hour, and, after heavy punishment, triumphantly pulled down their opponent as terriers pull down a jackal.

'Now,' gasped Jakin, 'I'll give you what-for.' He proceeded to pound the man's features while Lew stamped on the outlying portions of his anatomy. Chivalry is not a strong point in the composition of the average drummer-boy. He fights, as do his betters, to make his mark.

Ghastly was the ruin that escaped, and awful was the wrath of the Bazar-Sergeant. Awful too was the scene in Orderly-room when the two reprobates appeared to answer the charge of half-murdering a 'civilian.' The Bazar-Sergeant thirsted for a criminal action, and his son lied. The boys stood to attention while the black clouds of evidence accumulated.

'You little devils are more trouble than the rest of the Regiment put together,' said the Colonel angrily. 'One might as well admonish thistledown, and I can't well put you in cells or under stoppages. You must be birched again.'

'Beg y' pardon, Sir. Can't we say nothin' in our own defence, Sir?' shrilled Jakin.

'Hey! What? Are you going to argue with *me*?' said the Colonel.

'No, Sir,' said Lew. 'But if a man come to you, Sir, and said he was going to report you, Sir, for 'aving a bit of a turn-up with a friend, Sir, an' wanted to get money out o' *you*, Sir —'

The Orderly-room exploded in a roar of laughter. 'Well?' said the Colonel.

'That was what that measly *jarnwar* there did, Sir, and 'e'd 'a' *done* it, Sir, if we 'adn't prevented 'im. We didn't 'it 'im much, Sir. 'E 'adn't no manner o' right to interfere with us, Sir. I don't mind bein' birched by the Drum-Major, Sir, nor yet reported by any *Corp*'ral, but I'm – but I don't think it's fair, Sir, for a civilian to come an' talk over a man in the Army.'

A second shout of laughter shook the Orderly-room, but the Colonel was grave.

'What sort of characters have these boys?' he asked of the Regimental Sergeant-Major.

'Accordin' to the Bandmaster, Sir,' returned that revered official – the only soul in the Regiment whom the boys feared – 'they do everything *but* lie, Sir.'

'Is it like we'd go for that man for fun, Sir?' said Lew, pointing to the plaintiff.

'Oh, admonished – admonished!' said the Colonel testily, and when the boys had gone he read the Bazar-Sergeant's son a lecture on the sin of unprofitable meddling, and gave orders that the Bandmaster should keep the Drums in better discipline.

'If either of you come to practice again with so much as a scratch on your two ugly little faces,' thundered the Bandmaster, 'I'll tell the Drum-Major to take the skin off your backs. Understand that, you young devils.'

Then he repented of his speech for just the length of time that Lew, looking like a seraph in red worsted embellishments, took the place of one of the trumpets – in hospital – and rendered the echo of a battle-piece. Lew certainly was a musician, and had often in his more exalted moments expressed a yearning to master every instrument of the Band.

'There's nothing to prevent your becoming a Bandmaster, Lew,' said the Bandmaster, who had composed waltzes of his own, and worked day and night in the interests of the Band.

'What did he say?' demanded Jakin after practice.

'Said I might be a bloomin' Bandmaster, an' be asked in to 'ave a glass o' sherry wine on Mess-nights.'

'Ho! Said you might be a bloomin' noncombatant, did 'e! That's just about wot 'e would say. When I've put in my boy's service – it's a bloomin' shame that doesn't count for pension – I'll take on as a privit. Then I'll be a Lance in a year – knowin' what I know about the ins an' outs o' things. In three years I'll be a bloomin' Sergeant. I won't marry then, not I! I'll 'old on and learn the orf'cers' ways an' apply for exchange into a reg'ment that doesn't know all about me. Then I'll be a bloomin' orf'cer. Then I'll ask you to 'ave a glass o' sherry wine, *Mister* Lew, an' you'll bloomin' well 'ave to stay in the hanty-room while the Mess-Sergeant brings it to your dirty 'ands.'

'S'pose I'm going to be a Bandmaster? Not I, quite. I'll be a orf'cer too. There's nothin' like takin' to a thing an' stickin' to it, the Schoolmaster says. The Reg'ment don't go 'ome for another seven years. I'll be a Lance then or near to.'

Thus the boys discussed their futures, and conducted themselves piously for a week. That is to say, Lew started a flirtation with the Colour-Sergeant's daughter, aged thirteen – 'not,' as he explained to Jakin, 'with any intention o' matrimony, but by way o' keep in' my 'and in.' And the black-haired Cris Delighan enjoyed that flirtation more than previous ones, and the other drummer-boys raged furiously together, and Jakin preached sermons on the dangers of bein' tangled along o' petticoats.

But neither love nor virtue would have held Lew long in the paths of propriety had not the rumour gone abroad that the Regiment was to be sent on active service, to take part in a war which, for the sake of brevity, we will call 'The War of the Lost Tribes.'

The barracks had the rumour almost before the Mess-room, and of all the nine hundred men in barracks, not ten had seen a shot fired in anger. The Colonel had, twenty years ago, assisted at a Frontier expedition; one of the Majors had seen service at the Cape; a confirmed deserter in E Company had helped to clear streets in

Ireland; but that was all. The Regiment had been put by for many years. The overwhelming mass of its rank and file had from three to four years' service; the non-commissioned officers were under thirty years old; and men and sergeants alike had forgotten to speak of the stories written in brief upon the Colours – the New Colours that had been formally blessed by an Archbishop in England ere the Regiment came away.

They wanted to go to the Front – they were enthusiastically anxious to go – but they had no knowledge of what war meant, and there was none to tell them. They were an educated regiment, the percentage of school-certificates in their ranks was high, and most of the men could do more than read and write. They had been recruited in loyal observance of the territorial idea; but they themselves had no notion of that idea. They were made up of drafts from an over-populated manufacturing district. The system had put flesh and muscle upon their small bones, but it could not put heart into the sons of those who for generations had done overmuch work for overscanty pay, had sweated in drying-rooms, stooped over looms, coughed among white-lead, and shivered on lime-barges. The men had found food and rest in the Army, and now they were going to fight 'niggers' – people who ran away if you shook a stick at them. Wherefore they cheered lustily when the rumour ran, and the shrewd, clerkly non-commissioned officers speculated on the chances of *batta* and of saving their pay. At Headquarters men said: 'The Fore and Fit have never been under fire within the last generation. Let us, therefore, break them in easily by setting them to guard lines of communication.' And this would have been done but for the fact that British Regiments were wanted – badly wanted – at the Front, and there were doubtful Native Regiments that could fill the minor duties. 'Brigade 'em with two strong Regiments,' said Headquarters. 'They may be knocked about a bit, but they'll learn their business before they come through. Nothing like a night-alarm and a little cutting-up of stragglers to make a Regiment smart in the field. Wait till they've had half a dozen sentries' throats cut.'

The Colonel wrote with delight that the temper of his men was excellent, that the Regiment was all that could be wished, and as sound as a bell. The Majors smiled with a sober joy, and the subalterns waltzed in pairs down the Mess-room after dinner, and nearly shot themselves at revolver-practice. But there was consternation in the hearts of Jakin and Lew. What was to be done with the Drums? Would the Band go to the Front? How many of the Drums would accompany the Regiment?

They took counsel together, sitting in a tree and smoking.

'It's more than a bloomin' toss-up they'll leave us be'ind at the Depôt with the women. You'll like that,' said Jakin sarcastically.

''Cause o' Cris, y' mean? Wot's a woman, or a 'ole bloomin' Depôt o' women, 'longside o' the chanst of field-service? You know I'm as keen on goin' as you,' said Lew.

'Wish I was a bloomin' bugler,' said Jakin sadly. 'They'll take Tom Kidd along, that I can plaster a wall with, an' like as not they won't take us.'

'Then let's go an' make Tom Kidd so bloomin' sick 'e can't bugle no more. You 'old 'is 'ands an' I'll kick him,' said Lew, wriggling on the branch.

'That ain't no good neither. We ain't the sort o' characters to presoom on our rep'tations – they're bad. If they have the Band at the Depôt we don't go, and no error *there*. If they take the Band we may get cast for medical unfitness. Are you medical fit, Piggy?' said Jakin, digging Lew in the ribs with force.

'Yus,' said Lew with an oath. 'The Doctor says your 'eart's weak through smokin' on an empty stummick. Throw a chest an' I'll try yer.'

Jakin threw out his chest, which Lew smote with all his might. Jakin turned very pale, gasped, crowed, screwed up his eyes, and said – 'That's all right.'

'You'll do,' said Lew. 'I've 'eard o' men dying when you 'it 'em fair on the breastbone.'

'Don't bring us no nearer goin', though,' said Jakin. 'Do you know where we're ordered?'

'Gawd knows, an' 'E won't split on a pal. Somewheres up to the Front to kill Paythans – hairy big beggars that turn you inside out if they get 'old o' you. They say their women are good-looking, too.'

'Any loot?' asked the abandoned Jakin.

'Not a bloomin' anna, they say, unless you dig up the ground an' see what the niggers 'ave 'id. They're a poor lot.' Jakin stood upright on the branch and gazed across the plain.

'Lew,' said he, 'there's the Colonel coming. 'Colonel's a good old beggar. Let's go an' talk to 'im.'

Lew nearly fell out of the tree at the audacity of the suggestion. Like Jakin he feared not God, neither regarded he Man, but there are limits even to the audacity of a drummer-boy, and to speak to a Colonel was—

But Jakin had slid down the trunk and doubled in the direction of the Colonel. That officer was walking wrapped in thought and visions of a C.B. – yes, even a K.C.B., for had he not at command one of the best Regiments of the Line – the Fore and Fit? And he was aware of two small boys charging down upon him. Once before it had been solemnly reported to him that 'the Drums were in a state of mutiny,' Jakin and Lew being the ringleaders. This looked like an organised conspiracy. The boys halted at twenty yards, walked to the regulation four paces, and saluted together, each as well set-up as a ramrod and little taller.

The Colonel was in a genial mood; the boys appeared very forlorn and unprotected on the desolate plain, and one of them was handsome.

'Well!' said the Colonel, recognising them. 'Are you going to pull me down in the open? I'm sure I never interfere with you, even though' – he sniffed suspiciously – 'you have been smoking.'

It was time to strike while the iron was hot. Their hearts beat tumultuously.

'Beg y' pardon, Sir,' began Jakin. 'The Reg'ment's ordered on active service, Sir?'

'So I believe,' said the Colonel courteously.

'Is the Band goin', Sir?' said both together. Then, without pause, 'We're goin', Sir, ain't we?'

'You!' said the Colonel, stepping back the more fully to take in the two small figures. 'You! You'd die in the first march.'

'No, we wouldn't, Sir. We can march with the Reg'ment anywheres – p'rade an' anywhere else,' said Jakin.

'If Tom Kidd goes 'e'll shut up like a clasp-knife,' said Lew. 'Tom 'as very-close veins in both 'is legs, Sir.'

'Very how much?'

'Very-close veins, Sir. That's why they swells after long p'rade, Sir. If 'e can go, we can go, Sir.'

Again the Colonel looked at them long and intently.

'Yes, the Band is going,' he said as gravely as though he had been addressing a brother officer. 'Have you any parents, either of you two?'

'No, Sir,' rejoicingly from Lew and Jakin. 'We're both orphans, Sir. There's no one to be considered of on our account, Sir.'

'You poor little sprats, and you want to go up to the Front with the Regiment, do you? Why?'

'I've wore the Queen's Uniform for two years,' said Jakin. 'It's very 'ard, Sir, that a man don't get no recompense for doin' of 'is dooty, Sir.'

'An' – an' if I don't go, Sir,' interrupted Lew, 'the Bandmaster 'e says 'e'll catch an' make a bloo— a blessed musician o' me, Sir. Before I've seen any service, Sir.'

The Colonel made no answer for a long time. Then he said quietly: 'If you're passed by the Doctor I dare say you can go. I shouldn't smoke if I were you.'

The boys saluted and disappeared. The Colonel walked home and told the story to his wife, who nearly cried over it. The Colonel was well pleased. If that was the temper of the children, what would not the men do?

Jakin and Lew entered the boys' barrack-room with great stateliness, and refused to hold any conversation with their comrades for at least ten minutes. Then, bursting with pride, Jakin drawled: 'I've bin intervooin' the Colonel. Good old beggar is the Colonel. Says I to 'im, "Colonel," says I, "let me go to the Front, along o' the Reg'ment." – "To the Front you shall go," says 'e, "an' I only wish there was more like you among the dirty little devils that bang the bloomin' drums." Kidd, if you throw your 'courtrements at me for tellin' you the truth to your own advantage, your legs'll swell.'

None the less there was a Battle-Royal in the barrack-room, for the boys were consumed with envy and hate, and neither Jakin nor Lew behaved in conciliatory wise.

'I'm goin' out to say adoo to my girl,' said Lew, to cap the climax. 'Don't none o' you touch my kit because it's wanted for active service; me bein' specially invited to go by the Colonel.'

He strolled forth and whistled in the clump of trees at the back of the Married Quarters till Cris came to him, and, the preliminary kisses being given and taken, Lew began to explain the situation.

'I'm goin' to the Front with the Reg'ment,' he said valiantly.

'Piggy, you're a little liar,' said Cris, but her heart misgave her, for Lew was not in the habit of lying.

'Liar yourself, Cris,' said Lew, slipping an arm round her. 'I'm goin'. When the Reg'ment marches out you'll see me with 'em, all galliant and gay. Give us another kiss, Cris, on the strength of it.'

'If you'd on'y a-stayed at the Depôt – where you *ought* to ha' bin – you could get as many of 'em as – as you dam please,' whimpered Cris, putting up her mouth.

'It's 'ard, Cris. I grant you it's 'ard, But what's a man to do? If I'd a-stayed at the Depôt, you wouldn't think anything of me.'

'Like as not, but I'd 'ave you with me, Piggy. An' all the thinkin' in the world isn't like kissin'.'

'An' all the kissin' in the world isn't like 'avin' a medal to wear on the front o' your coat.'

'*You* won't get no medal.'

'Oh, yus, I shall though. Me an' Jakin are the only acting-drummers that'll be took along. All the rest is full men, an' we'll get our medals with them.'

'They might ha' taken anybody but you, Piggy. You'll get killed – you're so venturesome. Stay with me, Piggy darlin', down at the Depôt, an' I'll love you true, for ever.'

'Ain't you goin' to do that now, Cris? You said you was.'

'O' course I am, but th' other's more comfortable. Wait till you've growed a bit, Piggy. You aren't no taller than me now.'

'I've bin in the Army for two years, an' I'm not goin' to get out of a chanst o' seein' service, an' don't you try to make me do so. I'll come back, Cris, an' when I take on as a man I'll marry you – marry you when I'm a Lance.'

'Promise, Piggy.'

Lew reflected on the future as arranged by Jakin a short time previously, but Cris's mouth was very near to his own.

'I promise, s'elp me Gawd!' said he.

Cris slid an arm round his neck.

'I won't 'old you back no more, Piggy. Go away an' get your medal, an' I'll make you a new button-bag as nice as I know how,' she whispered.

'Put some o' your 'air into it, Cris, an' I'll keep it in my pocket so long's I'm alive.'

Then Cris wept anew, and the interview ended. Public feeling among the drummer-boys rose to fever pitch, and the lives of Jakin and Lew became unenviable. Not only had they been permitted to enlist two years before the regulation boy's age – fourteen – but, by virtue, it seemed, of their extreme youth, they were allowed to go to the Front – which thing had not happened to acting-drummers within the knowledge of boy. The Band which was to accompany the Regiment had been cut down to the regulation twenty men, the surplus returning to the ranks. Jakin and Lew were attached to the Band as supernumeraries, though they would much have preferred being company buglers.

'Don't matter much,' said Jakin after the medical inspection. 'Be thankful that we're 'lowed to go at all. The Doctor 'e said that if we could stand what we took from the Bazar-Sergeant's son we'd stand pretty nigh anything.'

'Which we will,' said Lew, looking tenderly at the ragged and ill-made housewife that Cris had given him, with a lock of her hair worked into a sprawling 'L' upon the cover.

'It was the best I could,' she sobbed. 'I wouldn't let mother nor the Sergeant's tailor 'elp me. Keep it always, Piggy, an' remember I love you true.'

They marched to the railway station, nine hundred and sixty strong, and every soul in cantonments turned out to see them go. The drummers gnashed their teeth at Jakin and Lew marching with the Band, the married women wept upon the platform, and the Regiment cheered its noble self black in the face.

'A nice level lot,' said the Colonel to the Second-in-Command as they watched the first four companies entraining.

'Fit to do anything,' said the Second-in-Command enthusiastically. 'But it seems to me they're a thought too young and tender for the work in hand. It's bitter cold up at the Front now.'

'They're sound enough,' said the Colonel. 'We must take our chance of sick casualties.'

So they went northward, ever northward, past droves and droves of camels, armies of camp-followers, and legions of laden mules, the throng thickening day by day, till with a shriek the train pulled up at a hopelessly congested junction where six lines of temporary track accommodated six forty-waggon trains; where whistles blew, Babus sweated, and Commissariat officers swore from dawn till far into the night, amid the wind-driven chaff of the fodder-bales and the lowing of a thousand steers.

'Hurry up – you're badly wanted at the Front,' was the message that greeted the Fore and Aft, and the occupants of the Red Cross carriages told the same tale.

''Tisn't so much the bloomin' fightin',' gasped a head-bound trooper of Hussars to a knot of admiring Fore and Afts. ''Tisn't so much the bloomin' fightin', though there's enough o' that. It's the bloomin' food an' the bloomin' climate. Frost all night 'cept when it hails, and b'iling sun all day, and the water stinks fit to knock you down. I got my 'ead chipped like a egg; I've got pneumonia too, an' my guts is all out o' order. 'Tain't no bloomin' picnic in those parts, I can tell you.'

'Wot are the niggers like?' demanded a private.

'There's some prisoners in that train yonder. Go an' look at 'em. They're the aristocracy o' the country. The common folk are a dashed sight uglier. If you want to know what they fight with, reach under my seat an' pull out the long knife that's there.'

They dragged out and beheld for the first time the grim, bone-handled, triangular Afghan knife. It was almost as long as Lew.

'That's the thing to jint ye,' said the trooper feebly. 'It can take off a man's arm at the shoulder as easy as slicing butter. I halved the beggar that used that un, but there's more of his likes up above. They don't understand thrustin', but they're devils to slice.'

The men strolled across the tracks to inspect the Afghan prisoners. They were unlike any 'niggers' that the Fore and Aft had ever met – these huge, black-haired, scowling sons of the Beni-Israel. As the men stared the Afghans spat freely and muttered one to another with lowered eyes.

'My eyes! Wot awful swine!' said Jakin, who was in the rear of the procession. 'Say, ole man, how you got *puckrowed*, eh? *Kiswasti* you wasn't hanged for your ugly face, hey?'

The tallest of the company turned, his leg-irons clanking at the movement, and stared at the boy. 'See!' he cried to his fellows in Pushto. 'They send children against us. What a people, and what fools!'

'*Hya*,' said Jakin, nodding his head cheerily. 'You go down-country. *Khana* get, *peenikapanee* get – live like a bloomin' Raja *ke marfik*. That's a better *bandobust* than baynit get it in your innards. Good-bye, ole man. Take care o' your beautiful figure-'ead, an' try to look *kushy*.'

The men laughed and fell in for their first march, when they began to realise that a soldier's life is not all beer and skittles. They were much impressed with the size and bestial ferocity of the niggers whom they had now learned to call 'Paythans,' and more with the exceeding discomfort of their own surroundings. Twenty old soldiers in the corps would have taught them how to make themselves moderately snug at night, but they had no old soldiers, and, as the troops on the line of march said, 'they lived like pigs.' They learned the heart-breaking cussedness of camp-kitchens and camels and the depravity of an E.P. tent and a wither-wrung mule. They studied animalculae in water, and developed a few cases of dysentery in their study.

At the end of their third march they were disagreeably surprised by the arrival in their camp of a hammered iron slug which, fired from a steady rest at seven hundred yards, flicked out the brains of a private seated by the fire. This robbed them of their peace for a night, and was the beginning of a long-range fire carefully calculated to that end. In the daytime they saw nothing except an unpleasant puff of smoke from a crag above the line of march. At night there were distant spurts of flame and occasional casualties, which set the whole camp blazing into the gloom and, occasionally, into opposite tents. Then they swore vehemently and vowed that this was magnificent but not war.

Indeed it was not. The Regiment could not halt for reprisals against the sharpshooters of the country-side. Its duty was to go forward and make connection with the Scotch and Gurkha troops with which it was brigaded. The Afghans knew this, and knew too, after their first tentative shots, that they were dealing with a raw regiment. Thereafter they devoted themselves to the task of keeping the Fore and Aft on the strain. Not for anything would they have taken equal liberties with a seasoned corps – with the wicked little Gurkhas, whose delight it was to lie out in the open on a dark night and stalk their stalkers – with the terrible big men dressed in women's clothes, who could be heard praying to their God in the night-watches, and whose peace of mind no amount of 'sniping' could shake – or with those vile Sikhs, who marched so ostentatiously unprepared and who dealt out such grim reward to those who tried to profit by that unpreparedness. This white regiment was different – quite different. It slept like a hog, and, like a hog, charged in every direction when it was roused. Its sentries walked with a footfall that could be heard for a quarter of a mile; would fire at anything that moved – even a driven donkey – and when they had once fired, could be scientifically 'rushed' and laid out a horror and an offence against the morning sun. Then there were camp-followers who straggled and could be cut up without fear. Their shrieks would disturb the white boys, and the loss of their services would inconvenience them sorely.

Thus, at every march, the hidden enemy became bolder and the Regiment writhed and twisted under attacks it could not avenge. The crowning triumph was a sudden night-rush ending in the cutting of many tent-ropes, the collapse of the sodden canvas, and a glorious knifing of the men who struggled and kicked below. It was a great deed, neatly carried out, and it shook the already shaken nerves of the Fore and Aft. All the courage that they had been required to exercise up to this point was the 'two o'clock in the morning courage'; and, so far, they had only succeeded in shooting their comrades and losing their sleep.

Sullen, discontented, cold, savage, sick, with their uniforms dulled and unclean, the Fore and Aft joined their Brigade.

'I hear you had a tough time of it coming up,' said the Brigadier. But when he saw the hospital-sheets his face fell.

'This is bad,' said he to himself. 'They're as rotten as sheep.' And aloud to the Colonel – 'I'm afraid we can't spare you just yet. We want all we have, else I should have given you ten days to recover in.'

The Colonel winced. 'On my honour, Sir,' he returned, 'there is not the least necessity to think of sparing us. My men have been rather mauled and upset without a fair return. They only want to go in somewhere where they can see what's before them.'

'Can't say I think much of the Fore and Fit,' said the Brigadier in confidence to his Brigade-Major. 'They've lost all their soldiering, and, by the trim of them, might have marched through the country from the other side. A more fagged-out set of men I never put eyes on.'

'Oh, they'll improve as the work goes on. The parade gloss has been rubbed off a little, but they'll put on field polish before long,' said the Brigade-Major. 'They've been mauled, and they don't quite understand it.'

They did not. All the hitting was on one side, and it was cruelly hard hitting with accessories that made them sick. There was also the real sickness that laid hold of a strong man and dragged him howling to the grave. Worst of all, their officers knew just as little of the country as the men themselves, and looked as if they did. The Fore and Aft were in a thoroughly unsatisfactory condition, but they believed that all would be well if they could once get a fair go-in at the enemy. Pot-shots up and down the valleys were unsatisfactory, and the bayonet never seemed to get a chance. Perhaps it was as well, for a long-limbed Afghan with a knife had a reach of eight feet, and could carry away lead that would disable three Englishmen.

The Fore and Aft would like some rifle-practice at the enemy – all seven hundred rifles blazing together. That wish showed the mood of the men.

The Gurkhas walked into their camp, and in broken, barrack-room English strove to fraternise with them: offered them pipes of tobacco and stood them treat at the canteen. But the Fore and Aft, not knowing much of the nature of the Gurkhas, treated them as they would treat any other 'niggers,' and the little men in green trotted back to their firm friends the Highlanders, and with many grins confided to them: 'That dam white regiment no dam use. Sulky – ugh! Dirty – ugh! *Hya*, any tot for Johnny?' Whereat the Highlanders smote the Gurkhas as to the head, and told them not to vilify a British Regiment, and the Gurkhas grinned cavernously, for the Highlanders were their elder brothers and entitled to the privileges of kinship. The common soldier who touches a Gurkha is more than likely to have his head sliced open.

Three days later the Brigadier arranged a battle according to the rules of war and the peculiarity of the Afghan temperament. The enemy were massing in inconvenient strength among the hills, and the moving of many green standards warned him that the tribes were 'up' in aid of the Afghan regular troops. A squadron and a half of Bengal Lancers represented the available Cavalry, and two screw-guns, borrowed from a column thirty miles away, the Artillery at the General's disposal.

'If they stand, as I've a very strong notion that they will, I fancy we shall see an infantry fight that will be worth watching,' said the Brigadier. 'We'll do it in style. Each regiment shall be played into action by its Band, and we'll hold the Cavalry in reserve.'

'For *all* the reserve?' somebody asked.

'For all the reserve; because we're going to crumple them up,' said the Brigadier, who was an extraordinary Brigadier, and did not believe in the value of a reserve when dealing with Asiatics. Indeed, when you come to think of it, had the British Army consistently waited for reserves in all its little affairs, the boundaries of Our Empire would have stopped at Brighton beach.

The battle was to be a glorious battle.

The three regiments debouching from three separate gorges, after duly crowning the heights above, were to converge from the centre, left, and right upon what we will call the Afghan army, then stationed towards the lower extremity of a flat-bottomed valley. Thus it will be seen that three sides of the valley practically belonged to the English, while the fourth was strictly Afghan property. In the event of defeat the Afghans had the rocky hills to fly to, where the fire from the guerrilla tribes in aid would cover their retreat. In the event of victory these same tribes would rush down and lend their weight to the rout of the British.

The screw-guns were to shell the head of each Afghan rush that was made in close formation, and the Cavalry, held in reserve in the right valley, were to gently stimulate the break-up which would follow on the combined attack. The Brigadier, sitting upon a rock overlooking the valley, would watch the battle unrolled at his feet. The Fore and Aft would debouch from the central gorge, the Gurkhas from the left, and the Highlanders from the right, for the reason that the left flank of the enemy seemed as though it required the most hammering. It was not every day that an Afghan force would take ground in the open, and the Brigadier was resolved to make the most of it.

'If we only had a few more men,' he said plaintively, 'we could surround the creatures and crumple 'em up thoroughly. As it is, I'm afraid we can only cut them up as they run. It's a great pity.'

The Fore and Aft had enjoyed unbroken peace for five days, and were beginning, in spite of dysentery, to recover their nerve. But they were not happy, for they did not know the work in hand, and had they known, would not have known how to do it. Throughout those five days in which old soldiers might have taught them the craft of the game, they discussed together their misadventures in the past – how such a one was alive at dawn and dead ere the dusk, and with what shrieks and struggles such another had given up his soul under the Afghan knife. Death was a new and horrible thing to the sons of mechanics who were used to die decently of zymotic disease; and their careful conservation in barracks had done nothing to make them look upon it with less dread.

Very early in the dawn the bugles began to blow, and the Fore and Aft, filled with a misguided enthusiasm, turned out without waiting for a cup of coffee and a biscuit; and were rewarded by being kept under arms in the cold while the other regiments leisurely prepared for the fray. All the world knows that it is ill taking the breeks off a Highlander. It is much iller to try to make him stir unless he is convinced of the necessity for haste.

The Fore and Aft waited, leaning upon their rifles and listening to the protests of their empty stomachs. The Colonel did his best to remedy the default of lining as soon as it was borne in upon him that the affair would not begin at once, and so well did he succeed that the coffee was just ready when – the men moved off, their Band leading. Even then there had been a mistake in time, and the Fore and Aft came out into the valley ten minutes before the proper hour. Their Band wheeled to the right after reaching the open, and retired behind a little rocky knoll still playing while the Regiment went past.

It was not a pleasant sight that opened on the uninstructed view, for the lower end of the valley appeared to be filled by an army in position – real and actual regiments attired in red coats, and – of this there was no doubt – firing Martini-Henry bullets which cut up the ground a hundred yards in front of the leading company. Over that pock-marked ground the Regiment had to pass, and it opened the ball with a general and profound courtesy to the piping pickets; ducking in perfect time, as though it had been brazed on a rod. Being half capable of thinking for itself, it fired a volley by the simple process of pitching its rifle into its shoulder and pulling the trigger. The bullets may have accounted for some of the watchers on the hill side, but they certainly did not affect the mass of enemy in front, while the noise of the rifles drowned any orders that might have been given.

'Good God!' said the Brigadier, sitting on the rock high above all. 'That Regiment has spoilt the whole show. Hurry up the others, and let the screw-guns get off.'

But the screw-guns, in working round the heights, had stumbled upon a wasp's nest of a small mud fort which they incontinently shelled at eight hundred yards, to the huge discomfort of the occupants, who were unaccustomed to weapons of such devilish precision.

The Fore and Aft continued to go forward, but with shortened stride. Where were the other regiments, and why did these niggers use Martinis? They took open order instinctively, lying down and firing at random, rushing a few paces forward and lying down again, according to the regulations. Once in this formation, each man felt himself desperately alone, and edged in towards his fellow for comfort's sake.

Then the crack of his neighbour's rifle at his ear led him to fire as rapidly as he could – again for the sake of the comfort of the noise. The reward was not long delayed. Five volleys plunged the files in banked smoke impenetrable to the eye, and the bullets began to take ground twenty or thirty yards in front of the firers, as the weight of the bayonet dragged down and to the right arms wearied with holding the kick of the leaping Martini. The Company Commanders peered helplessly through the smoke, the more nervous mechanically trying to fan it away with their helmets.

'High and to the left!' bawled a Captain till he was hoarse. 'No good! Cease firing, and let it drift away a bit.'

Three and four times the bugles shrieked the order, and when it was obeyed the Fore and Aft looked that their foe should be lying before them in mown swaths of men. A light wind drove the smoke to leeward, and showed the enemy still in position and apparently unaffected. A quarter of a ton of lead had been buried a furlong in front of them, as the ragged earth attested.

That was not demoralising to the Afghans, who have not European nerves. They were waiting for the mad riot to die down, and were firing quietly into the heart of the smoke. A private of the Fore and Aft spun up his company shrieking with agony, another was kicking the earth and gasping, and a third, ripped through the lower intestines by a jagged bullet, was calling aloud on his comrades to put him out of his pain. These were the casualties, and they were not soothing to hear or see. The smoke cleared to a dull haze.

Then the foe began to shout with a great shouting, and a mass – a black mass – detached itself from the main body, and rolled over the ground at horrid speed. It was composed of, perhaps, three hundred men, who would shout and fire and slash if the rush of their fifty comrades who were determined to die carried home. The fifty were Ghazis, half maddened with drugs and wholly mad with religious fanaticism. When they rushed the British fire ceased, and in the lull the order was given to close ranks and meet them with the bayonet.

Any one who knew the business could have told the Fore and Aft that the only way of dealing with a Ghazi rush is by volleys at long ranges; because a man who means to die, who desires to die, who will gain heaven by dying, must, in nine cases out of ten, kill a man who has a lingering prejudice in favour of life. Where they should have closed and gone forward, the Fore and Aft opened out and skirmished, and where they should have opened out and fired, they closed and waited.

A man dragged from his blankets half awake and unfed is never in a pleasant frame of mind. Nor does his happiness increase when he watches the whites of the eyes of three hundred six-foot fiends upon whose beards the foam is lying, upon whose tongues is a roar of wrath, and in whose hands are yard-long knives.

The Fore and Aft heard the Gurkha bugles bringing that regiment forward at the double, while the neighing of the Highland pipes came from the left. They strove to stay where they were, though the bayonets wavered down the line like the oars of a ragged boat. Then they felt body to body the amazing physical strength of their foes; a shriek of pain ended the rush, and the knives fell amid scenes not to be told. The men clubbed together and smote blindly – as often as not at their own fellows. Their front crumpled like paper, and the fifty Ghazis passed on; their backers, now drunk with success, fighting as madly as they.

Then the rear ranks were bidden to close up, and the subalterns dashed into the stew – alone. For the rear-ranks had heard the clamour in front, the yells and the howls of pain, and had seen the dark stale blood that makes afraid. They were not going to stay. It was the rushing of the camps over again. Let their officers go to Hell, if they chose; they would get away from the knives.

'Come on!' shrieked the subalterns, and their men, cursing them, drew back, each closing in to his neighbour and wheeling round.

Charteris and Devlin, subalterns of the last company, faced their death alone in the belief that their men would follow.

'You've killed me, you cowards,' sobbed Devlin and dropped, cut from the shoulder-strap to the centre of the chest; and a fresh detachment of his men retreating, always retreating, trampled him under foot as they made for the pass whence they had emerged.

> I kissed her in the kitchen and I kissed her in the hall
> Child'un, child'un, follow me!
> 'Oh Golly,' said the cook, 'is he gwine to kiss us all?'
> Halla – Halla – Halla – Hallelujah!

The Gurkhas were pouring through the left gorge and over the heights at the double to the invitation of their Regimental

Quick-step. The black rocks were crowned with dark green spiders as the bugles gave tongue jubilantly:–

> In the morning! In the morning by the bright light!
> When Gabriel blows his trumpet in the morning!

The Gurkha rear companies tripped and blundered over loose stones. The front files halted for a moment to take stock of the valley and to settle stray boot-laces. Then a happy little sigh of contentment soughed down the ranks, and it was as though the land smiled, for behold there below was the enemy, and it was to meet them that the Gurkhas had doubled so hastily. There was much enemy. There would be amusement. The little men hitched their *kukris* well to hand, and gaped expectantly at their officers as terriers grin ere the stone is cast for them to fetch. The Gurkhas' ground sloped downward to the valley, and they enjoyed a fair view of the proceedings. They sat upon the boulders to watch, for their officers were not going to waste their wind in assisting to repulse a Ghazi rush more than half a mile away. Let the white men look to their own front.

'Hi! yi!' said the Subadar-Major, who was sweating profusely. 'Dam fools yonder, stand close order! This is no time for close order, it is the time for volleys. Ugh!'

Horrified, amused, and indignant, the Gurkhas beheld the retirement of the Fore and Aft with a running chorus of oaths and commentaries.

'They run! The white men run! Colonel Sahib, may *we* also do a little running?' murmured Runbir Thappa, the Senior Jemadar.

But the Colonel would have none of it. 'Let the beggars be cut up a little,' said he wrathfully. 'Serves 'em right. They'll be prodded into facing round in a minute.' He looked through his field-glasses, and caught the glint of an officer's sword.

'Beating 'em with the flat – damned conscripts! How the Ghazis are walking into them!' said he.

The Fore and Aft, heading back, bore with them their officers. The narrowness of the pass forced the mob into solid formation, and the rear ranks delivered some sort of a wavering volley. The Ghazis drew off, for they did not know what reserve the gorge might hide. Moreover, it was never wise to chase white men too far. They returned as wolves return to cover, satisfied with the slaughter that they had done, and only stopping to slash at the wounded on the ground. A quarter of a mile had the Fore and Aft retreated, and now, jammed in the pass, was quivering with pain, shaken and demoralised with fear, while the officers, maddened beyond control, smote the men with the hilts and the flats of their swords.

'Get back! Get back, you cowards – you women! Right about face – column of companies, form – you hounds!' shouted the Colonel, and the subalterns swore aloud. But the Regiment wanted to go – to go anywhere out of the range of those merciless knives. It swayed to and fro irresolutely with shouts and outcries, while from the right the Gurkhas dropped volley after volley of cripple-stopper Snider bullets at long range into the mob of the Ghazis returning to their own troops.

The Fore and Aft Band, though protected from direct fire by the rocky knoll under which it had sat down, fled at the first rush. Jakin and Lew would have fled also, but their short legs left them fifty yards in the rear, and by the time the Band had mixed with the Regiment, they were painfully aware that they would have to close in alone and unsupported.

'Get back to that rock,' gasped Jakin. 'They won't see us there.'

And they returned to the scattered instruments of the Band, their hearts nearly bursting their ribs.

'Here's a nice show for *us*,' said Jakin, throwing himself full length on the ground. 'A bloomin' fine show for British Infantry! Oh, the devils! They've gone and left us alone here! Wot'll we do?'

Lew took possession of a cast-off water-bottle, which naturally was full of canteen rum, and drank till he coughed again.

'Drink,' said he shortly. 'They'll come back in a minute or two – you see.'

Jakin drank, but there was no sign of the Regiment's return. They could hear a dull clamour from the head of the valley of retreat, and saw the Ghazis slink back, quickening their pace as the Gurkhas fired at them.

'We're all that's left of the Band, an' we'll be cut up as sure as death,' said Jakin.

'I'll die game, then,' said Lew thickly, fumbling with his tiny drummer's sword. The drink was working on his brain as it was on Jakin's.

''Old on! I know something better than fightin',' said Jakin, stung by the splendour of a sudden thought due chiefly to rum. 'Tip our bloomin' cowards yonder the word to come back. The Paythan beggars are well away. Come on, Lew! We won't get hurt. Take the fife an' give me the drum. The Old Step for all your bloomin' guts are worth! There's a few of our men coming back now. Stand up, ye drunken little defaulter. By your right – quick march!'

He slipped the drum-sling over his shoulder, thrust the fife into Lew's hand, and the two boys marched out of the cover of the rock into the open, making a hideous hash of the first bars of the 'British Grenadiers.'

As Lew had said, a few of the Fore and Aft were coming back sullenly and shamefacedly under the stimulus of blows and abuse; their red coats shone at the head of the valley, and behind them were wavering bayonets. But between this shattered line and the enemy, who with Afghan suspicion feared that the hasty retreat meant an ambush, and had not moved therefore, lay half a mile of level ground dotted only by the wounded.

The tune settled into full swing and the boys kept shoulder to shoulder, Jakin banging the drum as one possessed. The one fife made a thin and pitiful squeaking, but the tune carried far, even to the Gurkhas.

'Come on, you dorgs!' muttered Jakin to himself. 'Are we to play for hever?' Lew was staring straight in front of him and marching more stiffly than ever he had done on parade.

And in bitter mockery of the distant mob, the old tune of the Old Line shrilled and rattled:–

> Some talk of Alexander,
> And some of Hercules;
> Of Hector and Lysander,
> And such great names as these!

There was a far-off clapping of hands from the Gurkhas, and a roar from the Highlanders in the distance, but never a shot was fired by British or Afghan. The two little red dots moved forward in the open parallel to the enemy's front.

> But of all the world's great heroes
> There's none that can compare,
> With a tow-row-row-row-row-row,
> To the British Grenadier!

The men of the Fore and Aft were gathering thick at the entrance into the plain. The Brigadier on the heights far above was speechless with rage. Still no movement from the enemy. The day stayed to watch the children.

Jakin halted and beat the long roll of the Assembly, while the fife squealed despairingly.

'Right about face! Hold up, Lew, you're drunk,' said Jakin. They wheeled and marched back:–

> Those heroes of antiquity
> Ne'er saw a cannon-ball,
> Nor knew the force o' powder,

'Here they come!' said Jakin. 'Go on, Lew':–

> To scare their foes withal!

The Fore and Aft were pouring out of the valley. What officers had said to men in that time of shame and humiliation will never be known; for neither officers nor men speak of it now.

'They are coming anew!' shouted a priest among the Afghans. 'Do not kill the boys! Take them alive, and they shall be of our faith.'

But the first volley had been fired, and Lew dropped on his face. Jakin stood for a minute, spun round and collapsed, as the Fore and Aft came forward, the curses of their officers in their ears, and in their hearts the shame of open shame.

Half the men had seen the drummers die, and they made no sign. They did not even shout. They doubled out straight across the plain in open order, and they did not fire.

'This,' said the Colonel of Gurkhas, softly, 'is the real attack, as it should have been delivered. Come on, my children.'

'Ulu-lu-lu-lu!' squealed the Gurkhas, and came down with a joyful clicking of *kukris* – those vicious Gurkha knives.

On the right there was no rush. The Highlanders, cannily commending their souls to God (for it matters as much to a dead man whether he has been shot in a Border scuffle or at Waterloo), opened out and fired according to their custom, that is to say without heat and without intervals, while the screw-guns, having disposed of the impertinent mud fort aforementioned, dropped shell after shell into the clusters round the flickering green standards on the heights.

'Charrging is an unfortunate necessity,' murmured the Colour-Sergeant of the right company of the Highlanders. 'It makes the men sweer so – but I am thinkin' that it will come to a charrge if these black devils stand much longer. Stewarrt, man, you're firing into the eye of the sun, and he'll not take any harm for Government ammuneetion. A foot lower and a great deal slower! What are the English doing? They're very quiet, there in the centre. Running again?'

The English were not running. They were hacking and hewing and stabbing, for though one white man is seldom physically a match for an Afghan in a sheepskin or wadded coat, yet, through the pressure of many white men behind, and a certain thirst for revenge in his heart, he becomes capable of doing much with both ends of his rifle. The Fore and Aft held their fire till one bullet could drive through five or six men, and the front of the Afghan force gave on the volley. They then selected their men, and slew them with deep gasps and short hacking coughs, and groanings of leather belts against strained bodies, and realised for the first time that an Afghan attacked is far less formidable than an Afghan attacking; which fact old soldiers might have told them.

But they had no old soldiers in their ranks.

The Gurkhas' stall at the bazar was the noisiest, for the men were engaged – to a nasty noise as of beef being cut on the block – with the *kukri*, which they preferred to the bayonet; well knowing how the Afghan hates the half-moon blade.

As the Afghans wavered, the green standards on the mountain moved down to assist them in a last rally. This was unwise. The Lancers, chafing in the right gorge, had thrice despatched their only subaltern as galloper to report on the progress of affairs. On the third occasion he returned, with a bullet-graze on his knee, swearing strange oaths in Hindustani, and saying that all things were ready. So that squadron swung round the right of the Highlanders with a wicked whistling of wind in the pennons of its lances, and fell upon the remnant just when, according to all the rules of war, it should have waited for the foe to show more signs of wavering.

But it was a dainty charge, deftly delivered, and it ended by the Cavalry finding itself at the head of the pass by which the Afghans intended to retreat; and down the track that the lances had made streamed two companies of the Highlanders, which was never intended by the Brigadier. The new development was successful. It detached the enemy from his base as a sponge is torn from a rock, and left him ringed about with fire in that pitiless plain. And as a sponge is chased round the bath-tub by the hand of the bather, so were the Afghans chased till they broke into little detachments much more difficult to dispose of than large masses.

'See!' quoth the Brigadier. 'Everything has come as I arranged. We've cut their base, and now we'll bucket 'em to pieces.'

A direct hammering was all that the Brigadier had dared to hope for, considering the size of the force at his disposal; but men who stand or fall by the errors of their opponents may be forgiven for turning Chance into Design. The bucketing went forward merrily. The Afghan forces were upon the run – the run of wearied wolves who snarl and bite over their shoulders. The red lances dipped by twos and threes, and, with a shriek, up rose the lance-butt, like a spar on a stormy sea, as the trooper cantering forward cleared his point. The Lancers kept between their prey and the steep hills, for all who could were trying to escape from the valley of death. The Highlanders gave the fugitives two hundred yards' law, and then brought them down, gasping and choking ere they could reach the protection of the boulders above. The Gurkhas followed suit; but the Fore and Aft were killing on their own account, for they had penned a mass of men between their bayonets and a wall of rock, and the flash of the rifles was lighting the wadded coats.

'We cannot hold them, Captain Sahib!' panted a Ressaidar of Lancers. 'Let us try the carbine. The lance is good, but it wastes time.'

They tried the carbine, and still the enemy melted away – fled up the hills by hundreds when there were only twenty bullets to stop them. On the heights the screw-guns ceased firing – they had run out of ammunition – and the Brigadier groaned, for the musketry fire could not sufficiently smash the retreat. Long before the last volleys were fired, the doolies were out in force looking for the wounded. The battle was over, and, but for want of fresh troops, the Afghans would have been wiped off the earth. As it was, they counted their dead by hundreds, and nowhere were the dead thicker than in the track of the Fore and Aft.

But the Regiment did not cheer with the Highlanders, nor did they dance uncouth dances with the Gurkhas among the dead. They looked under their brows at the Colonel as they leaned upon their rifles and panted.

'Get back to camp, you. Haven't you disgraced yourself enough for one day! Go and look to the wounded. It's all you're fit for,' said the Colonel. Yet for the past hour the Fore and Aft had been doing all that mortal commander could expect. They had lost heavily because they did not know how to set about their business with proper skill, but they had borne themselves gallantly, and this was their reward.

A young and sprightly Colour-Sergeant, who had begun to imagine himself a hero, offered his water-bottle to a Highlander whose tongue was black with thirst. 'I drink with no cowards,' answered the youngster huskily, and, turning to a Gurkha, said, '*Hya*, Johnny! Drink water got it?' The Gurkha grinned and passed his bottle. The Fore and Aft said no word.

They went back to camp when the field of strife had been a little mopped up and made presentable, and the Brigadier, who saw himself a Knight in three months, was the only soul who was complimentary to them. The Colonel was heartbroken, and the officers were savage and sullen.

'Well,' said the Brigadier, 'they are young troops, of course, and it was not unnatural that they should retire in disorder for a bit.'

'Oh, my only Aunt Maria!' murmured a junior Staff Officer. 'Retire in disorder! It was a bally run!'

'But they came again, as we all know,' cooed the Brigadier, the Colonel's ashy-white face before him, 'and they behaved as well as could possibly be expected. Behaved beautifully, indeed. I was watching them. It's not a matter to take to heart, Colonel. As some German General said of his men, they wanted to be shooted over a little, that was all.' To himself he said – 'Now they're blooded I can give 'em responsible work. It's as well that they got what they did. Teach 'em more than half a dozen rifle flirtations, that will – later – run alone and bite. Poor old Colonel, though.'

All that afternoon the heliograph winked and flickered on the hills, striving to tell the good news to a mountain forty miles away And in the evening there arrived, dusty, sweating, and sore, a misguided Correspondent who had gone out to assist at a trumpery village-burning, and who had read off the message from afar, cursing his luck the while.

'Let's have the details somehow – as full as ever you can, please. It's the first time I've ever been left this campaign,' said the Correspondent to the Brigadier; and the Brigadier, nothing loth, told him how an Army of Communication had been crumpled up, destroyed, and all but annihilated by the craft, strategy, wisdom, and foresight of the Brigadier.

But some say, and among these be the Gurkhas who watched on the hillside, that that battle was won by Jakin and Lew, whose little bodies were borne up just in time to fit two gaps at the head of the big ditch-grave for the dead under the heights of Jagai.

[First published in *Wee Willie Winkie and Other Child Stories*, Indian Railway Library No. 6 (Allahabad: A.H. Wheeler and Co., 1888).]

✠ ✠ ✠

This is one of the early Barrack-Room Ballads, comprising a British soldier's regretful lament at the harsh way he has treated his water-bearer, Gunga Din, who has recently been killed in battle.

GUNGA DIN

You MAY TALK o' gin and beer
When you're quartered safe out 'ere,
An' you're sent to penny-fights an' Aldershot it;
But when it comes to slaughter
You will do your work on water,
An' you'll lick the bloomin' boots of 'im that's got it.
Now in Injia's sunny clime,
Where I used to spend my time
A-servin' of 'Er Majesty the Queen,
Of all them blackfaced crew
The finest man I knew
Was our regimental *bhisti*, Gunga Din.
He was 'Din! Din! Din!
You limpin' lump o' brick-dust, Gunga Din!
Hi! slippery *hitherao*!
Water, get it! *Panee lao*!¹
You squidgy-nosed old idol, Gunga Din.'

The uniform 'e wore
Was nothin' much before,

An' rather less than 'arf o' that be'ind,
For a piece o' twisty rag
An' a goatskin water-bag
Was all the field-equipment 'e could find.
When the sweatin' troop-train lay
In a sidin' through the day,
Where the 'eat would make your bloomin' eyebrows crawl,
We shouted 'Harry By!'[2]
Till our throats were bricky-dry,
Then we wopped 'im 'cause 'e couldn't serve us all.
It was 'Din! Din! Din!
You 'eathen, where the mischief 'ave you been?
You put some *juldee*[3] in it
Or I'll *marrow*[4] you this minute
If you don't fill up my helmet, Gunga Din!'

'E would dot an' carry one
Till the longest day was done;
An' 'e didn't seem to know the use o' fear.
If we charged or broke or cut,
You could bet your bloomin' nut,
'E'd be waitin' fifty paces right flank rear.
With 'is *mussick*[5] on 'is back,
'E would skip with our attack,
An' watch us till the bugles made 'Retire',
An' for all 'is dirty 'ide
'E was white, clear white, inside
When 'e went to tend the wounded under fire!
It was 'Din! Din! Din!'
With the bullets kickin' dust-spots on the green.
When the cartridges ran out,
You could hear the front-files shout,
'Hi! ammunition-mules an' Gunga Din!'

I shan't forgit the night
When I dropped be'ind the fight
With a bullet where my belt-plate should 'a' been.
I was chokin' mad with thirst,
An' the man that spied me first
Was our good old grinnin', gruntin' Gunga Din.

'E lifted up my 'ead,
An' he plugged me where I bled,
An' 'e guv me 'arf-a-pint o' water-green:
It was crawlin' and it stunk,
But of all the drinks I've drunk,
I'm gratefullest to one from Gunga Din.
It was 'Din! Din! Din!
'Ere's a beggar with a bullet through 'is spleen;
'E's chawin' up the ground,
An' 'e's kickin' all around:
For Gawd's sake git the water, Gunga Din!'

'E carried me away
To where a dooli lay,
An' a bullet come an' drilled the beggar clean.
'E put me safe inside,
An' just before 'e died,
'I 'ope you liked your drink', sez Gunga Din.
So I'll meet 'im later on
At the place where 'e is gone –
Where it's always double drill and no canteen;
'E'll be squattin' on the coals
Givin' drink to poor damned souls,
An' I'll get a swig in hell from Gunga Din!
Yes, Din! Din! Din!
You Lazarushian-leather Gunga Din!
Though I've belted you and flayed you,
By the livin' Gawd that made you,
You're a better man than I am, Gunga Din!

¹ Bring water swiftly. ² Mr. Atkins's equivalent for 'O brother.' ³ Be quick.
⁴ Hit. ⁵ Water-skin. [These translations appear in texts approved by
Kipling.]

[First published in the *Scots Observer*, 7 June 1890, and then collected in
Ballads and Barrack-Room Ballads (1892).]

�֍ ✖ ✖

The Third Anglo-Burmese War of November 1885 led to the demise of the Konbaung dynasty and the consolidation of British rule throughout Burma. It made a particular mark on Kipling in Lahore since Burma was absorbed into the Raj as a province of India.

THE TAKING OF LUNGTUNGPEN

So we loosed a bloomin' volley,
 An' we made the beggars cut,
An' when our pouch was emptied out,
 We used the bloomin' butt.
  Ho! My!
  Don't yer come anigh,
When Tommy is a-playin' with the baynit an' the butt.

Barrack Room Ballad

MY FRIEND PRIVATE MULVANEY told me this, sitting on the parapet of the road to Dagshai, when we were hunting butterflies together. He had theories about the Army, and coloured clay pipes perfectly. He said that the young soldier is the best to work with, 'on account av the surpassing innocinse av the child.'

'Now, listen!' said Mulvaney, throwing himself full length on the wall in the sun. 'I'm a born scutt av the barrick-room! The Army's mate an' dhrink to me, bekaze I'm wan av the few that can't quit ut. I've put in sivinteen years, an' the pipeclay's in the marrow av me. Av I cud have kept out av wan big dhrink a month, I wud have been a Hon'ry Lift'nint by this time – a nuisince to my betthers, a laughin'-shtock to my equils, an' a curse to meself. Bein' fwhat I am, I'm Privit Mulvaney, wid no good-conduc' pay an' a devourin' thirst. Always barrin' me little frind Bobs Bahadur, I know as much about the Army as most men.'

I said something here.

'Wolseley be shot! Betune you an' me an' that butterfly net, he's a ramblin', incoherint sort av a divil, wid wan oi on the Quane an' the Coort, an' the other on his blessed silf-everlastin'ly playing Saysar and Alexandrier rowled into a lump. Now Bobs is a sinsible little man. Wid Bobs an' a few three-year-olds, I'd swape any army av the earth into a towel, an' throw it away afterwards. Faith, I'm not jokin'! 'Tis the bhoys – the raw bhoys – that don't know fwat a bullut manes, an' wudn't care av they did – that dhu the work. They're crammed wid bull-mate till they fairly *ramps* wid good livin'; and thin, av they don't fight, they blow each other's hids off. 'Tis the trut' I'm tellin' you. They shud be kept on water an' rice in the hot weather; but there'd be a mut'ny av 'twas done.

'Did ye iver hear how Privit Mulvaney tuk the town av Lungtungpen? I thought not! 'Twas the Lift'nint got the credit; but 'twas me planned the schame. A little before I was inviladed from Burma, me an' four-an'-twenty young wans undher a Lift'nint Brazenose, was ruinin' our dijeshins thryin' to catch dacoits. An' such double-ended divils I niver knew! 'Tis only a *dah* an' a Snider that makes a dacoit. Widout thim, he's a paceful cultivator, an' felony for to shoot. We hunted, an' we hunted, an' tuk fever an' elephints now an' again; but no dacoits. Evenshually, we *puckarowed* wan man. "Trate him tinderly," sez the Lift'nint. So I tuk him away into the jungle, wid the Burmese Interprut'r an' my clanin'-rod. Sez I to the man, "My paceful squireen," sez I, "you shquot on your hunkers an' dimonstrate to *my* frind here, where *your* frinds are whin they're at home?" Wid that I introjuced him to the clanin'-rod, an' he comminst to jabber; the Interprut'r interprutin' in betweens, an' me helpin' the Intilligince Departmint wid my clanin'-rod whin the man misremimbered.

'Prisintly, I learn that, acrost the river, about nine miles away, was a town just dhrippin' wid dahs, an' bohs an' arrows, an' dacoits, an' elephints, an' *jingles*. "Good!" sez I; "this office will now close!"

'That night I went to the Lift'nint an' communicates my information. I never thought much of Lift'nint Brazenose till that night. He was shtiff wid books an' the-ouries, an' all manner av thrimmin's no manner av use. "Town did ye say?" sez he. "Accordin' to the the-ouries av War, we shud wait for reinforcements." – "Faith!" thinks I, "we'd betther dig our graves thin"; for the nearest throops was up to their shtocks in the marshes out Mimbu way. "But," says the Lift'nint, "since 'tis a speshil case, I'll make an excepshin. We'll visit this Lungtungpen tonight."

'The bhoys was fairly woild wid deloight whin I tould 'em; an', by this an' that, they wint through the jungle like buck-rabbits. About midnight we come to the shtrame which I had clane forgot to minshin to my orficer. I was on, ahead, wid four bhoys, an' I thought that the Lift'nint might want to the-ourise. "Shtrip bhoys!" sez I. "Shtrip to the buff, an' shwim in where glory waits!" – "But I *can't* shwim!" sez two av thim. "To think I should live to hear that from a bhoy wid a board-school edukashin!" sez I. "Take a lump av timbher, an' me an' Conolly here will ferry ye over, ye young ladies!"

'We got an ould tree-trunk, an' pushed off wid the kits an' the rifles on it. The night was chokin' dhark, an' just as we was fairly embarked, I heard the Lift'nint behind av me callin' out. "There's a bit av a *nullah* here, Sorr," sez I, "but I can feel the bottom already." So I cud, for I was not a yard from the bank.

'"Bit av a *nullah*! Bit av an eshtury!" sez the Lift'nint. "Go on, ye mad Irishman! Shtrip bhoys!" I heard him laugh; an' the bhoys begun shtrippin' an' rollin' a log into the wather to put their kits on. So me an' Conolly shtruck out through the warm wather wid our log, an' the rest come on behind.

'That shtrame was miles woide! Orth'ris, on the rear-rank log, whispers we had got into the Thames below Sheerness by mistake. "Kape on shwimmin', ye little blayguard," sez I, "an' don't go pokin' your dirty jokes at the Irriwaddy." – "Silince, men!" sings out the Lift'nint. So we shwum on into the black dhark, wid our chests on the logs, trustin' in the Saints an' the luck av the British Army.

'Evenshually we hit ground – a bit av sand – an' a man. I put my heel on the back av him. He skreeched an' ran.

'"*Now* we've done it!" sez Lift'nint Brazenose. "Where the Divil *is* Lungtungpen?" There was about a minute and a half to wait. The bhoys laid a hould av their rifles an' some thried to put their belts on; we was marchin' wid fixed baynits av coorse. Thin we knew where Lungtungpen was; for we had hit the river-wall av it in the dhark, an' the whole town blazed wid thim messin' *jingles* an' Sniders like a cat's back on a frosty night. They was firin' all ways at wanst; but over our hids into the shtrame.

'"Have you got your rifles?" sez Brazenose, "Got 'em!" sez Orth'ris. "I've got that thief Mulvaney's for all my back-pay, an' she'll kick my heart sick wid that blunderin' long shtock av hers" – "Go on!" yells Brazenose, whippin' his sword out. "Go on an' take the town! An' the Lord have mercy on our sowls!"

'Thin the bhoys gave wan devastatin' howl, an' pranced into the dhark, feelin' for the town, an blindin' and stiffin' like Cavalry Ridin' Masters whin the grass pricked their bare legs. I hammered wid the butt at some bamboo-thing that felt wake, an' the rest come an' hammered contagious, while the *jingles* was jingling, an' feroshus yells from inside was shplittin' our ears. We was too close under the wall for thim to hurt us.

'Evenshually, the thing, whatever ut was, bruk; an' the six-and-twinty av us tumbled, wan after the other, naked as we was borrun, into the town of Lungtungpen. There was a *melly* av a sumpshus kind for a whoile; but whether they tuk us, all white an' wet, for a new breed av' divll, or a new kind av dacoit, I don't know. They ran as though we was both, an' we wint into thim, baynit an' butt, shriekin' wid laughin'. There was torches in the shtreets, an' I saw little Orth'ris rubbin' his showlther ivry time he loosed my longshtock Martini; an' Brazenose walkin' into the gang wid his sword, like Diarmid av the Gowlden Collar – barring he hadn't a stitch av clothin' on him. We diskivered elephints wid dacoits under their bellies, an', what wid wan thing an another, we was busy till mornin' takin' possession av the town of Lungtungpen.

'Thin we halted an' formed up, the wimmen howlin' in the houses an' Lift'nint Brazenose blushin' pink in the light av the mornin' sun. 'Twas the most ondasint p'rade I iver tuk a hand in. Foive-and-twenty privits an' an orficer av the Line in review ordher, an' not as much as wud dust a fife betune 'em all in the way of clothin'! Eight av us had their belts an' pouches on; but the rest had gone in wid a handful of cartridges an' the skin God gave thim. *They* was as naked as Vanus.

'"Number off from the right!" sez the Lift'nint. "Odd numbers fall out to dress; even numbers pathrol the town till relieved by the dressing party." Let me tell you, pathrollin' a town wid nothing on is an ex*pay*rience. I pathrolled for tin minutes, an' begad, before 'twas over, I blushed. The women laughed so. I niver blushed before or since; but I blushed all over my carkiss thin. Orth'ris didn't pathrol. He sez only, "Portsmith Barricks an' the 'Ard av a Sunday!" Thin he lay down an' rowled any ways wid laughin'.

'Whin we was all dhressed we counted the dead – sivinty-foive dacoits besides wounded. We tuk five elephints, a hunder' an' sivinty Sniders, two hunder' dahs, and a lot av other burglarious thruck. Not a man av us was hurt – excep' maybe the Lift'nint, an' he from the shock to his dasincy.

'The Headman av Lungtungpen, who surrinder'd himself, asked the Interprut'r – "Av the English fight like that wid their clo'es off, what in the wurruld do they do wid their clo'es on?" Orth'ris began rowlin' his eyes an' crackin' his fingers an' dancin' a step-dance for to impress the Headman. He ran to his house; an' we spint the rest av the day carryin' the Lift'nint on our showlthers round the town, an' playin' wid the Burmese babies – fat, little, brown little divils, as pretty as picturs.

'Whin I was inviladed for the dysent'ry to India, I sez to the Lift'nint, "Sorr," sez I, "you've the makin's in you av a great man; but, av you'll let an ould sodger spake, you're too fond of the-ourisin'." He shuk hands wid me and sez, "Hit high, hit low, there's no plasin' you, Mulvaney. You've seen me waltzin' through Luntungpen like a Red Injin widout the war-paint, any you say I'm too fond of the-ourisin'?" – "Sorr," sez I, for I loved the bhoy, "I wud waltz wid you in that condishin through *Hell*, an' so wud the rest av the men!" Thin I wint downshtrame in the flat an' left him my blessin'. May the Saints carry ut where ut shud go, for he was a fine upstandin' young orficer.

'To reshume. Fwhat I've said jist shows the use av three-year-olds. Wud fifty seasoned sodgers have taken Lungtungpen in the dhark that way? No! They'd know the risk av fever and chill; let alone the shootin'. Two hundher' might have done ut. But the three-year-olds know little an' care less; an' where there's no fear there's no danger. Catch thim young, feed thim high, an' by the honour av that great, little man Bobs, behind a good orficer, 'tisn't only dacoits they'd smash wid their clo'es off – 'tis Continental Ar-r-r-mies! They tuk Lungtungpen nakid; an' they'd take St. Pethersburg in their dhrawers! Begad, they would that!

'Here's your pipe, Sorr. Shmoke her tinderly wid honey-dew, afther letting the reek av the Canteen plug die away. But 'tis no good, thanks to you all the same, fillin' my pouch wid your chopped hay. Canteen baccy's like the Army; it shpoils a man's taste for moilder things.'

So saying, Mulvaney took up his butterfly-net, and returned to barracks.

[First published in the *Civil and Military Gazette*, 11 April 1887, and then collected in *Plain Tales from the Hills* (1888).]

✠ ✠ ✠

These lines were first published as an epigraph to a story of the same name in the book version of *Plain Tales from the Hills* in 1888.

THE ROUT OF THE WHITE HUSSARS

IT WAS NOT IN the open fight
We threw away the sword,
But in the lonely watching
In the darkness by the ford.
The waters lapped, the night-wind blew,
Full-armed the Fear was born and grew,
And we were flying ere we knew
From panic in the night.

[First published in *Plain Tales from the Hills* (1888).]

RETURN TO ENGLAND

This is an early Barrack-Room Ballad which is sometimes said to have been based on the execution of Private Flaxman of the Leicestershire Regiment in Lucknow in 1887.

DANNY DEEVER

'WHAT ARE THE BUGLES blowin' for?' said Files-on-Parade.
'To turn you out, to turn you out', the Colour-Sergeant said.
'What makes you look so white, so white?' said Files-on-Parade.
'I'm dreadin' what I've got to watch', the Colour-Sergeant said.
For they're hangin' Danny Deever, you can hear the Dead March
     play,
The regiment's in 'ollow square – they're hangin' him to-day;
They've taken of his buttons off an' cut his stripes away,
An' they're hangin' Danny Deever in the mornin'.

'What makes the rear-rank breathe so 'ard?' said Files-on-Parade.
'It's bitter cold, it's bitter cold', the Colour-Sergeant said.
'What makes that front-rank man fall down?' said Files-on-Parade.
'A touch o' sun, a touch o' sun', the Colour-Sergeant said.
They are hangin' Danny Deever, they are marchin' of 'im round,
They 'ave 'alted Danny Deever by 'is coffin on the ground;

An' 'e'll swing in 'arf a minute for a sneakin' shootin' hound –
O they're hangin' Danny Deever in the mornin'!

"Is cot was right-'and cot to mine', said Files-on-Parade.
"E's sleepin' out an' far to-night', the Colour-Sergeant said.
'I've drunk 'is beer a score o' times', said Files-on-Parade.
"E's drinkin' bitter beer alone', the Colour-Sergeant said.
They are hangin' Danny Deever, you must mark 'im to 'is place,
For 'e shot a comrade sleepin' – you must look 'im in the face;
Nine 'undred of 'is county an' the regiment's disgrace,
While they're hangin' Danny Deever in the mornin'.

'What's that so black agin' the sun?' said Files-on-Parade.
'It's Danny fightin' 'ard for life', the Colour-Sergeant said.
'What's that that whimpers over'ead?' said Files-on-Parade.
'It's Danny's soul that's passin' now', the Colour-Sergeant said.
For they're done with Danny Deever, you can 'ear the quickstep
    play,
The regiment's in column, an' they're marchin' us away;
Ho! the young recruits are shakin', an' they'll want their beer
    to-day,
After hangin' Danny Deever in the mornin'.

[First published in the *Scots Observer*, 22 February 1890.]

✠   ✠   ✠

The screw-guns of this poem were muzzle-loaded field guns
which, because of their size, were carried in two parts – the
breach and chase, each weighing approximately 200 lbs (90 kgs),
which were then screwed together. They were invented in the late
1870s and manufactured at the Armstrong company's Elswick
Ordnance Works on the River Tyne. Each gun was transported
by a team of five mules and required a support team of nine men.

SCREW-GUNS

SMOKIN' MY PIPE ON the mountings, sniffin' the mornin' cool,
I walks in my old brown gaiters along o' my old brown mule,

With seventy gunners be'ind me, an' never a beggar forgets
It's only the pick of the Army that handles the dear little pets –
    'Tss! 'Tss!
For you all love the screw-guns – the screw-guns they all love
    you!
So when we call round with a few guns, o' course you will know
    what to do – hoo! hoo!
Jest send in your Chief an' surrender – it's worse if you fights or
    you runs:
You can go where you please, you can skid up the trees, but you
    don't get away from the guns!

They sends us along where the roads are, but mostly we goes
    where they ain't:
We'd climb up the side of a sign-board an' trust to the stick o' the
    paint:
We've chivied the Naga an' Looshai, we've give the Afreedeeman
    fits,
For we fancies ourselves at two thousand, we guns that are built in
    two bits – 'Tss! 'Tss!
For you all love the screw-guns …

If a man doesn't work, why, we drills 'im an' teaches 'im 'ow to
    behave;
If a beggar can't march, why, we kills 'im an' rattles 'im into 'is
    grave.
You've got to stand up to our business an' spring without
    snatchin' or fuss.
D'you say that you sweat with the field-guns?
By God, you must lather with us – 'Tss! 'Tss!
For you all love the screw-guns …

The eagles is screamin' around us, the river's a-moanin' below,
We're clear o' the pine an' the oak-scrub, we're out on the rocks an'
    the snow,
An' the wind is as thin as a whip-lash what carries away to the
    plains
The rattle an' stamp o' the lead-mules – the jinglety-jink o' the
    chains – 'Tss! 'Tss!
For you all love the screw-guns …

There's a wheel on the Horns o' the Mornin', an' a wheel on the
    edge o' the Pit,
An' a drop into nothin' beneath you as straight as a beggar can spit:
With the sweat runnin' out o' your shirt-sleeves, an' the sun off the
    snow in your face,
An' 'arf o' the men on the drag-ropes to hold the old gun in 'er
    place – 'Tss! 'Tss!
For you all love the screw-guns …

Smokin' my pipe on the mountings, sniffin' the mornin' cool,
I climbs in my old brown gaiters along o' my old brown mule.
The monkey can say what our road was – the wild-goat 'e knows
    where we passed.
Stand easy, you long-eared old darlin's! Out drag-ropes! With
    shrapnel! Hold fast – 'Tss! 'Tss!
For you all love the screw-guns – the screw-guns they all love you!
So when we take tea with a few guns, o' course you will know
    what to do – hoo! hoo!
Jest send in your Chief an' surrender – it's worse if you fights or
    you runs:
You may hide in the caves, they'll be only your graves, but you
    can't get away from the guns!

[First published in the *Scots Observer*, 12 April 1890.]

❈ ❈ ❈

**Gentlemen-rankers were soldiers who enlisted in the ranks
although, by education or background, they might be expected
to serve as officers. They often signed up in the ranks as a result
of some scandal. The chorus of this poem is well-known as part of
the Whiffenpoof Song, which has been sung at Yale University
since the early twentieth century.**

GENTLEMEN-RANKERS

To THE LEGION OF the lost ones, to the cohort of the damned,
To my brethren in their sorrow overseas,

Sings a gentleman of England cleanly bred, machinely crammed,
And a trooper of the Empress, if you please.
Yea, a trooper of the forces who has run his own six horses,
And faith he went the pace and went it blind,
And the world was more than kin while he held the ready tin,
But to-day the Sergeant's something less than kind.
We're poor little lambs who've lost our way,
Baa! Baa! Baa!
We're little black sheep who've gone astray,
Baa-aa-aa!
Gentlemen-rankers out on the spree,
Damned from here to Eternity,
God ha' mercy on such as we,
Baa! Yah! Bah!

Oh, it's sweet to sweat through stables, sweet to empty kitchen slops,
And it's sweet to hear the tales the troopers tell,
To dance with blowzy housemaids at the regimental hops
And thrash the cad who says you waltz too well.
Yes, it makes you cock-a-hoop to be 'Rider' to your troop,
And branded with a blasted worsted spur,
When you envy, O how keenly, one poor Tommy being cleanly
Who blacks your boots and sometimes calls you 'Sir'.

If the home we never write to, and the oaths we never keep,
And all we know most distant and most dear,
Across the snoring barrack-room return to break our sleep,
Can you blame us if we soak ourselves in beer?
When the drunken comrade mutters and the great guard-lantern
    gutters
And the horror of our fall is written plain,
Every secret, self-revealing on the aching white-washed ceiling,
Do you wonder that we drug ourselves from pain?

We have done with Hope and Honour, we are lost to Love and Truth,
We are dropping down the ladder rung by rung,
And the measure of our torment is the measure of our youth.
God help us, for we knew the worst too young!
Our shame is clean repentance for the crime that brought the
    sentence,

Our pride it is to know no spur of pride,
And the Curse of Reuben holds us till an alien turf enfolds us
And we die, and none can tell them where we died.
We're poor little lambs who've lost our way,
Baa! Baa! Baa!
We're little black sheep who've gone astray,
Baa–aa–aa!
Gentlemen-rankers out on the spree,
Damned from here to Eternity,
God ha' mercy on such as we,
Baa! Yah! Bah!

[First published in *Ballads and Barrack-Room Ballads* (1892).]

✠   ✠   ✠

Attitudes to looting on the battlefield – for long an accepted practice in British army life – were changing, since 'with English morals' they no longer suited.

LOOT

IF YOU'VE EVER STOLE a pheasant-egg be'ind the keeper's back,
If you've ever snigged the washin' from the line,
If you've ever crammed a gander in your bloomin' 'aversack,
You will understand this little song o' mine.
But the service rules are 'ard, an' from such we are debarred,
For the same with English morals does not suit.
(*Cornet*: Toot! toot!)
W'y, they call a man a robber if 'e stuffs 'is marchin' clobber
With the –
(*Chorus*) Loo! loo! Lulu! lulu! Loo! loo! Loot! loot! loot!
Ow the loot!
Bloomin' loot!
That's the thing to make the boys git up an' shoot!
It's the same with dogs an' men,
If you'd make 'em come again
Clap 'em forward with a Loo! loo! Lulu! Loot!

(*ff*) Whoopee! Tear 'im, puppy! Loo! loo! Lulu! Loot! loot! loot!

If you've knocked a nigger edgeways when 'e's thrustin' for your
    life,
You must leave 'im very careful where 'e fell;
An' may thank your stars an' gaiters if you didn't feel 'is knife
That you ain't told off to bury 'im as well.
Then the sweatin' Tommies wonder as they spade the beggars under
Why lootin' should be entered as a crime;
So if my song you'll 'ear, I will learn you plain an' clear
'Ow to pay yourself for fightin' overtime.
(*Chorus*) With the loot, …

Now remember when you're 'acking round a gilded Burma god
That 'is eyes is very often precious stones;
An' if you treat a nigger to a dose o' cleanin'-rod
'E's like to show you everything 'e owns.
When 'e won't prodooce no more, pour some water on the floor
Where you 'ear it answer 'ollow to the boot
(*Cornet*: Toot! toot!) –
When the ground begins to sink, shove your baynick down the
    chink,
An' you're sure to touch the –
(*Chorus*) Loo! loo! Lulu! Loot! loot! loot!
Ow the loot! …

When from 'ouse to 'ouse you're 'unting, you must always work in
    pairs –
It 'alves the gain, but safer you will find –
For a single man gets bottled on them twisty-wisty stairs,
An' a woman comes and clobs 'im from be'ind.
When you've turned 'em inside out, an' it seems beyond a doubt
As if there weren't enough to dust a flute
(*Cornet*: Toot! toot!)
Before you sling your 'ook, at the 'ousetops take a look,
For it's underneath the tiles they 'ide the loot.
(*Chorus*) Ow the loot! …

You can mostly square a Sergint an' a Quartermaster too,
If you only take the proper way to go;

I could never keep my pickin's, but I've learned you all I knew –
An' don't you never say I told you so.
An' now I'll bid good-bye, for I'm gettin' rather dry,
An' I see another tunin' up to toot
(*Cornet*: Toot! toot!) –
So 'ere's good-luck to those that wears the Widow's clo'es,
An' the Devil send 'em all they want o' loot!
(*Chorus*) Yes, the loot,
Bloomin' loot!
In the tunic an' the mess-tin an' the boot!
It's the same with dogs an' men,
If you'd make 'em come again
(*ff*) Whoop 'em forward with a Loo! loo! Lulu! Loot! loot! loot!
Heeya! Sick 'im, puppy! Loo! loo! Lulu! Loot! loot! loot!

[First published in the *Scots Observer*, 29 March 1890.]

❈   ❈   ❈

This is a generic Barrack-Room Ballad about the hardships of
a soldier's existence, made memorable by its lines about being
'wounded and left on Afghanistan's plains'. These were much
quoted during Operation Enduring Freedom, the US-led NATO
invasion of Afghanistan from October 2001.

THE YOUNG BRITISH SOLDIER

WHEN THE 'ARF-MADE RECRUITY goes out to the East
'E acts like a babe an' 'e drinks like a beast,
An' 'e wonders because 'e is frequent deceased
Ere 'e's fit for to serve as a soldier.
Serve, serve, serve as a soldier,
Serve, serve, serve as a soldier,
Serve, serve, serve as a soldier,
So-oldier *OF* the Queen!

Now all you recruities what's drafted to-day,
You shut up your rag-box an' 'ark to my lay,

An' I'll sing you a soldier as far as I may:
A soldier what's fit for a soldier.
Fit, fit, fit for a soldier …

First mind you steer clear o' the grog-sellers' huts,
For they sell you Fixed Bay'nets that rots out your guts –
Ay, drink that 'ud eat the live steel from your butts –
An' it's bad for the young British soldier.
Bad, bad, bad for the soldier …

When the cholera comes – as it will past a doubt –
Keep out of the wet and don't go on the shout,
For the sickness gets in as the liquor dies out,
An' it crumples the young British soldier.
Crum-, crum-, crumples the soldier …

But the worst o' your foes is the sun over'ead:
You *must* wear your 'elmet for all that is said:
If 'e finds you uncovered 'e'll knock you down dead,
An' you'll die like a fool of a soldier.
Fool, fool, fool of a soldier …

If you're cast for fatigue by a sergeant unkind,
Don't grouse like a woman nor crack on nor blind;
Be handy and civil, and then you will find
That it's beer for the young British soldier.
Beer, beer, beer for the soldier …

Now, if you must marry, take care she is old –
A troop-sergeant's widow's the nicest I'm told,
For beauty won't help if your rations is cold,
Nor love ain't enough for a soldier.
'Nough, 'nough, 'nough for a soldier …

If the wife should go wrong with a comrade, be loath
To shoot when you catch 'em – you'll swing, on my oath! –
Make 'im take 'er and keep 'er: that's Hell for them both,
An' you're shut o' the curse of a soldier.
Curse, curse, curse of a soldier …

When first under fire an' you're wishful to duck,
Don't look nor take 'eed at the man that is struck,
Be thankful you're livin', and trust to your luck
And march to your front like a soldier.
Front, front, front like a soldier ...

When 'arf of your bullets fly wide in the ditch,
Don't call your Martini a cross-eyed old bitch;
She's human as you are – you treat her as sich,
An' she'll fight for the young British soldier.
Fight, fight, fight for the soldier ...

When shakin' their bustles like ladies so fine,
The guns o' the enemy wheel into line,
Shoot low at the limbers an' don't mind the shine,
For noise never startles the soldier.
Start-, start-, startles the soldier ...

If your officer's dead and the sergeants look white,
Remember it's ruin to run from a fight:
So take open order, lie down, and sit tight,
And wait for supports like a soldier.
Wait, wait, wait like a soldier ...

When you're wounded and left on Afghanistan's plains,
And the women come out to cut up what remains,
Jest roll to your rifle and blow out your brains
An' go to your Gawd like a soldier.
Go, go, go like a soldier,
Go, go, go like a soldier,
Go, go, go like a soldier,
So-oldier *of* the Queen!

[First published in the *Scots Observer*, 28 June 1890.]

This is another colourful epigraph – this time from Kipling's novel *The Light That Failed*, which focused on General Wolseley's expedition against the Mahdi (in relief of General Gordon) in Sudan in 1884–5.

RIDE TO KANDAHAR

THEN WE BROUGHT THE lances down – then the trumpets blew –
When we went to Kandahar, ridin' two an' two.
Ridin' – ridin' – ridin' two an' two!
Ta-ra-ra-ra-ra-ra-a!
All the way to Kandahar,
Ridin' two an' two.

[First published as 'Barrack-Room Ballad' in *The Light That Failed* in *Lippincott's Monthly Magazine*, January 1891.]

✠ ✠ ✠

Here we learn more about the realities of life in the British army ranks, as rendered in the Barrack-Room Ballads.

ROUTE MARCHING

WE'RE MARCHIN' ON RELIEF over Injia's sunny plains,
A little front o' Christmas-time an' just be'ind the Rains;
Ho! get away you bullock-man, you've 'eard the bugle blowed,
There's a regiment a-comin' down the Grand Trunk Road;
With its best foot first
And the road a-sliding past,
An' every bloomin' campin'-ground exactly like the last;
While the Big Drum says,
With 'is '*rowdy-dowdy-dow!*' –
'*Kiko kissywarsti* don't you *hamsher argy jow*?'[1]

Oh, there's them Injian temples to admire when you see,
There's the peacock round the corner an' the monkey up the tree,
An' there's that rummy silver grass a-wavin' in the wind,
An' the old Grand Trunk a-trailin' like a rifle-sling be'ind.
While it's best foot first …

At half-past five's Revelly, an' our tents they down must come,
Like a lot of button mushrooms when you pick 'em up at 'ome.
But it's over in a minute, an' at six the column starts,
While the women and the kiddies sit an' shiver in the carts.
An' it's best foot first …

Oh, then it's open order, an' we lights our pipes an' sings,
An' we talks about our rations an' a lot of other things,
An' we thinks o' friends in England, an' we wonders what they're at,
An' 'ow they would admire for to hear us sling the *bat*.
An' it's best foot first …

It's none so bad o' Sunday, when you're lyin' at your ease,
To watch the kites a-wheelin' round them feather-'eaded trees,
For although there ain't no women, yet there ain't no barrick-yards,
So the orficers goes shootin' an' the men they plays at cards.
Till it's best foot first …

So 'ark an' 'eed, you rookies, which is always grumblin' sore,
There's worser things than marchin' from Umballa to Cawnpore;
An' if your 'eels are blistered an' they feels to 'urt like 'ell,
You drop some tallow in your socks an' that will make 'em well.
For it's best foot first …

We're marchin' on relief over Injia's coral strand,
Eight 'undred fightin' Englishmen, the Colonel, and the Band;
Ho! get away you bullock-man, you've 'eard the bugle blowed,
There's a regiment a-comin' down the Grand Trunk Road;
With its best foot first
And the road a-sliding past,
An' every bloomin' campin'-ground exactly like the last;
While the Big Drum says,
With 'is '*rowdy-dowdy-dow!*' –
'*Kiko kissywarsti* don't you *hamsher argy jow*?'

    ¹ Why don't you get on?

[First published in *Ballads and Barrack-Room Ballads* (1892).]

A 'shillin' a day' was the pension money paid to retired or veteran soldiers.

SHILLIN' A DAY

My name is O'Kelly, I've heard the Revelly
From Birr to Bareilly, from Leeds to Lahore,
Hong-Kong and Peshawur,
Lucknow and Etawah,
And fifty-five more all endin' in 'pore'.
Black Death and his quickness, the depth and the thickness,
Of sorrow and sickness I've known on my way,
But I'm old and I'm nervis,
I'm cast from the Service,
And all I deserve is a shillin' a day.
(*Chorus*) Shillin' a day,
Bloomin' good pay –
Lucky to touch it, a shillin' a day!

Oh, it drives me half crazy to think of the days I
Went slap for the Ghazi, my sword at my side,
When we rode Hell-for-leather
Both squadrons together,
That didn't care whether we lived or we died.
But it's no use despairin', my wife must go charin'
An' me commissairin' the pay-bills to better,
So if me you be'old
In the wet and the cold,
By the Grand Metropold, won't you give me a letter?
(*Full chorus*) Give 'im a letter –
'Can't do no better,
Late Troop-Sergeant-Major an' – runs with a letter!
Think what 'e's been,
Think what 'e's seen,
Think of his pension an'–

GAWD SAVE THE QUEEN.

[First published in *Ballads and Barrack-Room Ballads* (1892).]

✠ ✠ ✠

After returning to Britain in 1889, Kipling continued writing about his 'Soldiers Three'. The story 'The Courting of Dinah Shadd', in which this poem appears, told of Mulvaney's often disastrous love affairs while serving on active duty.

PRIVATE ORTHERIS'S SONG

My girl she give me the go onst,
    When I was a London lad;
An' I went on the drink for a fortnight,
    An' then I went to the bad.
The Queen she give me a shillin'
    To fight for 'er over the seas;
But Guv'ment built me a fever-trap,
    An' Injia give me disease.

(*Chorus*) Ho! don't you 'eed what a girl says,
    An' don't you go for the beer;
But I was an ass when I was at grass,
    An' that is why I'm 'ere.

I fired a shot at a Afghan,
    The beggar 'e fired again,
An' I lay on my bed with a 'ole in my 'ed,
    An' missed the next campaign!
I up with my gun at a Burman
    Who carried a bloomin' dah,
But the cartridge stuck and the bay'nit bruk,
    An' all I got was the scar.

(*Chorus*) Ho! don't you aim at a Afghan,
When you stand on the skyline clear;
    An' don't you go for a Burman
If none o' your friends is near.

I served my time for a Corp'ral,
    An' wetted my stripes with pop,

For I went on the bend with a intimate friend,
    An' finished the night in the 'shop.'
I served my time for a Sergeant;
    The Colonel 'e sez 'No!
The most you'll see is a full C.B.'
    An'... very next night 'twas so!

(*Chorus*) Ho! don't you go for a Corp'ral
    Unless your 'ed is clear;
But I was an ass when I was at grass,
    An' that is why I'm 'ere.

I've tasted the luck o' the Army
    In barrack an' camp an' clink,
An' I lost my tip through the bloomin' trip
    Along o' the women an' drink.
I'm down at the heel o' my service,
    An' when I am laid on the shelf,
My very worst friend from beginning to end
    By the blood of a mouse was myself!

(*Chorus*) Ho! don't you 'eed what a girl says,
    An' don't you go for the beer;
But I was an ass when I was at grass,
    An' that is why I'm 'ere!

[First published in 'The Courting of Dinah Shadd', *Macmillan's Magazine*, March 1890, later collected in *Life's Handicap* (London: Macmillan, 1891).]

✠   ✠   ✠

This early Barrack-Room Ballad provides the authentic voice of the British regular soldier, who had been known as 'Tommy' or 'Tommy Atkins' in common parlance since the Napoloeonic Wars.

TOMMY

I WENT INTO A public-'ouse to get a pint o' beer,
The publican 'e up an' sez, 'We serve no red-coats here.'

The girls be'ind the bar they laughed an' giggled fit to die,
I outs into the street again an' to myself sez I:
O it's Tommy this, an' Tommy that, an' 'Tommy, go away';
But it's 'Thank you, Mister Atkins', when the band begins to play,
The band begins to play, my boys, the band begins to play,
O it's 'Thank you, Mister Atkins', when the band begins to play.

I went into a theatre as sober as could be,
They gave a drunk civilian room, but 'adn't none for me;
They sent me to the gallery or round the music-'alls,
But when it comes to fightin', Lord! they'll shove me in the stalls!
For it's Tommy this, an' Tommy that, an' 'Tommy, wait outside';
But it's 'Special train for Atkins' when the trooper's on the tide,
The troopship's on the tide, my boys, the troopship's on the tide,
O it's 'Special train for Atkins' when the trooper's on the tide.

Yes, makin' mock o' uniforms that guard you while you sleep
Is cheaper than them uniforms, an' they're starvation cheap;
An' hustlin' drunken soldiers when they're goin' large a bit
Is five times better business than paradin' in full kit.
Then it's Tommy this, an' Tommy that, an' 'Tommy, 'ow's yer
    soul?'
But it's 'Thin red line of 'eroes' when the drums begin to roll,
The drums begin to roll, my boys, the drums begin to roll,
O it's 'Thin red line of 'eroes' when the drums begin to roll.

We aren't no thin red 'eroes, nor we aren't no blackguards too,
But single men in barricks, most remarkable like you;
An' if sometimes our conduck isn't all your fancy paints,
Why, single men in barricks don't grow into plaster saints;
While it's Tommy this, an' Tommy that, an' 'Tommy, fall be'ind',
But it's 'Please to walk in front, sir', when there's trouble in the
    wind,
There's trouble in the wind, my boys, there's trouble in the wind,
O it's 'Please to walk in front, sir', when there's trouble in the wind.

You talk o' better food for us, an' schools, an' fires, an' all:
We'll wait for extry rations if you treat us rational.
Don't mess about the cook-room slops, but prove it to our face
The Widow's Uniform is not the soldier-man's disgrace.

For it's Tommy this, an' Tommy that, an' 'Chuck him out, the
    brute!'
But it's 'Saviour of 'is country' when the guns begin to shoot;
An' it's Tommy this, an' Tommy that, an' anything you please;
An' Tommy ain't a bloomin' fool – you bet that Tommy sees!

[First published in the *Scots Observer*, 1 March 1890.]

EGYPT AND SUDAN

This is another Barrack-Room Ballad where Kipling pays tribute to the martial and human qualities of the soldiers that the British fought against – in this case in the expedition against the Mahdi in Sudan in 1884–5.

FUZZY-WUZZY

(Soudan Expeditionary Force)

WE'VE FOUGHT WITH MANY men acrost the seas,
An' some of 'em was brave an' some was not:
The Paythan an' the Zulu an' Burmese;
But the Fuzzy was the finest o' the lot.
We never got a ha'porth's change of 'im:
'E squatted in the scrub an' 'ocked our 'orses,
'E cut our sentries up at Sua*kim*,
An' 'e played the cat an' banjo with our forces.
So 'ere's *to* you, Fuzzy-Wuzzy, at your 'ome in the Soudan;
You're a pore benighted 'eathen but a first-class fightin' man;
We gives you your certificate, an' if you want it signed
We'll come an' 'ave a romp with you whenever you're inclined.

We took our chanst among the Khyber 'ills,
The Boers knocked us silly at a mile,

The Burman give us Irriwaddy chills,
An' a Zulu *impi* dished us up in style:
But all we ever got from such as they
Was pop to what the Fuzzy made us swaller;
We 'eld our bloomin' own, the papers say,
But man for man the Fuzzy knocked us 'oller.
Then 'ere's *to* you, Fuzzy-Wuzzy, an' the missis and the kid;
Our orders was to break you, an' of course we went an' did.
We sloshed you with Martinis, an' it wasn't 'ardly fair;
But for all the odds agin' you, Fuzzy-Wuz, you broke the square.

'E 'asn't got no papers of 'is own,
'E 'asn't got no medals nor rewards,
So we must certify the skill 'e's shown
In usin' of 'is long two-'anded swords:
When 'e's 'oppin' in an' out among the bush
With 'is coffin-'eaded shield an' shovel-spear,
An 'appy day with Fuzzy on the rush
Will last an 'ealthy Tommy for a year.
So 'ere's *to* you, Fuzzy-Wuzzy, an' your friends which are no more,
If we 'adn't lost some messmates we would 'elp you to deplore;
But give an' take's the gospel, an' we'll call the bargain fair,
For if you 'ave lost more than us, you crumpled up the square!

'E rushes at the smoke when we let drive,
An', before we know, 'e's 'ackin' at our 'ead;
'E's all 'ot sand an' ginger when alive,
An' 'e's generally shammin' when 'e's dead.
'E's a daisy, 'e's a ducky, 'e's a lamb!
'E's a injia-rubber idiot on the spree,
'E's the on'y thing that doesn't give a damn
For a Regiment o' British Infantree!
So 'ere's *to* you, Fuzzy-Wuzzy, at your 'ome in the Soudan;
You're a pore benighted 'eathen but a first-class fightin' man;
An' 'ere's *to* you, Fuzzy-Wuzzy, with your 'ayrick 'ead of 'air –
You big black boundin' beggar – for you broke a British square!

[First published in the *Scots Observer*, 15 March 1890.]

✠ ✠ ✠

Back in London after spending seven years in India, Kipling wanted to write a novel. *The Light that Failed* **was a complex story about an artist's professional and romantic life, set against a backdrop of the 1884-5 expedition against the Sudanese Mahdi.**

THE LIGHT THAT FAILED

DICK FOLLOWED TORPENHOW WHEREVER the latter's fancy chose to lead him, and between the two they managed to accomplish some work that almost satisfied themselves. It was not an easy life in any way, and under its influence the two were drawn very closely together, for they ate from the same dish, they shared the same water-bottle, and, most binding tie of all, their mails went off together. It was Dick who managed to make gloriously drunk a telegraph-clerk in a palm hut far beyond the Second Cataract, and, while the man lay in bliss on the floor, possessed himself of some laboriously acquired exclusive information, forwarded by a confiding correspondent of an opposition syndicate, made a careful duplicate of the matter, and brought the result to Torpenhow, who said that all was fair in love or war correspondence, and built an excellent descriptive article from his rival's riotous waste of words. It was Torpenhow who – but the tale of their adventures, together and apart, from Philx to the waste wilderness of Herawi and Muella, would fill many books. They had been penned into a square side by side, in deadly fear of being shot by over-excited soldiers; they had fought with baggage-camels in the chill dawn; they had jogged along in silence under blinding sun on indefatigable little Egyptian horses; and they had floundered on the shallows of the Nile when the whale-boat in which they had found a berth chose to hit a hidden rock and rip out half her bottom-planks.

Now they were sitting on the sand-bank, and the whale-boats were bringing up the remainder of the column.

'Yes,' said Torpenhow, as he put the last rude stitches into his over-long-neglected gear, 'it has been a beautiful business.'

'The patch or the campaign?' said Dick. 'Don't think much of either, myself.'

'You want the *Eurylas* brought up above the Third Cataract, don't you? and eighty-one-ton guns at Jakdul? Now, *I'm* quite satisfied with my breeches.' He turned round gravely to exhibit himself, after the manner of a clown.

'It's very pretty. Specially the lettering on the sack. G.B.T. Government Bullock Train. That's a sack from India.'

'It's my initials, – Gilbert Belling Torpenhow. I stole the cloth on purpose. What the mischief are the camel-corps doing yonder?' Torpenhow shaded his eyes and looked across the scrub-strewn gravel.

A bugle blew furiously, and the men on the bank hurried to their arms and accoutrements.

'"Pisan soldiery surprised while bathing,"' remarked Dick calmly. 'D'you remember the picture? It's by Michael Angelo; all beginners copy it. That scrub's alive with enemy.'

The camel-corps on the bank yelled to the infantry to come to them, and a hoarse shouting down the river showed that the remainder of the column had wind of the trouble and was hastening to take share in it. As swiftly as a reach of still water is crisped by the wind, the rock-strewn ridges and scrub-topped hills were troubled and alive with armed men. Mercifully, it occurred to these to stand far off for a time, to shout and gesticulate joyously. One man even delivered himself of a long story. The camel-corps did not fire. They were only too glad of a little breathing-space, until some sort of square could be formed. The men on the sand-bank ran to their side; and the whale-boats, as they toiled up within shouting distance, were thrust into the nearest bank and emptied of all save the sick and a few men to guard them. The Arab orator ceased his outcries, and his friends howled.

'They look like the Mahdi's men,' said Torpenhow, elbowing himself into the crush of the square; 'but what thousands of 'em there are! The tribes hereabout aren't against us, I know.'

'Then the Mahdi's taken another town,' said Dick, 'and set all these yelping devils free to chaw us up. Lend us your glass.'

'Our scouts should have told us of this. We've been trapped,' said a subaltern. 'Aren't the camel-guns ever going to begin? Hurry up, you men!'

There was no need for any order. The men flung themselves panting against the sides of the square, for they had good reason to know that whoso was left outside when the fighting began would very probably die in an extremely unpleasant fashion. The little hundred-and-fifty-pound camel-guns posted at one corner of the square opened the ball as the square moved forward by its right to get possession of a knoll of rising ground. All had fought in this manner many times before, and there was no novelty in the entertainment: always the same hot and stifling formation, the smell of dust and leather, the same boltlike rush of the enemy, the same pressure on the weakest side of the square, the few minutes of desperate hand-to-hand scuffle, and then the silence of the desert, broken only by the yells of those whom the handful of cavalry attempted to pursue. They had grown careless. The camel-guns spoke at intervals, and the square slouched forward amid the protests of the camels. Then came the attack of three thousand men who had not learned from books that it is impossible for troops in close order to attack against breechloading fire. A few dropping shots heralded their approach, and a few horsemen led, but the bulk of the force was naked humanity, mad with rage, and armed with the spear and the sword. The instinct of the desert, where there is always much war, told them that the right flank of the square was the weakest, for they swung clear of the front. The camel-guns shelled them as they passed; and opened for an instant lanes through their midst, most like those quick-closing vistas in a Kentish hop-garden seen when the train races by at full speed; and the infantry fire, held till the opportune moment, dropped them in close-packed hundreds. No civilised troops in the world could have endured the hell through which they came, the living leaping high to avoid the dying who clutched at their heels, the wounded cursing and staggering forward, till they fell – a torrent black as the sliding water above a mill-dam – full on the right flank of the square. Then the line of the dusty troops and the faint blue desert sky overhead went out in rolling smoke, and the little stones on the heated ground and the tinder-dry clumps of scrub became matters of surpassing interest, for men measured their agonised retreat and recovery by these things, counting mechanically and hewing their way back to chosen pebble and branch. There was no semblance of any concerted fighting. For aught the men knew, the enemy might be attempting all four sides of the square at once. Their business was to destroy what lay in front of them, to bayonet in the back those who passed over them, and, dying, to drag down the slayer till he could be knocked on the head by some avenging gunbutt.

Dick waited quietly with Torpenhow and a young doctor till the stress became unendurable. There was no hope of attending to the wounded till the attack was repulsed, so the three moved forward gingerly towards the weakest side. There was a rush from without, the short *hough-hough* of the stabbing spears, and a man on a horse, followed by thirty or forty others, dashed through, yelling and hacking. The right flank of the square sucked in after them, and the other sides sent help. The wounded, who knew that they had but a few hours more to live, caught at the enemy's feet and brought them down, or, staggering to a discarded rifle, fired blindly into the scuffle that raged in the centre of the square. Dick was conscious that somebody had cut him violently across his helmet, that he had fired his revolver into a black, foam-flecked face which forthwith ceased to bear any resemblance to a face, and that Torpenhow had gone down under an Arab whom he had tried to 'collar low,' and was turning over and over with his captive, feeling for the man's eyes. The doctor was jabbing at a venture with a bayonet, and a helmetless soldier was firing over Dick's shoulder: the flying grains of powder stung his cheek. It was to Torpenhow that Dick turned by instinct. The representative of the Central Southern Syndicate had shaken himself clear of his enemy, and rose, wiping his thumb on his trousers. The Arab, both hands to his forehead, screamed aloud, then snatched up his spear and rushed at Torpenhow, who was panting under shelter of Dick's revolver. Dick fired twice, and the man dropped limply. His upturned face lacked one eye. The musketry-fire redoubled, but cheers mingled with it. The rush had failed, and the enemy were flying. If the heart of the square were shambles, the ground beyond was a butcher's shop. Dick thrust his way forward between the maddened men. The remnant of the enemy were retiring, as the few – the very few – English cavalry rode down the laggards.

Beyond the lines of the dead, a broad blood-stained Arab spear cast aside in the retreat lay across a stump of scrub, and beyond this again the illimitable dark levels of the desert. The sun caught the steel and turned it into a savage red disc. Some one behind him was saying, 'Ah, get away, you brute!' Dick raised his revolver and pointed towards the desert. His eye was held by the red splash in the distance, and the clamour about him seemed to die down to a very far-away whisper, like the whisper of a level sea. There was the revolver and the red light, ... and the voice of some one scaring something away, exactly as had fallen somewhere before – probably in a past life. Dick waited for what should happen afterwards. Something seemed to crack inside his head, and for an instant he stood in the dark – a darkness that stung. He fired at random, and the bullet went out, across the desert as he muttered, 'Spoilt my aim. There aren't any more cartridges. We shall have to run home.' He put his hand to his head and brought it away covered with blood.

'Old man, you're cut rather badly,' said Torpenhow. 'I owe you something for this business. Thanks. Stand up! I say, you can't be ill here.'

Dick had fallen stiffly on Torpenhow's shoulder, and was muttering something about aiming low and to the left. Then he sank to the ground and was silent. Torpenhow dragged him off to a doctor and sat down to work out an account of what he was pleased to call 'a sanguinary battle, in which our arms had acquitted themselves,' etc.

All that night, when the troops were encamped by the whale-boats, a black figure danced in the strong moonlight on the sand-bar and shouted that Khartoum the accursed one was dead – was dead – was dead – that two steamers were rock-staked on the Nile outside the city, and that of all their crews there remained not one; and Khartoum was dead – was dead – was dead!

But Torpenhow took no heed. He was watching Dick, who was calling aloud to the restless Nile for Maisie – and again Maisie!

'Behold a phenomenon,' said Torpenhow, rearranging the blanket. 'Here is a man, presumably human, who mentions the name of one woman only. And I've seen a good deal of delirium, too – Dick, here's some fizzy drink.'

'Thank you, Maisie,' said Dick.

[First published as *The Light that Failed* in *Lipincott's Monthly Magazine*, January 1891, and then in book form (London: Macmillan 1891).]

BACK IN ENGLAND, 1890s

Bobs was General (from 1895 Field Marshal) Sir Frederick Roberts (later the 1st Earl Roberts), whom Kipling had got to know as commander-in-chief in India. Roberts, who had fought in the Indian Mutiny, made his name with his march from Kabul to raise the Siege of Kandahar in 1880. This provided a boost to British ambitions in Afghanistan since, in the wake of the British disaster at Maiwand, it saw off the threat of an Afghan pretender Ayub Khan, who was thought to be sympathetic to the Russians, and paved the way for a pro-British Amir Abdur Rahman (who, as reported by Kipling above, was received in a Durbar by Lord Dufferin in 1885). Roberts was later recalled to lead the British forces in the Boer War in 1899. He was a particular hero of Kipling's.

BOBS

(Field Marshal Lord Roberts of Kandahar)

THERE'S A LITTLE RED-FACED man,
Which is Bobs,
Rides the talliest 'orse 'e can –
Our Bobs.
If it bucks or kicks or rears,

'E can sit for twenty years
With a smile round both 'is ears –
Can't yer, Bobs?

Then 'ere's to Bobs Bahadur – little Bobs, Bobs, Bobs!
'E's our *pukka* Kandaharder –
Fightin' Bobs, Bobs, Bobs!
'E's the Dook of *Aggy Chel*;
'E's the man that done us well,
An' we'll follow 'im to 'ell –
Won't we, Bobs?

If a limber's slipped a trace,
'Ook on Bobs.
If a marker's lost 'is place,
Dress by Bobs.
For 'e's eyes all up 'is coat,
An' a bugle in 'is throat,
An' you will not play the goat
Under Bobs.

'E's a little down on drink
Chaplain Bobs;
But it keeps us outer Clink –
Don't it, Bobs?
So we will not complain
Tho' 'e's water on the brain,
If 'e leads us straight again –
Blue-light Bobs.

If you stood 'im on 'is head,
Father Bobs,
You could spill a quart of lead
Outer Bobs.
'E's been at it thirty years,
An-amassin' soveneers
In the way o' slugs an' spears –
Ain't yer Bobs?

What 'e does not know o' war,
Gen'ral Bobs,
You cun arst the shop next door –
Can't they, Bobs?
Oh, 'e's little but he's wise;
'E's terror for 'is size,
An' – 'e – does – not – advertise –
Do yer, Bobs?

Now they've made a blooimin' Lord
Outer Bobs,
Which was but 'is fair reward –
Weren't it, Bobs?
So 'e'll wear a coronet
Where 'is 'elmet used to set;
But we know you won't forget –
Will yer, Bobs?

Then 'ere's to Bobs Bahadur – little Bobs, Bobs, Bobs,
Pocket-Wellin'ton an' *'arder* –
Fightin' Bobs, Bobs, Bobs!
This ain't no bloomin' ode,
But you've 'elped the soldier's load,
An' for benefits bestowed,
Bless yer, Bobs!

[First published in the *Pall Mall Magazine,* December 1893.]

In this poem an experienced soldier is addressing a band of new recruits on how to get along in the army. The Battle of Minden was fought in Prussia in August 1759 as part of the Seven Years War. It pitched an Anglo-German force headed by Field Marshal Ferdinand, Duke of Brunswick, against the French.

THE MEN THAT FOUGHT AT MINDEN

A Song of Instruction

THE MEN THAT FOUGHT at Minden, they was rookies in their time –
So was them that fought at Waterloo!
All the 'ole command, yuss, from Minden to Maiwand,
They was once dam' sweeps like you!

Then do not be discouraged, 'Eaven is your 'elper,
We'll learn you not to forget;
An' you mustn't swear an' curse, or you'll only catch it worse,
For we'll make you soldiers yet!

The men that fought at Minden, they 'ad stocks beneath their chins,
Six inch 'igh an' more;
But fatigue it was their pride, and they *would* not be denied
To clean the cook-'ouse floor.

The men that fought at Minden, they had anarchistic bombs
Served to 'em by name of 'and-grenades;
But they got it in the eye (same as you will by-an'-by)
When they clubbed their field-parades.

The men that fought at Minden, they 'ad buttons up an' down,
Two-an'-twenty dozen of 'em told;
But they didn't grouse an' shirk at an hour's extry work,
They kept 'em bright as gold.

The men that fought at Minden, they was armed with musketoons,
Also, they was drilled by 'alberdiers;
I don't know what they were, but the sergeants took good care
They washed be'ind their ears.

The men that fought at Minden, they 'ad ever cash in 'and
Which they did not bank nor save,
But spent it gay an' free on their betters – such as me –
For the good advice I gave.

The men that fought at Minden, they was civil – yuss, they was –
Never didn't talk o' rights an' wrongs,
But they got it with the toe (same as you will get it – so!) –
For interrupting songs.

The men that fought at Minden, they was several other things
Which I don't remember clear;
But *that's* the reason why, now the six-year men are dry,
The rooks will stand the beer!

Then do not be discouraged, 'Eaven is your 'elper,
We'll learn you not to forget;
An' you mustn't swear an' curse, or you'll only catch it worse,
For we'll make you soldiers yet!

Soldiers yet, if you've got it in you –
All for the sake of the Core;
Soldiers yet, if we 'ave to skin you –
Run an' get the beer, Johnny Raw – Johnny Raw!
Ho! run an' get the beer, Johnny Raw!

[First published in the *Pall Mall Gazette*, 9 May 1895.]

This is one of the 16 service songs published in 1903 at the end of Kipling's post-Boer War collection *The Five Nations*, this poem celebrates the Royal Artillery which, at the behest of King William IV in 1833, adopted the word 'Ubique' meaning 'Everywhere' to add to its long-standing motto *Quo Fas et Gloria ducunt* – Where Right and Glory lead.

UBIQUE

THERE IS A WORD you often see, pronounce it as you may –
'You bike,' 'you bikwe,' 'ubbikwe' – alludin' to R.A.
It serves 'Orse, Field, an' Garrison as motto for a crest,
An' when you've found out all it means I'll tell you 'alf the rest.

Ubique means the long-range Krupp be'ind the low-range 'ill –
Ubique means you'll pick it up an', while you do stand, still.
Ubique means you've caught the flash an' timed it by the sound.
Ubique means five gunners' 'ash before you've loosed a round.

Ubique means Blue Fuse,¹ an' make the 'ole to sink the trail.
Ubique means stand up an' take the Mauser's 'alf-mile 'ail.
Ubique means the crazy team not God nor man can 'old.
Ubique means that 'orse's scream which turns your innards cold.

Ubique means 'Bank, 'Olborn, Bank – a penny all the way –
The soothin' jingle-bump-an'-clank from day to peaceful day.
Ubique means 'They've caught De Wet, an' now we sha'n't be long.'
Ubique means 'I much regret, the beggar's going strong!'

Ubique means the tearin' drift where, breech-blocks jammed with mud,
The khaki muzzles duck an' lift across the khaki flood.
Ubique means the dancing plain that changes rocks to Boers.
Ubique means the mirage again an' shellin' all outdoors.

Ubique means 'Entrain at once for Grootdefeatfontein'!
Ubique means 'Off-load your guns' – at midnight in the rain!
Ubique means 'More mounted men. Return all guns to store.'
Ubique means the R.A.M.R. Infantillery Corps!

Ubique means the warnin' grunt the perished linesman knows,
When o'er 'is strung an' sufferin' front the shrapnel sprays 'is foes,
An' as their firin' dies away the 'usky whisper runs
From lips that 'aven't drunk all day: 'The Guns! Thank Gawd, the
    Guns!'

Extreme, depressed, point-blank or short, end-first or any'ow,
From Colesberg Kop to Quagga's Poort – from Ninety-Nine till now –
By what I've 'eard the others tell an' I in spots 'ave seen,
There's nothin' this side 'Eaven or 'Ell Ubique doesn't mean!

¹ Extreme range.

[First published in *The Five Nations* (London: Methuen, 1903).]

**This is Kipling's paean to the work of the sappers, or Royal
Engineers.**

SAPPERS

WHEN THE WATERS WERE dried an' the Earth did appear,
('It's all one,' says the Sapper),
The Lord He created the Engineer,
Her Majesty's Royal Engineer,
With the rank and pay of a Sapper!

When the Flood come along for an extra monsoon,
'Twas Noah constructed the first pontoon
To the plans of Her Majesty's, etc.

But after fatigue in the wet an' the sun,
Old Noah got drunk, which he wouldn't ha' done
If he'd trained with, etc.

When the Tower o' Babel had mixed up men's *bat*,
Some clever civilian was managing that,
An' none of, etc.

When the Jews had a fight at the foot of a hill,
Young Joshua ordered the sun to stand still,
For he was a Captain of Engineers, etc.

When the Children of Israel made bricks without straw,
They were learnin' the regular work of our Corps,
The work of, etc.

For ever since then, if a war they would wage,
Behold us a-shinin' on history's page –
First page for, etc.

We lay down their sidings an' help 'em entrain,
An' we sweep up their mess through the bloomin' campaign,
In the style of, etc.

They send us in front with a fuse an' a mine
To blow up the gates that are rushed by the Line,
But bent by, etc.

They send us behind with a pick an' a spade,
To dig for the guns of a bullock-brigade
Which has asked for, etc.

We work under escort in trousers and shirt,
An' the heathen they plug us tail-up in the dirt,
Annoying, etc.

We blast out the rock an' we shovel the mud,
We make 'em good roads an' – they roll down the *khud*,
Reporting, etc.

We make 'em their bridges, their wells, an' their huts,
An' the telegraph-wire the enemy cuts,
An' it's blamed on, etc.

An' when we return, an' from war we would cease,
They grudge us adornin' the billets of peace,
Which are kept for, etc.

We build 'em nice barracks – they swear they are bad,
That our Colonels are Methodist, married or mad,
Insultin', etc.

They haven't no manners nor gratitude too,
For the more that we help 'em, the less will they do,
But mock at, etc.

Now the Line's but a man with a gun in his hand,
An' Cavalry's only what horses can stand,
When helped by, etc.

Artillery moves by the leave o' the ground,
But *we* are the men that do something all round,
For *we* are, etc.

I have stated it plain, an' my argument's thus
('It's all one,' says the Sapper),
There's only one Corps which is perfect – that's us;
An' they call us Her Majesty's Engineers,
Her Majesty's Royal Engineers,
With the rank and pay of a Sapper!

[First published in *The Seven Seas* (London: Methuen, 1896).]

✠　✠　✠

This is another poem commemorating the Battle of Maiwand in 1880 – and in particular the role of the Royal Berkshire Regiment, which happened to be stationed in Bermuda when Kipling visited in 1894.

THAT DAY

IT GOT BEYOND ALL orders an' it got beyond all 'ope;
It got to shammin' wounded an' retirin' from the 'alt.
'Ole companies was lookin' for the nearest road to slope;
It were just a bloomin' knock-out – an' our fault!

Now there ain't no chorus 'ere to give,
Nor there ain't no band to play;
An' I wish I was dead 'fore I done what I did,
Or seen what I seed that day!

We was sick o' bein' punished, an' we let 'em know it, too;
An' a company-commander up an' 'it us with a sword,
An' some one shouted "Ook it!' an' it come to *sove-ki-poo*,
An' we chucked our rifles from us – O my Gawd!

There was thirty dead an' wounded on the ground we wouldn't
    keep –
No, there wasn't more than twenty when the front begun to go;
But, Christ! along the line o' flight they cut us up like sheep,
An' that was all we gained by doin' so.

I 'eard the knives be'ind me, but I dursn't face my man,
Nor I don't know where I went to, 'cause I didn't 'alt to see,
Till I 'eard a beggar squealin' out for quarter as 'e ran,
An' I thought I knew the voice an' – it was me!

We was 'idin' under bedsteads more than 'arf a march away;
We was lyin' up like rabbits all about the countryside;
An' the major cursed 'is Maker 'cause 'e lived to see that day,
An' the colonel broke 'is sword acrost, an' cried.

We was rotten 'fore we started – we was never disci*plined*;
We made it out a favour if an order was obeyed;
Yes, every little drummer 'ad 'is rights an' wrongs to mind,
So we had to pay for teachin' – an' we paid!

The papers 'id it 'andsome, but you know the Army knows;
We was put to groomin' camels till the regiments withdrew,
An' they gave us each a medal for subduin' England's foes,
An' I 'ope you like my song – because it's true!

An' there ain't no chorus 'ere to give,
Nor there ain't no band to play;
But I wish I was dead 'fore I done what I did,
Or seen what I seed that day!

[First published in the *Pall Mall Gazette*, 25 April 1895.]

✠ ✠ ✠

This is one of Kipling's best-known poems, commemorating Queen Victoria's Diamond Jubilee in 1897. It was written after he had witnessed the naval review in June that year, when 165 vessels were assembled at Spithead. Although celebrating the Jubilee, he also wanted to warn against imperial pride. He was unsatisfied with what he wrote and consigned it to the waste-paper basket, from where it was retrieved by Caroline Norton, a family friend who was visiting from America. Kipling sent it to *The Times*, stating that he would not require payment.

RECESSIONAL

June 22, 1897

GOD OF OUR FATHERS, known of old –
Lord of our far-flung battle-line –
Beneath whose awful Hand we hold
Dominion over palm and pine –
Lord God of Hosts, be with us yet,
Lest we forget, lest we forget!

The tumult and the shouting dies –
The captains and the kings depart –
Still stands Thine ancient sacrifice,
An humble and a contrite heart.
Lord God of Hosts, be with us yet,
Lest we forget, lest we forget!

Far-call'd our navies melt away –
On dune and headland sinks the fire –
Lo, all our pomp of yesterday
Is one with Nineveh and Tyre!
Judge of the Nations, spare us yet,
Lest we forget, lest we forget!

If, drunk with sight of power, we loose
Wild tongues that have not Thee in awe –

Such boasting as the Gentiles use
Or lesser breeds without the Law –
Lord God of Hosts, be with us yet,
Lest we forget, lest we forget!

For heathen heart that puts her trust
In reeking tube and iron shard –
All valiant dust that builds on dust,
And guarding calls not Thee to guard –
For frantic boast and foolish word,
Thy Mercy on Thy People, Lord!

[First published in *The Times*, 17 July 1897.]

✠　✠　✠

This controversial poem lent support to the United States and
its newfound imperial mission following its war against Spain
in 1898. As a result of the Treaty of Paris in October that year,
Washington gained control of Cuba, Puerto Rico, Guam and the
Philippines.

THE WHITE MAN'S BURDEN

TAKE UP THE WHITE Man's burden –
Send forth the best ye breed –
Go bind your sons to exile
To serve your captives' need;
To wait in heavy harness
On fluttered folk and wild –
Your new-caught, sullen peoples,
Half devil and half child.

Take up the White Man's burden –
In patience to abide,
To veil the threat of terror
And check the show of pride;
By open speech and simple,

An hundred times made plain.
To seek another's profit,
And work another's gain.

Take up the White Man's burden –
The savage wars of peace –
Fill full the mouth of Famine
And bid the sickness cease;
And when your goal is nearest
The end for others sought,
Watch Sloth and heathen Folly
Bring all your hope to nought.

Take up the White Man's burden –
No tawdry rule of kings,
But toil of serf and sweeper –
The tale of common things.
The ports ye shall not enter,
The roads ye shall not tread,
Go make them with your living,
And mark them with your dead!

Take up the White Man's burden –
And reap his old reward:
The blame of those ye better,
The hate of those ye guard –
The cry of hosts ye humour
(Ah, slowly!) toward the light:–
'Why brought ye us from bondage,
'Our loved Egyptian night?'

Take up the White Man's burden –
Ye dare not stoop to less –
Nor call too loud on freedom
To cloak your weariness;
By all ye cry or whisper,
By all ye leave or do,
The silent, sullen peoples
Shall weigh your Gods and you.

Take up the White Man's burden –
Have done with childish days –
The lightly proffered laurel,
The easy, ungrudged praise.
Comes now, to search your manhood
Through all the thankless years,
Cold-edged with dear-bought wisdom,
The judgment of your peers!

[First published in *The Times* and *Literature*, 4 February 1899.]

SOUTH AFRICA

Kipling wrote this popular poem to raise money for the families of soldiers who had gone to fight in the Boer War (1899–1902). He freed them from copyright, so they were widely reproduced and sung. Over £300,000 was raised for the cause.

THE ABSENT-MINDED BEGGAR

WHEN YOU'VE SHOUTED 'RULE Britannia,' when you've sung 'God
    Save the Queen,'
    When you've finished killing Kruger with your mouth,
Will you kindly drop a shilling in my little tambourine
    For a gentleman in khaki going South?
He's an absent-minded beggar, and his weaknesses are great –
    But we and Paul must take him as we find him –
He is out on active service, wiping something of a slate –
    And he's left a lot of little things behind him!
Duke's son – cook's son – son of a hundred kings –
    (Fifty thousand horse and foot going to Table Bay!)
Each of 'em doing his country's work
    (and who's to look after his things?)
Pass the hat for your credit's sake,
        and pay – pay – pay!

There are girls he married secret, asking no permission to,
    For he knew he wouldn't get it if he did.

There is gas and coals and vittles, and the house-rent falling due,
  And it's more than rather likely there's a kid.
There are girls he walked with casual. They'll be sorry now he's
    gone,
  For an absent-minded beggar they will find him,
But it ain't the time for sermons with the winter coming on.
  We must help the girl that Tommy's left behind him!
Cook's son – Duke's son – son of a belted Earl –
  Son of Lambeth publican – it's all the same today!
Each of them doing the country's work
  (and who's to look after the girl?)
Pass the hat for your credit's sake,
    and pay – pay – pay!

They are families by thousands, far too proud to beg or speak,
  And they'll put their sticks and bedding up the spout,
And they'll live on half o' nothing, paid 'em punctual once a
    week,
  'Cause the man that earns the wage is ordered out.
He's an absent-minded beggar, but he heard his country call,
  And his reg'ment didn't need to send to find him!
He chucked his job and joined it – so the job before us all
  Is to help the home that Tommy's left behind him!
Duke's job – cook's job – gardener, baronet, groom,
  Mews or palace or paper-shop, there's someone gone away!
Each of 'em doing his country's work
  (and who's to look after the room?)
Pass the hat for your credit's sake,
    and pay – pay – pay!

Let us manage so as later, we can look him in the face,
  And tell him – what he'd very much prefer –
That, while he saved the Empire, his employer saved his place,
  And his mates (that's you and me) looked out for *her*.
He's an absent-minded beggar and he may forget it all,
  But we do not want his kiddies to remind him
That we sent 'em to the workhouse while their daddy hammered
    Paul,
  So we'll help the homes that Tommy left behind him!
Cook's home – Duke's home – home of millionaire,

(Fifty thousand horse and foot going to Table Bay!)
Each of 'em doing his country's work
    (and what have you got to spare?)
Pass the hat for your credit's sake
        and pay – pay – pay!

[First published in the *Daily Mail*, 31 October 1899.]

✠ ✠ ✠

**The Battle of Kari (or Karee) took place on 28 March 1900, some
12 miles north of Bloemfontein. Kipling was accompanied by
Bennet Burleigh, a well-known war correspondent working for
the *Daily Telegraph*.**

UNDER FIRE AT KARI SIDING

BY THE TIME THAT I returned to Bloemfontein the populace had
it that eighty thousand Boers were closing in on the town at once,
and the Press Censor (Lord Stanley, now Derby) was besieged with
persons anxious to telegraph to Cape Town. To him a non-Aryan
pushed a domestic wire 'weather here changeable.' Stanley, himself
a little worried for the fate of some of his friends in that ambuscaded
column, rebuked the gentleman.

The Sardine was right about the 'bill-sticking' expeditions. Wandering columns had been sent round the country to show how kind
the British desired to be to the misguided Boer. But the Transvaal
Boer, not being a town-bird, was unimpressed by the 'fall' of the Free
State capital, and ran loose on the veldt with his pony and Mauser.

So there had to be a battle, which was called the Battle of Kari
Siding. All the staff of the Bloemfontein Friend attended. I was put
in a Cape cart, with native driver, containing most of the drinks,
and with me was a well-known war-correspondent. The enormous
pale landscape swallowed up seven thousand troops without a
sign, along a front of seven miles. On our way we passed a collection of neat, deep and empty trenches well undercut for shelter
on the shrapnel side. A young Guards officer, recently promoted
to Brevet-Major – and rather sore with the paper that we had

printed it Branch – studied them interestedly. They were the first dim lines of the dug-out, but his and our eyes were held. The Hun had designed them secundum artem, but the Boer had preferred the open within reach of his pony. At last we came to a lone farm-house in a vale adorned with no less than five white flags. Beyond the ridge was a sputter of musketry and now and then the whoop of a field-piece. 'Here,' said my guide and guardian, 'we get out and walk. Our driver will wait for us at the farm-house.' But the driver loudly objected. 'No, sar. They shoot. They shoot me.' 'But they are white-flagged all over,' we said. 'Yess, sar. That why,' was his answer, and he preferred to take his mules down into a decently remote donga and wait our return.

The farm-house (you will see in a little why I am so detailed) held two men and, I think, two women, who received us disinterestedly. We went on into a vacant world full of sunshine and distances, where now and again a single bullet sang to himself. What I most objected to was the sensation of being under aimed fire – being, as it were, required as a head. 'What are they doing this for?' I asked my friend. 'Because they think we are the Something Light Horse. They ought to be just under this slope.' I prayed that the particularly Something Light Horse would go elsewhere, which they presently did, for the aimed fire slackened and a wandering Colonial, bored to extinction, turned up with news from a far flank. 'No; nothing doing and no one to see.' Then more cracklings and a most cautious move forward to the lip of a large hollow where sheep were grazing. Some of them began to drop and kick. 'That's both sides trying sighting-shots,' said my companion. 'What range do you make it?' I asked. 'Eight hundred, at the nearest. That's close quarters nowadays. You'll never see anything closer than this. Modern rifles make it impossible. We're hung up till something cracks somewhere.' There was a decent lull for meals on both sides, interrupted now and again by sputters. Then one indubitable shell – ridiculously like a pip-squeak in that vastness but throwing up much dirt. 'Krupp! Four- or six-pounder at extreme range,' said the expert. 'They still think we're the — Light Horse. They'll come to be fairly regular from now on.' Sure enough, every twenty minutes or so, one judgmatic shell pitched on our slope. We waited, seeing nothing in the emptiness, and hearing only a faint murmur as of wind along gas-jets, running in and out of the unconcerned hills.

Then pom-poms opened. These were nasty little one-pounders, ten in a belt (which usually jammed about the sixth round). On soft ground they merely thudded. On rock-face the shell breaks up and yowls like a cat. My friend for the first time seemed interested. 'If these are their pom-poms, it's Pretoria for us,' was his diagnosis. I looked behind me – the whole length of South Africa down to Cape Town – and it seemed very far. I felt that I could have covered it in five minutes under fair conditions, but – not with those aimed shots up my back. The pom-poms opened again at a bare rock-reef that gave the shells full value. For about two minutes a file of racing ponies, their tails and their riders' heads well down, showed and vanished northward. 'Our pom-poms,' said the correspondent. 'Le Gallais, I expect. Now we shan't be long.' All this time the absurd Krupp was faithfully feeling for us, vice-Light Horse, and, given a few more hours, might perhaps hit one of us. Then to the left, almost under us, a small piece of hanging woodland filled and fumed with our shrapnel much as a man's moustache fills with cigarette-smoke. It was most impressive and lasted for quite twenty minutes. Then silence; then a movement of men and horses from our side up the slope, and the hangar our guns had been hammering spat steady fire at them. More Boer ponies on more skylines; a last flurry of pom-poms on the right and a little frieze of far-off meek-tailed ponies, already out of rifle range.

'Maffeesh,' said the correspondent, and fell to writing on his knee. 'We've shifted 'em.'

Leaving our infantry to follow men on ponyback towards the Equator, we returned to the farm-house. In the donga where he was waiting someone squibbed off a rifle just after we took our seats, and our driver flogged out over the rocks to the danger of our sacred bottles.

Then Bloemfontein, and Gwynne storming in late with his accounts complete – one hundred and twenty-five casualties, and the general opinion that 'French was a bit of a butcher' and a tale of the General commanding the cavalry who absolutely refused to break up his horses by galloping them across raw rock – 'not for any dam' Boer.'

Months later, I got a cutting from an American paper, on information from Geneva – even then a pest-house of propaganda – describing how I and some officers – names, date, and place correct – had entered a farm-house where we found two men and three women. We had dragged the women from under the bed where they had taken refuge (I assure you that no Tantie Sannie of that day could bestow herself beneath any known bed) and, giving them a hundred yards' start, had shot them down as they ran.

Even then, the beastliness struck me as more comic than significant. But by that time I ought to have known that it was the Hun's reflection of his own face as he spied at our back-windows. He had thrown in the 'hundred yards' start' touch as a tribute to our national sense of fair play.

From the business point of view the war was ridiculous. We charged ourselves step by step with the care and maintenance of all Boerdom – women and children included. Whence horrible tales of our atrocities in the concentration-camps.

One of the most widely exploited charges was our deliberate cruelty in making prisoners' tents and quarters open to the north. A Miss Hobhouse among others was loud in this matter, but she was to be excused.

We were showing off our newly-built little 'Woolsack' to a great lady on her way upcountry, where a residence was being built for her. At the larder the wife pointed out that it faced south – that quarter being the coldest when one is south of the Equator. The great lady considered the heresy for a moment. Then, with the British sniff which abolishes the absurd, 'Hmm! I shan't allow that to make any difference to me.'

Some Army and Navy Stores Lists were introduced into the prisoners' camps, and the women returned to civil life with a knowledge of corsets, stockings, toilet-cases, and other accessories frowned upon by their clergymen and their husbands. Qua women they were not very lovely, but they made their men fight, and they knew well how to fight on their own lines.

In the give-and-take of our work our troops got to gauge the merits of the commando-leaders they were facing. As I remember the scale, De Wet, with two hundred and fifty men, was to be taken seriously. With twice that number he was likely to fall over his own feet. Smuts (of Cambridge), warring, men assured me, in a black suit, trousers rucked to the knees, and a top-hat, could handle five hundred but, beyond that, got muddled. And so with the others. I had the felicity of meeting Smuts as a British General, at the Ritz during the Great War. Meditating on things seen and suffered, he said that being hunted about the veldt on a pony made a man think quickly, and that perhaps Mr. Balfour (as he was then) would have been better for the same experience.

Each commando had its own reputation in the field, and the grizzlier their beards the greater our respect. There was an elderly contingent from Wakkerstroom which demanded most cautious handling. They shot, as you might say, for the pot. The young men were not so good. And there were foreign contingents who insisted on fighting after the manner of Europe. These the Boers wisely put in the forefront of the battle and kept away from. In one affair the Zarps – the Transvaal Police – fought brilliantly and were nearly all killed. But they were Swedes for the most part, and we were sorry.

Occasionally foreign prisoners were gathered in. Among them I remember a Frenchman who had joined for pure logical hatred of England, but, being a professional, could not resist telling us how we ought to wage the war. He was quite sound but rather cantankerous.

The 'war' became an unpleasing compost of 'political considerations,' social reform, and housing; maternity-work and variegated absurdities. It is possible, though I doubt it, that first and last we may have killed four thousand Boers. Our own casualties, mainly from preventible disease, must have been six times as many.

The junior officers agreed that the experience ought to be a 'first-class dress-parade for Armageddon,' but their practical conclusions were misleading. Long-range, aimed rifle-fire would do the work of the future; troops would never get nearer each other than half a mile, and Mounted Infantry would be vital. This was because, having found men on foot cannot overtake men on ponies, we created eighty thousand of as good Mounted Infantry as the world had seen. For these Western Europe had no use. Artillery preparation of wire-works, such as were not at Magersfontein, was rather overlooked in the reformers' schemes, on account of the difficulty of bringing up ammunition by horse-power. The pom-poms, and Lord Dundonald's galloping light gun-carriages, ate up their own weight in shell in three or four minutes.

In the ramshackle hotel at Bloemfontein, where the correspondents lived and the officers dropped in, one heard free and fierce debate as points came up, but – since no one dreamt of the internal-combustion engine that was to stand the world on its thick head, and since our wireless apparatus did not work in those landscapes – we were all beating the air.

Eventually the 'war' petered out on political lines. Brother Boer – and all ranks called him that – would do everything except die. Our men did not see why they should perish chasing stray commandoes, or festering in block-houses, and there followed a sort of demoralising 'handy-pandy' of alternate surrenders complicated by exchange of Army tobacco for Boer brandy which was bad for both sides.

At long last, we were left apologising to a deeply-indignant people, whom we had been nursing and doctoring for a year or two; and who now expected, and received, all manner of free gifts and appliances for the farming they had never practised. We put them in a position to uphold and expand their primitive lust for racial domination, and thanked God we were 'rid of a knave.'

[First published in *Something of Myself* (London: Macmillan, 1937).]

✠   ✠   ✠

The early months of the Boer War put British soldiers through thousands of miles of forced marches. Kipling's poem expresses his sympathy with their hardship. It also reflects the fact that George Allen, the businessman who brought Kipling back to India to work on his newspaper, the *Civil and Military Gazette*, in 1882, had a thriving business manufacturing leather and boots for the army.

BOOTS

Infantry Columns

WE'RE FOOT – SLOG – SLOG – slog – sloggin' over Africa –
Foot – foot – foot – foot – sloggin' over Africa –
(Boots – boots – boots – boots – movin' up an' down again!)
There's no discharge in the war!

Seven – six – eleven – five – nine-an'-twenty mile to-day –
Four – eleven – seventeen – thirty-two the day before –
(Boots – boots – boots – boots – movin' up an' down again!)
There's no discharge in the war!

Don't – don't – don't – don't – look at what's in front of you.
(Boots – boots – boots – boots – movin' up an' down again);
Men – men – men – men – men go mad with watchin' 'em,
An' there's no discharge in the war!

Try – try – try – try – to think o' something different –
Oh – my – God – keep – me from goin' lunatic!
(Boots – boots – boots – boots – movin' up an' down again!)
There's no discharge in the war!

Count – count – count – count – the bullets in the bandoliers.
If – your – eyes – drop – they will get atop o' you!
(Boots – boots – boots – boots – movin' up an' down again) –
There's no discharge in the war!

We – can – stick – out – 'unger, thirst, an' weariness,
But – not – not – not – not the chronic sight of 'em –
Boot – boots – boots – boots – movin' up an' down again,
An' there's no discharge in the war!

'Taint – so – bad – by – day because o' company,
But night – brings – long – strings – o' forty thousand million
Boots – boots – boots – boots – movin' up an' down again.
There's no discharge in the war!

I – 'ave – marched – six – weeks in 'Ell an' certify
It – is – not – fire – devils, dark, or anything,
But boots – boots – boots – boots – movin' up an' down again,
An' there's no discharge in the war!

[First published in *The Five Nations* (1903).]

This is a fine example of Kipling getting into the mind of a soldier whose whole world picture has been changed by his military service abroad.

CHANT-PAGAN

English Irregular, Discharged

ME THAT 'AVE BEEN what I've been –
Me that 'ave gone where I've gone –
Me that 'ave seen what I've seen –
'Ow can I ever take on
With awful old England again,
An' 'ouses both sides of the street,
And 'edges two sides of the lane,
And the parson an' gentry between,
An' touchin' my 'at when we meet –
Me that 'ave been what I've been?

Me that 'ave watched 'arf a world
'Eave up all shiny with dew,
Kopje on kop to the sun,
An' as soon as the mist let 'em through
Our 'elios winkin' like fun –
Three sides of a ninety-mile square,
Over valleys as big as a shire –
'Are ye there? Are ye there? Are ye there?'
An' then the blind drum of our fire ...
An' I'm rollin' 'is lawns for the Squire,
Me!

Me that 'ave rode through the dark
Forty mile, often, on end,
Along the Ma'ollisberg Range,
With only the stars for my mark
An' only the night for my friend,
An' things runnin' off as you pass,
An' things jumpin' up in the grass,
An' the silence, the shine an' the size

Of the 'igh, unexpressible skies –
I am takin' some letters almost
As much as a mile to the post,
An' 'mind you come back with the change!'
Me!

Me that saw Barberton took
When we dropped through the clouds on their 'ead,
An' they 'ove the guns over and fled –
Me that was through Di'mond 'Ill,
An' Pieters an' Springs an' Belfast –
From Dundee to Vereeniging all –
Me that stuck out to the last
(An' five bloomin' bars on my chest) –
I am doin' my Sunday-school best,
By the 'elp of the Squire an' 'is wife
(Not to mention the 'ousemaid an' cook),
To come in an' 'ands up an' be still,
An' honestly work for my bread,
My livin' in that state of life
To which it shall please God to call
Me!

Me that 'ave followed my trade
In the place where the Lightnin's are made;
'Twixt the Rains and the Sun and the Moon –
Me that lay down an' got up
Three years with the sky for my roof –
That 'ave ridden my 'unger an' thirst
Six thousand raw mile on the hoof,
With the Vaal and the Orange for cup,
An' the Brandwater Basin for dish –
Oh! it's 'ard to be'ave as they wish
(Too 'ard, an' a little too soon),
I'll 'ave to think over it first –
Me!

I will arise an' get 'ence –
I will trek South and make sure
If it's only my fancy or not

That the sunshine of England is pale,
And the breezes of England are stale,
An' there's something gone small with the lot.
For I know of a sun an' a wind,
An' some plains and a mountain be'ind,
An' some graves by a barb-wire fence,
An' a Dutchman I've fought 'oo might give
Me a job where I ever inclined
To look in an' offsaddle an' live
Where there's neither a road nor a tree –
But only my Maker an' me,
An I think it will kill me or cure,
So I think I will go there an' see.

[First published in *The Five Nations* (1903).]

✠ ✠ ✠

At the time Lichtenberg was a small village in the western
Transvaal. Some of its trees were cut down by the Boers in 1901 to
make it easier to defend.

LICHTENBERG

(New South Wales Contingent)

SMELLS ARE SURER THAN sounds or sights
To make your heart-strings crack –
They start those awful voices o' nights
That whisper, 'Old man, come back!'
That must be why the big things pass
And the little things remain,
Like the smell of the wattle by Lichtenberg,
Riding in, in the rain.

There was some silly fire on the flank
And the small wet drizzling down –
There were the sold-out shops and the bank

And the wet, wide-open town;
And we were doing escort-duty
To somebody's baggage-train,
And I smelt wattle by Lichtenberg –
Riding in, in the rain.

It was all Australia to me –
All I had found or missed:
Every face I was crazy to see,
And every woman I'd kissed:
All that I shouldn't ha' done, God knows!
(As He knows I'll do it again),
That smell of the wattle round Lichtenberg,
Riding in, in the rain!

And I saw Sydney the same as ever,
The picnics and brass-bands;
And my little homestead on Hunter River
And my new vines joining hands.
It all came over me in one act
Quick as a shot through the brain –
With the smell of the wattle round Lichtenberg,
Riding in, in the rain.

I have forgotten a hundred fights,
But one I shall not forget –
With the raindrops bunging up my sights
And my eyes bunged up with wet;
And through the crack and the stink of the cordite
(Ah Christ! My country again!)
The smell of the wattle by Lichtenberg,
Riding in, in the rain!

[First published in *The Five Nations* (1903).]

The Yeomanry was composed of (mainly) volunteer cavalry regiments, originally established to defend Britain at the time of the Napoleonic Wars. This poem refers to the amalgamated Imperial Yeomanry which fought in the Boer War. A kopje is a small usually rocky hill which sticks up on the flat African veld.

TWO KOPJES

(Made Yeomanry towards the End of the Boer War)

ONLY TWO AFRICAN KOPJES,
Only the cart-tracks that wind
Empty and open between 'em,
Only the Transvaal behind;
Only an Aldershot column
Marching to conquer the land …
Only a sudden and solemn
Visit, unarmed, to the Rand.

Then scorn not the African kopje,
The kopje that smiles in the heat,
The wholly unoccupied kopje,
The home of Cornelius and Piet.
You can never be sure of your kopje,
But of this be you blooming well sure,
A kopje is always a kopje,
And a Boojer is always a Boer!

Only two African kopjes,
Only the vultures above,
Only baboons – at the bottom,
Only some buck on the move;
Only a Kensington draper
Only pretending to scout …
Only bad news for the paper,
Only another knock-out.

Then mock not the African kopje,
And rub not your flank on its side,

The silent and simmering kopje,
The kopje beloved by the guide.
You can never be, etc.

Only two African kopjes,
Only the dust of their wheels,
Only a bolted commando,
Only our guns at their heels …
Only a little barb-wire,
Only a natural fort,
Only 'by sections retire,'
Only 'regret to report!'

Then mock not the African kopje,
Especially when it is twins,
One sharp and one table-topped kopje
For that's where the trouble begins.
You never can be, etc.

Only two African kopjes
Baited the same as before –
Only we've had it so often,
Only we're taking no more …
Only a wave to our troopers,
Only our flanks swinging past,
Only a dozen voorloopers,
Only we've learned it at last!

Then mock not the African kopje,
But take off your hat to the same,
The patient, impartial old kopje,
The kopje that taught us the game!
For all that we knew in the Columns,
And all they've forgot on the Staff,
We learned at the Fight o' Two Kopjes,
Which lasted two years an' a half.

O mock not the African kopje,
Not even when peace has been signed –
The kopje that isn't a kopje –

The kopje that copies its kind.
You can never be sure of your kopje,
But of this be you blooming well sure,
That a kopje is always a kopje,
And a Boojer is always a Boer!

[First published in *The Five Nations* (1903).]

✠ ✠ ✠

This poem does not refer to anyone in particular, but again shows Kipling's empathy with the courage and endurance of everyone under arms, even those fighting against the British.

PIET

(Regular of the Line)

I DO NOT LOVE my Empire's foes,
  Nor call 'em angels; still,
What *is* the sense of 'atin' those
  'Oom you are paid to kill?

So, barrin' all that foreign lot
Which only joined for spite,
Myself, I'd just as soon as not
Respect the man I fight.

Ah there, Piet! – 'is trousies to 'is knees,
'Is coat-tails lyin' level in the bullet-sprinkled breeze;
'E does not lose 'is rifle an' 'e does not lose 'is seat,
I've known a lot o' people ride a dam' sight worse than Piet.

I've 'eard 'im cryin' from the ground
Like Abel's blood of old,
An' skirmished out to look, an' found
The beggar nearly cold.

I've waited on till 'e was dead
(Which couldn't 'elp 'im much),
But many grateful things 'e's said
To me for doin' such.

Ah there, Piet! whose time 'as come to die,
'Is carcase past rebellion, but 'is eyes inquirin' why.
Though dressed in stolen uniform with badge o' rank complete,
I've known a lot o' fellers go a dam' sight worse than Piet.

An' when there wasn't aught to do
But camp and cattle-guards,
I've fought with 'im the 'ole day through
At fifteen 'undred yards;

Long afternoons o' lyin' still,
An' 'earin' as you lay
The bullets swish from 'ill to 'ill
Like scythes among the 'ay.

Ah there, Piet! – be'ind 'is stony kop.
With 'is Boer bread an' biltong, an' 'is flask of awful Dop;
'Is Mauser for amusement an' 'is pony for retreat,
I've known a lot o' fellers shoot a dam' sight worse than Piet.

He's shoved 'is rifle 'neath my nose
Before I'd time to think,
An' borrowed all my Sunday clo'es
An' sent me 'ome in pink.

[First published in *The Five Nations* (1903).]

After arriving in South Africa in February 1900, Kipling took a Red Cross ambulance train which travelled over 600 miles from the Cape to the Modder River to pick up casualties after the Battle of Paardeberg and back again.

WITH NUMBER THREE

A journey with a hospital train from Cape Town to the north during the South African War
April 1900

All the world over, nursing their scars,
Sit the poor fighting-men broke in our wars
Sit the poor fighting-men, surly and grim,
Mocking the lilt of the conquerors' hymn.
Dust of the battle o'erwhelmed them and hid
Fame never found them for aught that they did.
Wounded and spent, to the lazar they drew,
Lining the road where the legions went through.
Sons of the Laurel, that press to your meed
Worthy God's pity most ye that succeed
Ye that tread triumphing crowned toward the stars,
Pity poor fighting-men broke in our wars!

THE SUN HAD FADED the Red Cross on her panels almost to brick colour; had warped her woodwork and blistered her paint. For three months she had jackalled behind the army – now at Belmont, now at Magersfontein, now at Rensburg, and in that time had carried over thirteen hundred sick and wounded. In her appointments, her doctors, her two Nursing Sisters, and her nineteen orderlies there was neither veneer nor pretence, coquetry of uniforms, nor the suspicion of official side. She was starkly set for the work in hand, her gear worn smooth by use and habit, detailed for certain business only, and to that business most strictly attending.

Since she started from no known platform I came aboard early, and while we lay silent as a ship in port, the big stock-pot purring in the kitchen, the bottles clicking in the pharmacy as the doctor counted them over, I felt that peace had never been in our generation

– that Number Three Hospital Train – iodoform-scented, washed, scrubbed, and scoured – had plied since the beginning of time.

Know now that hospital trains have the right of way over all traffic, and since their crews feed aboard them, need only stop to water and change engines. We slipped out of Cape Town into the twilight at a steady twenty-five mile an hour on our six-hundred-mile journey North. Some day you in England will realise what it means to handle armies and their supplies over this distance on a single three-foot-six line. The war has been a war of shunting and side-tracking, of telegraphs and time-tables; so we may hope that the railway men, who have worked like devils, will not be overlooked when the decorations fall ripe.

Because the line runs through Cape Colony, and because Cape Colony is – we have the highest authority for it – loyally trying to be 'neutral', every bridge, every culvert, every point at which the line may be cut or blown up is guarded by a little detachment of armed men. These are drawn chiefly from local corps, such as the Duke of Edinburgh's Own Volunteer Rifles. They do not like the work; they love still less the 'loyalty' which has made the fatigue necessary.

Said a dust-spotted, begrimed Sergeant of the 'Duke's' as Number Three, double-headed, panted up the Hex River pass into the Karroo, 'We've been here since November. I don't mind telling you we're pretty sick of it. We haven't had a look-in at the Front yet. We sit here and patrol the line. Lovely work!'

The setting of the picture hardly varied a hair's breadth. A single track, lifting and dancing in the heat, the brown, hairless hills dusted with split stones, the sleek mirages, the knots of khaki figures, the dingy tents, repeated themselves as though we were running in circles. Here was a water-tank. Number Three drank of it, sucking thirstily; here a speckle of tin houses and a refreshment-room, which we had no need to enter; here a new-laid siding. Number Three flung them all behind her; but for the men with rifles, the red-eyed, bristlebearded, disgusted track-watchers there was no escape.

Suddenly we overhauled a train-load of horses, Bhownagar's and Jamnagar's gifts to the war; stolid saises and a sowar or two in charge.

'Whence dost thou come?'

'From Bombay, with a Sahib.' (The man looked like a Hyderabadi, but he had taken off most of his clothes.

'Dost thou know the name of this land?'

'No.'

'Dost thou know whither thou goest?'

'I do not know.'

'What, then, dost thou do?'

'I go with my Sahib.'

Great is the East, serene and immutable! We left them feeding and watering as the order was.

A few miles farther on – forty or fifty are of no account in this huge place – were guns, infantry, and buck-wagons, rumbling towards De Aar, and, I think, New South Wales Lancers. Then, a Victorian contingent camped by the wayside, happier than the 'Duke's' because they were nearer the Front, but wrathful in that certain Canadians still farther up the line had had the audacity to make a camp called Maple Leaf. They wanted news of the Burma Military Police, long men on little fat ponies like clockwork mice, recently landed, and vanished. Corps have a knack of disappearing bodily in this country. Of the Burmans I knew nothing, but could furnish information more or less accurate of some Malay Light Horse lately seen in Cape Town, and of some Yeomanry details.

'Ah,' said Australia, with a rifle, by the water-tank, 'wait till you see our Queensland bushmen. My word! They're something.'

Then he expressed a private and unprintable opinion about those arrogant Canucks up the line, which opinion, twisted the other way, I got back again from a Canadian, an Eastern Province man, a few hours later.

Strictly in confidence, I may tell you that the Colonial Corps are riding just the least little bit in the world jealous. They have each the honour of a new country to uphold, and it is neck and neck between them. So I sat joyously on the rear platform while Number Three ran the links of Empire through my hands. English of the Midlands, Cockney, Scots, Irish, Welsh, Queenslander, Victorian, and Canadian, one after another, we picked them up and dropped them with a flying word.

There was nothing wrong with that chain, and by the same token, it seemed to have got hold of something at last, for a truckload of Boer prisoners slid by in charge of what looked like a few disreputable bearded veldt-cornets.

'Ho!' said an orderly critically. 'And where did you pick them up?'

'Round Paardeberg. There's more to follow. Most of these is Transvaalers.'

'That's all right,' said the orderly.

The Army, you see, is collecting Transvaalers, and has come a long way for samples. 'An' which might be prisoner and which is guard?'

Said the veldt-cornet with a battered helmet, 'I'm a sergeant of Northamptons in charge.'

'Oh, you are, are you? Then what are you doin' with Labby's friends? Take 'em along. Mr. Labouchere won't be pleased at you.'

But the Sergeant was mightily pleased, save that his prisoners had not washed for some time. He said so. Then we drew to the home of lies, which is De Aar – a junction, the pivot of many of our manoeuvres and a telegraph centre.

It smelt like Umballa platform in the hot weather, and they kept a hell there of fifty half-naked telegraph operators, sweating under the blazing kerosene lamps, each man with two pairs of hands and some extra ears. Outside was thick darkness, and the shunting of trucks – thousands of trucks: but the steady boom of the racing instruments beat through all other noises like the noise of hiving bees.

There was some need to work, and, at least, one very good reason in the shape of a big saloon that glided past us in the night, a lit window revealing just a chair and a neat empty table. The Sirdar (Lord Kitchener) was on the move; going down to Naauwpoort to arrange surprises, and it is not at all healthy to be idle when Kitchener passes by. Therefore, and before this war is over, you will hear all sorts of baseless tales from a certain type of officer who has been made to work: and you must not believe them.

After De Aar time-tables ceased. We were cut adrift on the Sargasso Sea of accumulated rolling-stock between that place and Orange River. Here the rumours begin. There had been a killing – a big killing – the first satisfactory killing – at Paardeberg, up the Modder. Roberts held Cronje in a ring of fire burning day and night. That was none of our concern. We had some news that many wounded waited for us at Modder – thirty officers, at least, and twice as many men – all more or less bad cases.

Here and there one could catch the name of a dead man, and the Sister's lips tightened. Was So-and-so alive? Well, he was a week ago someone had seen him. And Such-another? Oh, Such-another had been buried a week back. Could Number Three go ahead?

Oh yes; but there was a block at the Modder, and Kimberley was sending down a full train.

Number Three whistled madly. Her business was to get up, load, and get away again. Belmont, with the bullet-holes through the station name-board, interested her not, nor Graspan either. She had been that road too often hot on the heels of the very fight itself. She checked despairingly, fifth in a line of long trains on the red smear of Modder Plain. The old bridge, wrecked by the Boers, was now all but repaired.

At present, Number Three would go over the trestle, but as to when Number Three would get across, authority could not say, and whistling was just waste of steam. Merciful rain had laid the dust which normally lies ten inches thick, and one could look all across the brick-red land.

By this time you probably know more about Modder than I; will have seen a hundred photographs of the naked, coverless plain that tilts to the thin line of trees and the dirty little river; lifting again northwards, as a slow wave of the Atlantic lifts, towards Shooter's Hill, where the naval gun played. North of this again, a bluish lump in the morning light, rises Magersfontein. At that precise moment – but the camp fills and empties as quickly as the river – most of our men were out with Roberts nearly thirty miles to the westward. Vast empty acreages showed where their accommodation had stood. Men, horses, and wheels had wiped out every trace of herbage, and the diminishing perspective of their patient single files attested how far afield the camp-oxen had to go to graze. Horsemen by twos and threes wandered forth attacking interminable distances in which they were swallowed up. Sidings solid with trucks spurred left and right across the plain, and the trucks on the main line backed up to the very shoulders of the riveters repairing the bridge.

Number Three fought her way inch by inch, and was met by a little knot of Army Sisters. In civilisation their uniform is hideous, but out here one sees the use of the square-cut vermilion cape. Everything else is dust coloured, so a man need not ask where a Sister may be. She leaps to the eye across all the camp.

'And where are our wounded?' asks Number Three. 'Still coming in from Paardeberg. They're being dressed. You'll get them later. Where are your spare doctors?' We had come up with six surgeons taken from the big Wynberg and Rondebosch hospitals, where for months they had lived on a promise of work at the Front. They were not R.A.M.C. men, but house surgeons fresh from the Home hospitals, young, enthusiastic, and happy, though their baggage had been cut down to the thirty-five-pound scale, and they had not the ghost of a notion where they were going.

They were uncarted like stags on Modder platform, gazed awhile, met a man in authority, and were swiftly commandeered. Two or three doctors lay dead or wounded across the plains, and there was a hot press for the Medical Service.

Half a mile across the plain, behind the graves of the Highland Brigade, lay the hospital-tents, and thither loaded mule- and ox-wagons were heading. Like Number Three, they had been at the work a weary while. There came no surprise or bewilderment, hardly even any pity to the onlooker, as the big Red Crosses lurched and pitched. This, said the wagons, is the custom with the wounded. Stricken men are gathered as soon as possible by the bearer companies, whose casualty-list is a heavy one. They are dressed for the first time swiftly and efficiently; they are then put into the tilted wagons till they reach the hospital that sends them to the rail. The rail takes the badly wounded to Cape Town and the sea which leads to Netley.

This is the system, said the wagons, and here was the system all naked to the glaring day. Three nights had the wagons been on the road, rained upon, thundered over, and lightned about, jolted and jerked, and jarred; but the long and the short of it was that of eight hundred wounded the wagons had lost not one.

'Would the hospitals take delivery, please?' said the wagons, and they drew aside to rest; for their cattle were very, very tired.

As for Number Three? No, it would *not* be wise to visit Magersfontein. The train might be filled and sent away at any moment.

There was the old official ring about this, and I was not the least surprised that we waited eleven hours – time to have gone to Magersfontein and back on all fours. But I am glad I stayed by Number Three. It is early days to make that field of blood a showplace, and one can collect shells on other beaches when peace comes again.

The station was the centre of local society. The Staff, including a German prince, lived across the road in a battered caravanserai with scores of ponies tied to the veranda. The platform was banked with Red Cross cases, badly needed at Kimberley, and with mail bags badly needed by the men who came up, fingered them curiously, and slunk away. Business first, mails later. The telegraph office was a small edition of De Aar, hideously overworked. A knot of Sappers came up from the river, where they had been tamping ballast under new sidings. Other Sappers with 'R.P.R.' on their hats followed.

These last were the details of the Railway Pioneers, skilled mechanicians, and the like, of Johannesburg; and under the grime and the khaki one met a host of a certain weird dinner given in the Gold Reef city two years ago.

One gets used to privates with visiting-cards, and it is perfectly natural to discuss bacteriology, West African exploration, and the ethics of publishing, the intricacies of the Bankruptcy Act, and the prospects of the Labour party in South Australia with spurred troopers.

So it was not disconcerting to meet men of the Chitral siege, once prisoners in the hands of Omra Khan, old schoolmates, Indian Staff Corps men doing duty as 'tail-twisters' in the Transport, lost acquaintances of ten years ago, side by side with the fellow passenger of three weeks back, unrecognisable to-day under sunburn, hair, and dust.

It was only an undress rehearsal for the Day of Judgment.

A detail of Army Service men en route for Kimberley spread themselves at ease on their baggage, and chaffed a quartermaster-sergeant who had lost his sword but by the regulations was miserably tied to the empty scabbard till he could return the thing to store. A knot of excited Life Guards demanded news of French's division. 'Out since Sunday week and no news. We belong to 'em. We were sick. We want to rejoin. Do you know where he is?'

A Colonial suggested that cavalry divisions always suspend operations for the return of one corporal of horse and two dozen troopers.

A Gunner driver in a cart pored over a three-days-old Cape paper, for there is no news at the Modder. A man with a drawn face came out from nowhere and told a story. His wife had died at home of influenza: was dead and buried. His people could look after the children, thank God! But it hurt – it hurt cruelly. He spoke and vanished.

Half a mile up the line a private of Highlanders was cooking potatoes and semolina together. He was in luck. Had helped 'swipe' a Boer wagon overturned by our shell-fire, and picked up the semolina out of the dust.

A knot of officers had made themselves a rude messhouse in a roofless hut, with a blanket for shade. One of them wished to see a Sister of Number Three – to tell her that So-and-so was dead. A little gathering moved across the dust to look for the graves of the Highland Brigade. Even now the name-boards are split and blistered, and the date carries us back a thousand years. And so it went on, hour after hour, this procession of faces, this tangle of half-caught tales. Towards evening the remnants, as it were, of a battalion moved from the hospital tent in broken squads, one man supporting another.

They were our 'light' cases – men denied the merciful cushioning shock of severe wounds – in acute and annoying pain. They would go down to Naauwpoort by the Kimberley train, but first they must be called over.

They reached the platform haltingly; their uniforms were darkened in places by patches as of carelessly spilled varnish, and sometimes their trouser hems were gummy with the same stuff. They sat down by companies in the dust, half a score of regiments mixed. Their officers got them fruit and cigarettes; the more sound filled their companions' water-bottles. They chaffed greatly in undertones, but they did not say one single word which by any construction could be considered even coarse. They did not complain, they did not growl, they did not curse. They were going to Naauwpoort to get well. In a few days they would return. They had out-marched and out-manoeuvred their enemy – on a couple of biscuits a day, for they had also out-marched their provisions. Their companions were now attending to that enemy, and they were content.

On their departure Number Three waked to life. The wagons were coming from the hospitals. The doors of the cars flew back; orderlies went to their stretchers; the side-boards were ripped out of the bunks; the cook put the last flavouring to the big stock-pot; the Sisters stood to attention, each in her ward – a doctor and a Sister responsible for half a train apiece – and the blessed morphine needles were made ready. They want rest from pain, our wounded. Food and clean sheets will often bring it, but on occasion we must help Nature.

The worn, chipped, and scratched rifles clattered into the arm-racks, the thin dusty kits followed, and after them the loaded stretchers.

'Fractured thigh,' said an orderly. 'Which? Left or right?' said the Sister.

'Right,' said the man, and was slipped on his back accordingly, injured leg outside, where it could be got at easiest.

'Special,'said the orderly. Here was a clean stomach wound. He could eat milk and slops in a bunk marked to that effect, and the gentlemanly Mauser bullet would suffer him to live. Down the car he went, thinking nobly of his soul, and in no way approving of milk-diet. Entered one amputation below the right elbow, very cheery. Full diet for this amputation; but no full diet for yonder lung-shot, who cannot lie down without pain. Were there any sick?

There were no sick, and the doctors thanked Heaven. They would sooner bring down three trains of wounded than one of sick.

Dysentery that milks the heart out of a man and shames him before his kind; rheumatism, which is the seven devils of toothache, in the marrow of your bones; typhoid of the loaded breath and the silly eye, incontinent and consuming; pneumonia that stabs in the back and drives the poor soul, suffocating and bewildered, through the hells of delirium – we are clear of these for this journey, at least. The clean aseptic bullet-kiss and the shell-splinter is all our care.

Quietly and quickly, but above all quietly, come the stretchers.

Fractured shoulder; elbow joint; lung again from left to right, but nothing vital touched; shattered forearm (owner says explosive bullet); two head-cases, but both will live. Eye, head, and neck; upper arm; thigh again; two or three clean shots through the thigh (owners very hungry); shoulder smashed and top of finger shot off (owner much annoyed over this little extra); forearm again, and 'Please, sir, me bandages are pinchin' me horrid.'

It isn't the bandages, but the doctor does not say so. He exhibits the merciful squirt, and the bandages miraculously loosen themselves.

Now come the Officers.

One Colonel, bearded like the heavy swell of the 'Sixties; another Colonel (the Highlanders must have been catching it); a Major; a bearded Captain (on investigation this turns out to be a Lieutenant, aged twenty-three, when he is shaved); and a sprinkling of subalterns and doctors. In each man's bed is a bag holding shirt, pyjamas, towel, brush, sponge, soap, and toothbrush. They call it the Good Hope bag, but it was evidently invented by a thoughtful she-angel.

Man after man shakes off or is helped out of the creased, dusty, greasy, blood-stained khaki and nestles into the luxury of clean body-clothes between clean sheets. They have rest; now they must have food, thick soup for choice, if they will only stay awake to drink it; and milk and brandy for the stomach and lung people.

Theoretically, six hundred miles of rail should be bad for wounded men. Practically it does them all the good in the world.

In the first place, they are cleanly and honourably out of it. Not for weeks the sun and the dust, the foul water, and the weary marching; the booted sleep, and the plug-plug of the rifle-butt against the shoulder.

Many of them will be permanently lost. The ship will take them to England; they will find their billets waiting, and they will return to live before the faces of their fathers.

Moreover, these are they who have come out of a winning fight. Cronje's end is certain. They left the guns pounding the soul out of his laager by the Modder.

It is not as was that terrible journey after Magersfontein, when doctors and Sisters had to sit up with weeping men – men who had been killed in heaps of a sudden one day and damned in heaps by their General the next – men who tried to explain but broke down and turned their faces to the wall and cried miserably and hopelessly.

Number Three's Staff will remember that Magersfontein trip as long as they live.

This is distinctly a better business. They are going off to sleep, like tired children, already – thirty-one officers and sixty-six men. They will be different people tomorrow. The doctors look at the Sisters and nod joyously. A good train-load; no one will be lost, and that little end car for once need not do duty as a mortuary.

Number Twenty-seven wants something solid to eat. Number Twenty-seven won't get it. He is shot through the stomach, and it is a miracle that he is not under the Modder dirt. He can have some more milk and brandy ...

'Please, Sister, there's a Colonel hoppin' about the alley-way.'

A Sister advances to cut him off. Mere doctors are helpless here. They dare not herd Colonels like ostriches. Besides, he has one sound leg. He says so.

'But you are to get on to your back and lie down,' is the order.

'But, Please, Sister, I feel quite fit.'

'But I say so.'

A wave of her hand eliminates the Colonel. He will hop no more to-night.

A fractured Victorian (shoulder and collar-bone by the look of it) and a child with a slung arm have dodged the eye of authority for a few minutes, and *suadente diabolo* (but I knew Australians liked tea) are drinking tea in the Staff carriage.

The child is nineteen; he has one month's service; he does not appreciate a Sister's drawing comparisons between him and a seventeen-year-old middy, carted off the field at Graspan. It was his first engagement. He was scooping potted meat out of a can when the advance began. Then he was firing. A bullet hit his rifle on the trigger-guard, broke up, and continued through his hand, which is now extensively bandaged. It hurts a little.

'Of course it does if you let it hang down like that,' says the Sister; and she deftly loops up the sling while the child blushes adorably.

He argues impersonally on the advantages of retaining the forefinger of the right hand. Not his forefinger by name, but abstract forefinger. One wants it for shooting and writing, don't you know. Oh, there are a heap of things one can do with it.

Then the colour goes out of his face, and the Sister whirls him into bed.

The Victorian turns pale dun and thinks he will lie down.

One finds out later from other men that the child was a most plucky child, and would not take chloroform when they dressed him. His hand is horribly cut up, and his rifle in the rack is smashed across the stock. The nickel-nosed bullet has sunk a quarter of an inch into the steel trigger-guard. It would be unfair to steal that rifle.

The child is asleep. He looks about thirteen. Now the covers are drawn on the lamps; the night watches are set, and we take our last turn down the corridor.

A thunderstorm chases Number Three southward, the lightning spills all over the veldt, and the sun-warped roofs leak. Thirty or forty or fifty thousand men are lying tentless in this downpour, but it must be flooding out Cronje in the bed of the Modder.

Our children are here asleep – deeply and beautifully asleep – all except one man, whose eyes shine like the eyes of a prepared moth.

'What is the matter?'

'I haven't slept in these' – he picks up the sheet – 'since the third of November. It's too comfortable to sleep. Oh, Lord, it is comfortable.' He squirms luxuriously in his bunk.

Through the long night when we stop all voices are lowered. Footsteps halt before us and voices whisper: 'Have you any New South Wales Lancers, sir, please?'

'No, we have not. Have we any Oxfords? Yes, a Sergeant, but nobody is coming to wake up this train. Yes, we are full, but they are all doing well. No' – for the tenth time – 'there are no dying. They are in bed and asleep, and you must go away.' All this in tense whispers.

Doctors and Sisters call it an easy night. They are not actually on their feet or fanning a pneumonia case from eleven to six.

Well, they had their reward in the clean rain-washed morning when every runnel of the Karroo was bank full and the waste-water (some day we shall get big dams with a system to them) spilled away profligately. Our children were hungry – mutinously hungry. Officers fancied this and fancied that. Milk men wanted to know why they were not full-dieters, and full-dieters sent verbal messages by orderlies asking for more – much more.

'You won't get any breakfast till they are all fed,' said to me an orderly with a pyramid of porridge basins. 'You'd better fill up on Osborne biscuits. You see, 'arf of 'em 'aven't the use of their 'ands.'

So they stoked them – the "arf that 'adn't the use of their 'ands' – and they re-dressed their bandages, and they washed their little faces and combed their little hair, and then the cry went up for tobacco.

Some of the men had changed past recognition during the night. The lines of pain, the tense drawn expressions were gone. They had rested; their bellies were full; they were smoking. You must remember that a wounded man is not a sick man. He is generally in superb physical condition; he has been off all excess liquor for some months, and so responds readily to stimulants. His blood is clean, and he breathes the best of air. Give him half a chance, and he will clamber up again hand over fist.

Then, all animal needs satisfied, some of them wanted to send word home; and that was a full morning's job. The usual form ran: 'Dear Mother, Just a few lines to tell you I was hit at Paardeberg on Feb. 18th, when we fought Cronje. I was hit in such-and-such a place, but please do not worry about me, as I am coming on all right. It was a bit hard in the carts, but I am lying in bed in the train here, and we are all going down to the hospital, and I am quite comfortable, and I shall be all right in a few weeks, so please do not worry about me, because I am all right and doing well.'

Their first thought in every instance was that she should not worry. One man – a Celt, to be sure – launched into some description of the fight (I saw him later at Wynberg covering sheets and sheets) and a few others had business matters to adjust; but for the bulk, the word, the assurance, and the message of love, sufficed. Remember, it was not the Army that you and I know, but the Army of the People, heavily laced with Reservists, family folk, who have kiddies and businesses over the sea. Blacksmiths, gardeners, clubporters, and small shopkeepers were among those represented, and their physique was almost as admirable as their spirit.

One man only of all that train broke down – and small blame to him. He was a badly shotten 'lunger,' and there seemed no way to make him easy, sitting or lying. He got out his home-photos – the little tintypes that one carries in the inside pocket and the cruel home-sickness atop of the pain took him and broke him for a minute or two. I think he had come out of some well-ordered country-house, for he returned to the manner of the lodge-porter in his talk.

There were quiet men, deeply concerned for the probable loss of a working arm. There were mildly – oh, so mildly! – riotous men, who staggered about visiting from bunk to bunk. There were funny men, worth their weight in silver to the ward. There were just men admitting that their enemy up in a tree had sighted more quickly than they, 'but my section got him with four bullets, and he came down like a pheasant, sir.' There were silent men breathing quickly, counting each turn of the wheels; and there were doubting Thomases who needed particular information about Wynberg hospital.

I heard a good deal of all sorts, but I did not hear one word of complaint.

So it is in the base hospital. From at least a thousand wounded met at Rondebosch and Wynberg under fairly intimate circumstances, orderlies out of earshot and the talk running free, I did not gather one whimper.

A badly hit man – fracture or stomach – is, of course, glad he is going home – till the steamer comes round. Then he is not so pleased.

A slightly wounded man takes all the ward to witness that so soon as he is mended, wild horses won't keep him away from his family. Ten days later, he is lying – lying like a skirmish-line under pom-pom fire – to his doctor with intent to rejoin.

The hospitals have their own *esprit de corps*, and they are proud to be able to say they are all going back. But our boys counted rest before all things; and Number Three hurried them to it. Our little world on wheels had hardly come to know itself when we were halfway home. A little letter-writing; a small 'smoker' between two cool windows where wounded Colonels and subalterns met in pyjamas and talked over good men killed, while the idle rifles clicked in the rack behind; another ravenous meal or two ('Which will you 'ave, sir? Steak or rissole?' 'Oh, both. I've been dreaming of steaks since Jacobsdal!'; another and an easier night, and then the thrice-blessed firs of Wynberg, the waiting hooded ambulances, a good road, and Number One and Two Hospitals just round the corner.

Once more the business of the stretchers, the tally of fractures and perforations; the whispered cautions, and the louder words of good cheer. It is not in the official bond, but Number Three's Staff – a little worn with night-watching, dusty and heavy-eyed – will see the boys up to their beds. They know every one of the cases now, and a word or two in season will be profitable.

In an hour Number Three stands empty and stripped. Blankets, sheets, and bedding must be renewed; a hundred things go to the wash; and they swish and swill the floors.

To-morrow night her work begins again.

[First published in the *Daily Mail* on 21, 23, 24 and 25 April 1900.]

PRE-FIRST WORLD WAR

In this poem Kipling made his classic plea to Britain to learn the lessons of the South Africa War, in which he was afraid that the plucky Boers had almost succeeded in inflicting military embarrassment on his own often arrogant and deluded countrymen.

THE LESSON

1899–1902
(Boer War)

LET US ADMIT IT fairly, as a business people should,
We have had no end of a lesson: it will do us no end of good.

Not on a single issue, or in one direction or twain,
But conclusively, comprehensively, and several times and again,
Were all our most holy illusions knocked higher than Gilderoy's
   kite.
We have had a jolly good lesson, and it serves us jolly well right!

This was not bestowed us under the trees, nor yet in the shade of a
   tent,
But swingingly, over eleven degrees of a bare brown continent.

From Lamberts to Delagoa Bay, and from Pietersburg to Sutherland,
Fell the phenomenal lesson we learned – with a fullness accorded
   no other land.

It was our fault, and our very great fault, and not the judgment of
   Heaven.
We made an Army in our own image, on an island nine by seven,
Which faithfully mirrored its makers' ideals, equipment, and
   mental attitude –
And so we got our lesson: and we ought to accept it with gratitude.

We have spent two hundred million pounds to prove the fact once
   more,
That horses are quicker than men afoot, since two and two make four;
And horses have four legs, and men have two legs, and two into
   four goes twice,
And nothing over except our lesson – and very cheap at the price.

For remember (this our children shall know: we are too near for
   that knowledge)
Not our mere astonied camps, but Council and Creed and College –
All the obese, unchallenged old things that stifle and overlie us –
Have felt the effects of the lesson we got – an advantage no money
   could buy us!

Then let us develop this marvellous asset which we alone
   command,
And which, it may subsequently transpire, will be worth as much
   as the Rand.
Let us approach this pivotal fact in a humble yet hopeful mood –
We have had no end of a lesson, it will do us no end of good!

It was our fault, and our very great fault – and now we must turn
   it to use.
We have forty million reasons for failure, but not a single excuse.
So the more we work and the less we talk the better results we
   shall get –
We have had an Imperial lesson; it may make us an Empire yet!

[First published in *The Times*, 29 July 1901.]

✠ ✠ ✠

This is the first part of a two-part story in which Kipling continues to muse on the drawbacks of the old-style army. In unashamedly propagandist style he advocates a form of national service. He was already associated with his friend Lord Roberts's National Service League, which favoured conscription.

THE ARMY OF A DREAM

Part I

I SAT DOWN IN the Club smoking-room to fill a pipe.

. . . . .

It was entirely natural that I should be talking to 'Boy' Bayley. We had met first, twenty odd years ago, at the Indian mess of the Tyneside Tail-twisters. Our last meeting, I remembered, had been at the Mount Nelson Hotel, which was by no means India, and there we had talked half the night. Boy Bayley had gone up that week to the front, where I think he stayed a long, long time.

But now he had come back.

'Are you still a Tynesider?' I asked.

'I command the Imperial Guard Battalion of the old regiment, my son,' he replied.

'Guard which? They've been Fusiliers since Fontenoy. Don't pull my leg, Boy.'

'I said Guard, not Guard-s. The I.G. Battalion of the Tail-twisters. Does that make it any clearer?'

'Not in the least.'

'Then come over to mess and see for yourself. We aren't a step from barracks. Keep on my right side. I'm-I'm a bit deaf on the near.'

We left the Club together and crossed the street to a vast four-storied pile, which more resembled a Rowton lodging-house than a barrack. I could see no sentry at the gates.

'There ain't any,' said the Boy lightly. He led me into a many-tabled restaurant full of civilians and grey-green uniforms. At one end of the room, on a slightly raised dais, stood a big table.

'Here we are! We usually lunch here and dine in mess by our-selves. These are our chaps – but what am I thinking of? You must know most of 'em. Devine's my second in command now. There's old Luttrell – remember him at Cherat? – Burgard, Verschoyle (you were at school with him), Harrison, Pigeon, and Kyd.'

With the exception of the last I knew them all, but I could not remember that they had all been Tynesiders.

'I've never seen this sort of place,' I said, looking round. 'Half the men here are in plain clothes, and what are those women and children doing?'

'Eating, I hope,' Boy Bayley answered. 'Our canteens would never pay if it wasn't for the Line and Militia trade. When they were first started people looked on 'em rather as catsmeat-shops; but we got a duchess or two to lunch in 'em, and they've been grossly fashionable since.'

'So I see,' I answered. A woman of the type that shops at the Stores came up the room looking about her. A man in the dull-grey uniform of the corps rose up to meet her, piloted her to a place between three other uniforms, and there began a very merry little meal.

'I give it up,' I said. 'This is guilty splendour that I don't understand.'

'Quite simple,' said Burgard across the table. 'The barrack supplies breakfast, dinner, and tea on the Army scale to the Imperial Guard (which we call I.G.) when it's in barracks as well as to the Line and Militia. They can all invite their friends if they choose to pay for them. That's where we make our profits. Look!'

Near one of the doors were four or five tables crowded with workmen in the raiment of their callings. They ate steadily, but found time to jest with the uniforms about them; and when one o'clock clanged from a big half-built block of flats across the street, filed out.

'Those,' Devine explained, 'are either our Line or Militia men, as such entitled to the regulation whack at regulation cost. It's cheaper than they could buy it; an' they meet their friends too. A man'll walk a mile in his dinner-hour to mess with his own lot.'

'Wait a minute,' I pleaded. 'Will you tell me what those plumbers and plasterers and bricklayers, that I saw go out just now, have to do with what I was taught to call the Line?'

'Tell him,' said the Boy over his shoulder to Burgard. He was busy talking with the large Verschoyle, my old schoolmate.

'The Line comes next to the Guard. The Linesman's generally a town-bird who can't afford to be a Volunteer. He has to go into camp in an Area for two months his first year, six weeks his second, and a month the third. He gets about five bob a week the year round for that and for being on duty two days of the week, and for being liable to be ordered out to help the Guard in a row. He needn't live in barracks unless he wants to, and he and his family can feed at the regimental canteen at usual rates. The women like it.'

'All this,' I said politely, but intensely, 'is the raving of delirium. Where may your precious recruit who needn't live in barracks learn his drill?'

'At his precious school, my child, like the rest of us. The notion of allowing a human being to reach his twentieth year before asking him to put his feet in the first position *was* raving lunacy if you like!' Boy Bayley dived back into the conversation.

'Very good,' I said meekly. 'I accept the virtuous plumber who puts in two months of his valuable time at Aldershot—'

'Aldershot!' The table exploded. I felt a little annoyed.

'A camp in an Area is not exactly Aldershot,' said Burgard. 'The Line isn't exactly what you fancy. Some of them even come to *us*!'

'You recruit from 'em?'

'I beg your pardon,' said Devine with mock solemnity. 'The Guard doesn't recruit. It selects.'

'It would,' I said, 'with a Spiers and Pond restaurant; pretty girls to play with; and—'

'A room apiece, four bob a day and all found,' said Verschoyle. 'Don't forget that.'

'Of course!' I said. 'It probably beats off recruits with a club.'

'No, with the ballot-box,' said Verschoyle, laughing. 'At least in all R.C. companies.'

'I didn't know Roman Catholics were so particular,' I ventured.

They grinned. 'R.C. companies,' said the Boy, 'mean Right of Choice. When a company has been very good and pious for a long time it may, if the C.O. thinks fit, choose its own men – all same one-piecee Club. All our companies are R.C.s, and, as the battalion is making up a few vacancies ere starting once more on the wild and trackless "heef" into the Areas, the Linesman is here in force to-day sucking up to our non-coms.'

'Would some one mind explaining to me the meaning of every other word you've used,' I said. 'What's a trackless "heef"? What's an Area? What's everything generally?' I asked.

'Oh, "heef's" part of the British Constitution,' said the Boy. 'It began long ago when they first mapped out the big military

manoeuvring grounds – we call 'em Areas for short – where the
I.G. spend two-thirds of their time and the other regiments get their
training. It was slang originally for beef on the hoof, because in the
Military Areas two-thirds of your meat-rations at least are handed
over to you on the hoof, and you make your own arrangements. The
word "heef" became a parable for camping in the Military Areas
and all its miseries. There are two Areas in Ireland, one in Wales for
hill-work, a couple in Scotland, and a sort of parade-ground in the
Lake District; but the real working Areas are in India, Africa, and
Australia, and so on.'

'And what do you do there?'

'We "heef" under service conditions, which are rather like hard
work. We "heef" in an English Area for about a year, coming into
barracks for one month to make up wastage. Then we may "heef"
foreign for another year or eighteen months. Then we do sea-time
in the war boats—'

'What-t?' I said.

'Sea-time,' Bayley repeated. 'Just like Marines, to learn about the
big guns and how to embark and disembark quick. Then we come
back to our territorial headquarters for six months, to educate the
Line and Volunteer camps, to go to Hythe, to keep abreast of any
new ideas, and then we fill up vacancies. We call those six months
"Schools." Then we begin all over again, thus: Home "heef," foreign
"heef," sea-time, schools. "Heefing" isn't precisely luxurious, but
it's on "heef" that we make our head-money.'

'Or lose it,' said the sallow Pigeon, and all laughed, as men will,
at regimental jokes.

'The Dove never lets me forget that,' said Boy Bayley. 'It
happened last March. We were out in the Second Northern Area
at the top end of Scotland where a lot of those silly deer-forests
used to be. I'd sooner "heef" in the middle of Australia myself – or
Athabasca, with all respect to The Dove; he's a native of those parts.
We were camped somewhere near Caithness, and the Armity (that's
the combined Navy and Army Board which runs our show) sent us
about eight hundred raw remounts to break in to keep us warm.?'

'Why horses for a foot regiment?'

'I.G.s don't foot it unless they're obliged to. No have gee-gee how
can move? I'll show you later. Well, as I was saying, we broke those
beasts in on compressed forage and small boxspurs, and then we
started across Scotland to Applecross to hand 'em over to a horse-

depot there. It was snowing cruel, and we didn't know the country overmuch. You remember the 30th – the old East Lancashire – at Mian Mir? Their Guard Battalion had been "heefing" round those parts for six months. We thought they'd be snowed up all quiet and comfy, but Burden, their C.O., got wind of our coming, and sent spies in to Eshcol.'

'Confound him!' said Luttrell, who was fat and well-liking. 'I entertained one of 'em – in a red worsted comforter – under Bean Derig. He said he was a crofter. 'Gave him a drink too.'

'I don't mind admitting,' said the Boy, 'that, what with the cold and the remounts, we were moving rather base-over-apex. Burden bottled us under Sghurr Mhor in a snowstorm. He stampeded half the horses, cut off a lot of us in a snowbank, and generally rubbed our noses in the dirt.'

'Was he allowed to do that?' I said.

'There is no peace in a Military Area. If we'd beaten him off or got away without losing anyone, we'd have been entitled to a day's pay from every man engaged against us. But we didn't. He cut off fifty of ours, held 'em as prisoners for the regulation three days, and then sent in his bill – three days' pay for each man taken. Fifty men at twelve bob a head, plus five pounds for The Dove as a captured officer, and Kyd here, his junior, three, made about forty quid to Burden and Co. They crowed over us horrid.'

'Couldn't you have appealed to an umpire or – or something?'

'We could, but we talked it over with the men and decided to pay and look happy. We were fairly had. The 30th knew every foot of Sghurr Mhor. I spent three days huntin' 'em in the snow, but they went off on our remounts about twenty mile that night.'

'Do you always do this sham-fight business?' I asked.

'Once inside an Area you must look after yourself; but I tell you that a fight which means that every man-Jack of us may lose a week's pay isn't so dam-sham after all. It keeps the men nippy. Still, in the long run, it's like whist on a P. and O. It comes out fairly level if you play long enough. Now and again, though, one gets a present – say, when a Line regiment's out on the "heef," and signifies that it's ready to abide by the rules of the game. You mustn't take head-money from a Line regiment in an Area unless it says that it'll play you; but, after a week or two, those clever Linesmen always think they see a chance of making a pot, and send in their compliments to the nearest I.G. Then the fun begins.

We caught a Line regiment single-handed about two years ago in Ireland – caught it on the hop between a bog and a beach. It had just moved in to join its brigade, and we made a forty-two-mile march in fourteen hours, and cut it off, lock, stock, and barrel. It went to ground like a badger – I *will* say those Line regiments can dig – but we got out privily by night and broke up the only road it could expect to get its baggage and company-guns along. Then we blew up a bridge that some Sappers had made for experimental purposes (*they* were rather stuffy about it) on its line of retreat, while we lay up in the mountains and signalled for the A.C. of those parts.'

'Who's an A.C.?' I asked.

'The Adjustment Committee – the umpires of the Military Areas. They're a set of superannuated old aunts of colonels kept for the purpose, but they occasionally combine to do justice. Our A.C. came, saw our dispositions, and said it was a sanguinary massa*cree* for the Line, and that we were entitled to our full pound of flesh – head-money for one whole regiment, with equipment, four company-guns, and all kit! At Line rates this worked out as one fat cheque for two hundred and fifty. Not bad!'

'But we had to pay the Sappers seventy-four quid for blowing their patent bridge to pieces,' Devine interpolated. 'That was a swindle.'

'That's true,' the Boy went on, 'but the Adjustment Committee gave our helpless victims a talking-to that was worth another hundred to hear.'

'But isn't there a lot of unfairness in this head-money system?' I asked.

'"Can't have everything perfect,' said the Boy. 'Head-money is an attempt at payment by results, and it gives the men a direct interest in their job. Three times out of five, of course, the A.C. will disallow both sides' claim, but there's always the chance of bringing off a coup.'

'Do all regiments do it?'

'Heavily. The Line pays a bob per prisoner and the Militia ninepence, not to mention side-bets which are what really keep the men keen. It isn't supposed to be done by the Volunteers, but they gamble worse than anyone. Why, the very kids do it when they go to First Camp at Aldershot or Salisbury.'

'Head-money's a national institution – like betting,' said Burgard.

'I should say it was,' said Pigeon suddenly. 'I was roped in the other day as an Adjustment Committee by the Kemptown Board School. I was riding under the Brighton racecourse, and I heard the whistle goin' for umpire – the regulation, two longs and two shorts. I didn't take any notice till an infant about a yard high jumped up from a furze-patch and shouted: "Guard! Guard! Come 'ere! I want you *per*-fessionally. Alf says 'e ain't outflanked. Ain't 'e a liar? Come an' look 'ow I've posted my men." You bet I looked! The young demon trotted by my stirrup and showed me his whole army (twenty of 'em) laid out under cover as nicely as you please round a cowhouse in a hollow. He kept on shouting: "I've drew Alf into there. 'Is persition ain't tenable. Say it ain't tenable, Guard!" I rode round the position, and Alf with his army came out of his cowhouse an' sat on the roof and protested like a – like a Militia Colonel; but the facts were in favour of my friend and I umpired according. Well, Alf abode by my decision. I explained it to him at length, and he solemnly paid up his head-money – farthing points if you please!'

'Did they pay you umpire's fee?' said Kyd. 'I umpired a whole afternoon once for a village school at home, and they stood me a bottle of hot ginger beer.'

'I compromised on a halfpenny – a sticky one – or I'd have hurt their feelings,' said Pigeon gravely. 'But I gave 'em sixpence back.'

'How were they manœuvring and what with?' I asked.

'Oh, by whistle and hand-signal. They had the dummy Board School guns and flags for positions, but they were rushing their attack much too quick for that open country. I told 'em so, and they admitted it.'

'But who taught 'em?' I said.

'They had learned in their schools, of course, like the rest of us. They were all of 'em over ten; and squad-drill begins when they're eight. They knew their company-drill a heap better than they knew their King's English.'

'How much drill do the boys put in?' I asked.

'All boys begin physical drill to music in the Board Schools when they're six; squad-drill, one hour a week, when they're eight; company-drill when they're ten, for an hour and a half a week. Between ten and twelve they get battalion-drill of a sort. They take the rifle at twelve and record their first target-score at thirteen. That's what the Code lays down. But it's worked very loosely so long as a boy comes up to the standard of his age.'

'In Canada we don't need your physical-drill. We're born fit,' said Pigeon, 'and our ten-year-olds could knock spots out of your twelve-year-olds.'

'I may as well explain,' said the Boy, 'that The Dove is our "swop" officer. He's an untamed Huskie from Nootka Sound when he's at home. An I.G. Corps exchanges one officer every two years with a Canadian or Australian or African Guard Corps. We've had a year of our Dove, an' we shall be sorry to lose him. He humbles our insular pride. Meantime, Morten, our "swop" in Canada, keeps the ferocious Canuck humble. When Pij goes we shall swop Kyd, who's next on the roster, for a Cornstalk or a Maori. But about the education-drill. A boy can't attend First Camp, as we call it, till he is a trained boy and holds his First Musketry certificate. The Education Code says he must be fourteen, and the boys usually go to First Camp at about that age. Of course, they've been to their little private camps and Boys' Fresh Air Camps and public-school picnics while they were at school, but First Camp is where the young drafts all meet – generally at Aldershot in this part of the world. First Camp lasts a week or ten days, and the boys are looked over for vaccination and worked lightly in brigades with lots of blank cartridge. Second Camp – that's for the fifteen- to eighteen-year-olds – lasts ten days or a fortnight, and that includes a final medical examination. Men don't like to be chucked out on medical certificate much – nowadays. I assure you Second Camp, at Salisbury, say, is an experience for a young I.G. Officer. We're told off to 'em in rotation. A wilderness of monkeys isn't in it. The kids are apt to think 'emselves soldiers, and we have to take the edge off 'em with lots of picquet-work and night attacks.'

'And what happens after Second Camp?'

'It's hard to explain. Our system is so illogical. Theoretically, the boys needn't show up for the next three or four years after Second Camp. They are supposed to be making their way in life. Actually, the young doctor or lawyer or engineer joins a Volunteer battalion that sticks to the minimum of camp – ten days per annum. That gives him a holiday in the open air, and now that men have taken to endowing their Volunteer drill-halls with baths and libraries he finds, if he can't run to a Club, that his own drill-hall is an efficient substitute. He meets men there who'll be useful to him later, and he keeps himself in touch with what's going on while he's studying for his profession. The town-birds – such as the chemist's assistant, clerk, plumber, mechanic, electrician, and so forth – generally put in for their town Volunteer corps as soon as they begin to walk out with the girls. They like takin' their true-loves to our restaurants. Look yonder!' I followed his gaze, and saw across the room a man and a maid at a far table, forgetting in each other's eyes the good food on their plates.

'So it is,' said I. 'Go ahead.'

'Then, too, we have some town Volunteer corps that lay them-selves out to attract promising youths of nineteen or twenty, and make much of 'em on condition that they join their Line battalion and play for their county. Under the new county qualifications – birth or three years' residence – that means a great deal in League matches, and the same in County cricket.'

'By Jove, that's a good notion,' I cried. 'Who invented it?'

'C.B. Fry – long ago. He said, in his paper, that County cricket and County volunteering ought to be on the same footing – unpaid and genuine. "No cricketer no corps. No corps no cricketer" was his watchword. There was a row among the pros at first, but C.B. won, and later the League had to come in. They said at first it would ruin the gate; but when County matches began to be *pukka* county, *plus* inter-regimental, affairs the gate trebled, and as two-thirds of the gate goes to the regiments supplying the teams some Volunteer corps fairly wallow in cash. It's all unofficial, of course, but League Corps, as they call 'em, can take their pick of the Second Camper. Some corps ask ten guineas entrance-fee, and get it too, from the young bloods that want to shine in the arena. I told you we catered for all tastes. Now, as regards the Line proper, I believe the young artisan and mechanic puts in for that before he marries. He likes the two months' "heef" in his first year, and five bob a week is something to go on with between times.'

'Do they follow their trade while they're in the Line?' I demanded.

'Why not? How many well-paid artisans work more than four days a week anyhow? Remember a Linesman hasn't to be drilled in your sense of the word. He must have had at least eight years' grounding in that, as well as two or three years in his Volunteer battalion. He can sleep where he pleases. He can't leave town-limits without reporting himself, of course, but he can get leave if he wants it. He's on duty two days in the week as a rule, and he's liable to be invited out for garrison duty down the Mediterranean, but his benefit societies will insure him against that. I'll tell you about that later. If it's a hard winter and trade's slack, a lot of the bachelors are taken into the I.G. barracks (while the I.G. is out on the "heef") for theoretical instruction. Oh, I assure you the Line hasn't half a bad time of it.'

'Amazing!' I murmured. 'And what about the others?'

'The Volunteers? Observe the beauty of our system. We're a free people. We get up and slay the man who says we aren't. But as a little detail we never mention, if we don't volunteer in some corps or another – as combatants if we're fit, as non-combatants if we ain't – till we're thirty-five – we don't vote, and we don't get poor-relief, and the women don't love us.'

'Oh, that's the compulsion of it?' said I.

Bayley inclined his head gravely. 'That, Sir, is the compulsion. We voted the legal part of it ourselves in a fit of panic, and we have not yet rescinded our resolution! The women attend to the unofficial penalties. But being free British citizens—'

'*And* snobs,' put in Pigeon.

'The point is well taken, Pij – we have supplied ourselves with every sort and shape and make of Volunteer corps that you can imagine, and we've mixed the whole show up with our Oddfellows and our I.O.G.T.s and our Buffaloes, and our Burkes and our Debretts, not to mention Leagues and Athletic Clubs, till you can't tell t'other from which. You remember the young pup who used to look on soldiering as a favour done to his ungrateful country – the gun-poking, ferret-pettin', landed gentleman's offspring – the suckin' Facey Romford? Well, he generally joins a Foreign Service Corps when he leaves college.'

'Can Volunteers go foreign then?'

'Can't they just, if their C.O. *or* his wife has influence! The Armity will always send a well-connected F.S. corps out to help a Guard battalion in a small campaign. Otherwise F.S. corps make their own arrangements about camps. You see, the Military Areas are always open. They can "heef" there (and gamble on head-money) as long as their finances run to it; or they can apply to do sea-time in the ships. It's a cheap way for a young man to see the world, and if he's any good he can try to get into the Guard later.'

'The main point,' said Pigeon, 'is that F.S. corps are "swagger" – the correct thing. It 'ud never do to be drawn for the Militia, don't you know,' he drawled, trying to render the English voice.

'That's what happens to a chap who doesn't volunteer,' said Bayley. 'Well, after the F.S. corps (we've about forty of 'em)

come our territorial Volunteer battalions, and a man who can't
suit himself somewhere among 'em must be a shade difficult.
We've got those "League" corps I was talking about; and those
studious corps that just scrape through their ten days' camp; and
we've crack corps of highly-paid mechanics who can afford a
two months' "heef" in an interesting Area every other year; and
we've senior and junior scientific corps of earnest boilermakers
and fitters and engineers who read papers on high explosives,
and do their "heefing" in a wet picket-boat – mine-droppin' – at
the ports. Then we've heavy artillery – recruited from the big
manufacturing towns and ship-building yards – and ferocious
hard-ridin' Yeomanry (they *can* ride – now), genteel, semi-genteel,
and Hooligan corps, and so on and so forth till you come to the
Home Defence Establishment – the young chaps knocked out
under medical certificate at the Second Camp, but good enough to
sit behind hedges or clean up camp, and the old was-birds who've
served their time but don't care to drop out of the fun of the yearly
camps and the halls. They call 'emselves veterans and do fancy
shooting at Bisley, but, between you and me, they're mostly Fresh
Air Benefit Clubs. They contribute to the Volunteer journals and
tell the Guard that it's no good. But I like 'em. I shall be one of 'em
some day – a copper-nosed was-bird … So you see we're mixed to
a degree on the Volunteer side.'

'It sounds that way,' I ventured.

'You've overdone it, Bayley,' said Devine. 'You've missed our one
strong point.' He turned to me and continued: 'It's embarkation.
The Volunteers may be as mixed as the Colonel says, but they *are*
trained to go down to the sea in ships. You ought to see a big Bank
Holiday roll-out! We suspend most of the usual railway traffic
and turn on the military time-table – say on Friday at midnight.
By 4 a.m. the trains are running from every big centre in England
to the nearest port at two-minute intervals. As a rule, the Armity
meets us at the other end with shipping of sorts – Fleet Reserves or
regular men-of-war or hulks – anything you can stick a gang-plank
to. We pile the men on to the troop-decks, stack the rifles in the
racks, send down the sea-kit, steam about for a few hours, and land
'em somewhere. It's a good notion, because our army to be any use
must be an army of embarkation. Why, last Whit Monday we had
– how many were down at the dock-edge in the first eight hours?
Kyd, you're the Volunteer enthusiast last from school.'

'In the first ten hours over a hundred and eighteen thousand,' said Kyd across the table, 'with thirty-six thousand actually put in and taken out of ship. In the whole thirty-six hours we had close on ninety thousand men on the water and a hundred and thirty-three thousand on the quays fallen in with their sea-kit.'

'That must have been a sight,' I said.

'One didn't notice it much. It was scattered between Chatham, Dover, Portsmouth, Plymouth, Bristol, Liverpool, and so on, merely to give the inland men a chance to get rid of their breakfasts. We don't like to concentrate and try a big embarkation at any one point. It makes the Continent jumpy. Otherwise,' said Kyd, 'I believe we could get two hundred thousand men, with their kits, away on one tide.'

'What d'you want with so many?' I asked.

'*We* don't want one of 'em; but the Continent used to point out, every time relations were strained, that nothing would be easier than to raid England if they got command of the sea for a week. After a few years some genius discovered that it cut both ways, an' there was no reason why we, who are supposed to command the sea and own a few ships, should not organise our little raids in case of need. The notion caught on among the Volunteers – they were getting rather sick of manœuvres on dry land – and since then we haven't heard so much about raids from the Continent,' said Bayley.

'It's the offensive-defensive,' said Verschoyle, 'that they talk so much about. We learned it *all* from the Continent – bless 'em! They insisted on it so.'

'No, we learned it from the Fleet,' said Devine. 'The Mediterranean Fleet landed ten thousand marines and sailors, with guns, in twenty minutes once at manœuvres. That was long ago. I've seen the Fleet Reserve, and a few paddle-steamers hired for the day, land twenty-five thousand Volunteers at Bantry in four hours – half the men sea-sick too. You've no notion what a difference that sort of manœuvre makes in the calculations of our friends on the mainland. The Continent knows what invasion means. It's like dealing with a man whose nerve has been shaken. It doesn't cost much after all, and it makes us better friends with the great European family. We're as thick as thieves now.'

'Where does the Imperial Guard come in in all this gorgeousness?' I asked. 'You're unusual modest about yourselves.'

'As a matter of fact, we're supposed to go out and stay out. We're the permanently mobilised lot. I don't think there are more than eight I.G. battalions in England now. We're a hundred battalions all told. Mostly on the "heef" in India, Africa, and so forth.'

'A hundred thousand. Isn't that small allowance?' I suggested.

'You think so? One hundred thousand *men*, without a single case of venereal, and an average sick list of two per cent, permanently on a war footing? Well, perhaps you're right, but it's a useful little force to begin with while the others are getting ready. There's the native Indian Army also, which isn't a broken reed, and, since "no Volunteer no Vote" is the rule throughout the Empire, you will find a few men in Canada, Australia, and elsewhere, that are fairly hefty in their class.'

'But a hundred thousand isn't enough for garrison duty,' I persisted.

'A hundred thousand *sound* men, not sick boys, go quite a way,' said Pigeon.

'We expect the Line to garrison the Mediterranean Ports and thereabouts,' said Bayley. 'Don't sneer at the mechanic. He's deuced good stuff. He isn't rudely ordered out, because this ain't a military despotism, and we have to consider people's feelings. The Armity usually brackets three Line regiments together, and calls for men for six months or a year for Malta, Gib, or elsewhere, at a bob a day. Three battalions will give you nearly a whole battalion of bachelors between 'em. You fill up deficiencies with a call on the territorial Volunteer battalion, and away you go with what we call a Ports battalion. What's astonishing in that? Remember that in this country, where fifty per cent of the able-bodied males have got a pretty fair notion of soldiering, and, which is more, have all camped out in the open, you wake up the spirit of adventure in the young.'

'Not much adventure at Malta, Gib, or Cyprus,' I retorted. 'Don't they get sick of it?'

'But you don't realise that we treat 'em rather differently from the soldier of the past. You ought to go and see a Ports battalion drawn from a manufacturing centre growin' vines in Cyprus in its shirt sleeves; and at Gib, and Malta, of course, the battalions are working with the Fleet half the time.'

'It seems to me,' I said angrily, 'you are knocking *esprit de corps* on the head with all this Army–Navy fumble. It's as bad as—'

'I know what you're going to say. As bad as what Kitchener used to do when he believed that a thousand details picked up on the veldt were as good as a column of two regiments. In the old days, when drill was a sort of holy sacred art learned in old age, you'd be quite right. But remember *our* chaps are broke to drill from childhood, and the theory we work on is that a thousand trained Englishmen ought to be about as good as another thousand trained Englishmen. We've enlarged our horizon, that's all. Some day the Army and the Navy will be interchangeable.'

'You've enlarged it enough to fall out of, I think. Now where in all this mess of compulsory Volunteers—?'

'My dear boy, there's no compulsion. You've *got* to be drilled when you're a child, same as you've got to learn to read; and if you don't pretend to serve in some corps or other till you're thirty-five or medically chucked, you rank with lunatics, women, and minors. That's fair enough.'

'Compulsory conscripts,' I continued. 'Where, as I was going to say, does the Militia come in?'

'As I have said – for the men who can't afford volunteering. The Militia is recruited by ballot – pretty comprehensively too. Volunteers are exempt, but most men not otherwise accounted for are bagged by the Militia. They have to put in a minimum three weeks' camp every other year, and they get fifteen bob a week and their keep when they're at it, and some sort of a yearly fee, I've forgotten how much. 'Tisn't a showy service, but it's very useful. It keeps the mass of the men between twenty-five, say, and thirty-five moderately fit, and gives the Armity an excuse for having more equipment ready – in case of emergencies.'

'I don't think you're quite fair on the Militia,' drawled Verschoyle. 'They're better than we give 'em credit for. Don't you remember the Middle Moor Collieries strike?'

'Tell me,' I said quickly. Evidently the others knew.

'We-ell, it was no end of a pitmen's strike about eight years ago. There were twenty-five thousand men involved – Militia, of course. At the end of the first month – October – when things were looking rather blue, one of those clever Labour leaders got hold of the Militia Act and discovered that any Militia regiment could, by a two-thirds vote, go on "heef" in a Military Area in addition to its usual biennial camp. Two-and-twenty battalions of Geordies solemnly applied, and they were turned loose into the Irish and Scotch Areas under an I.G.

Brigadier who had private instructions to knock clinkers out of 'em. But the pitman is a strong and agile bird. He throve on snowdrifts and entrenching and draggin' guns through heather. *He* was being fed and clothed for nothing, besides having a chance of making head-money, and his strike-pay was going clear to his wife and family. You see? Wily man. But wachtabittje! When that "heef" finished in December the strike was still on. *Then* that same Labour leader found out, from the same Act, that if at any time more than thirty or forty men of a Militia regiment wished to volunteer to do sea-time and study big guns in the Fleet they were in no wise to be discouraged, but were to be taken on as opportunity offered and paid a bob a day. Accordingly, about January, Geordie began volunteering for sea-time – seven and eight hundred men out of each regiment. Anyhow it made up seventeen thousand men! It was a splendid chance and the Armity jumped at it. The Home and Channel Fleets and the North Sea and Cruiser Squadrons were strengthened with lame ducks from the Fleet Reserve, and between 'em with a little stretching and pushing they accommodated all of that young division.'

'Yes, but you've forgotten how we lied to the Continent about it. All Europe wanted to know what the dooce we were at,' said Boy Bayley, 'and the wretched Cabinet had to stump the country in the depths of winter explaining our new system of poor-relief. I beg your pardon, Verschoyle.'

'The Armity improvised naval manœuvres between Gib and Land's End, with frequent coalings and landings; ending in a cruise round England that fairly paralysed the pitmen. The first day out they wanted the Fleet stopped while they went ashore and killed their Labour leader, but they couldn't be obliged. Then they wanted to mutiny over the coaling – it was too like their own job. Oh, they had a lordly time! They came back – the combined Fleets anchored off Hull – with a nautical hitch to their breeches. They'd had a free fight at Gib with the Ports battalion there; they cleared out the town of Lagos; and they'd fought a pitched battle with the dockyard-mateys at Devonport. So they'd done 'emselves well, but they didn't want any more military life for a bit.'

'And the strike?'

'That ended, all right enough, when the strike-money came to an end. The pit-owners were furious. They said the Armity had wilfully prolonged the strike, and asked questions in the House. The Armity said that they had taken advantage of the crisis to put a six months' polish on fifteen thousand fine young men, and if the masters cared to come out on the same terms they'd be happy to do the same by them.'

'And then?'

'Palaver done set,' said Bayley. 'Everybody laughed.'

'I don't quite understand about this sea-time business,' I said. 'Is the Fleet open to take any regiment aboard?'

'Rather. The I.G. must, the Line can, the Militia may, and the Volunteers do put in sea-time. The Coast Volunteers began it, and the fashion is spreading inland. Under certain circumstances, as Verschoyle told you, a Volunteer or Militia regiment can vote whether it "heefs" wet or dry. If it votes wet and has influence (like some F.S. corps), it can sneak into the Channel or the Home Fleet and do a cruise round England or to Madeira or the North Sea. The regiment, of course, is distributed among the ships, and the Fleet dry-nurse 'em. It rather breaks up shore discipline, but it gives the inland men a bit of experience and, of course, it gives us a fairish supply of men behind the gun, in event of any strain on the Fleet. Some coast corps make a speciality of it, and compete for embarking and disembarking records. I believe some of the Tyneside engineerin' corps put ten per cent of their men through the Fleet engine-rooms. But there's no need to stay talking here all the afternoon. Come and see the I.G. in his lair – the miserable conscript driven up to the colours at the point of the bayonet.'

[First published in the *Morning Post*, 15–18 June 1904.]

✠ ✠ ✠

The first pitched battle of the English Civil War was fought at Edgehill in Warwickshire on 23 October 1642.

EDGEHILL FIGHT

NAKED AND GREY THE Cotswolds stand
Beneath the summer sun,
And the stubble fields on either hand
Where Stour and Avon run.

There is no change in the patient land
That has bred us every one.

She should have passed in cloud and fire
And saved us from this sin
Of war – red war – 'twixt child and sire,
Household and kith and kin,
In the heart of a sleepy Midland shire,
With the harvest scarcely in.

But there is no change as we meet at last
On the brow-head or the plain,
And the raw astonished ranks stand fast
To slay or to be slain
By the men they knew in the kindly past
That shall never come again –

By the men they met at dance or chase,
In the tavern or the hall,
At the justice bench and the market place,
At the cudgel play or brawl –
Of their own blood and speech and race,
Comrades or neighbours all!

More bitter than death this day must prove
Whichever way it go,
For the brothers of the maids we love
Make ready to lay low
Their sisters' sweethearts, as we move
Against our dearest foe.

Thank Heaven! At last the trumpets peal
Before our strength gives way.
For King or for the Commonweal–
No matter which they say,
The first dry rattle of new-drawn steel
Changes the world today!

[First published in C.R.L. Fletcher and Rudyard Kipling, *A School History of England* (Oxford: Clarendon Press, 1911).]

✠ ✠ ✠

Kipling was a great admirer of ancient Saxon ways. This poem suggests that the Normans, like the British in parts of their empire, should try to get to know those they had defeated – in this case, the Saxons.

NORMAN AND SAXON

'MY SON,' SAID THE Norman Baron, 'I am dying, and you will be heir
To all the broad acres in England that William gave me for my share
When we conquered the Saxon at Hastings, and a nice little handful it is.
But before you go over to rule it I want you to understand this:–

'The Saxon is not like us Normans. His manners are not so polite.
But he never means anything serious till he talks about justice and right.
When he stands like an ox in the furrow with his sullen set eyes on your own,
And grumbles, "This isn't fair dealings," my son, leave the Saxon alone.

'You can horsewhip your Gascony archers, or torture your Picardy spears,
But don't try that game on the Saxon; you'll have the whole brood round your ears.
From the richest old Thane in the county to the poorest chained serf in the field,
They'll be at you and on you like hornets, and, if you are wise, you will yield.

'But first you must master their language, their dialect, proverbs and songs.
Don't trust any clerk to interpret when they come with the tale of their wrongs.

Let them know that you know what they're saying; let them feel
    that you know what to say.
Yes, even when you want to go hunting, hear 'em out if it takes
    you all day.

'They'll drink every hour of the daylight and poach every hour of
    the dark,
It's the sport not the rabbits they're after (we've plenty of game in
    the park).
Don't hang them or cut off their fingers. That's wasteful as well as
    unkind,
For a hard-bitten, South-country poacher makes the best man-at-
    arms you can find.

'Appear with your wife and the children at their weddings and
    funerals and feasts.
Be polite but not friendly to Bishops; be good to all poor parish
    priests.
Say "we," "us" and "ours" when you're talking instead of "you
    fellows" and "I."
Don't ride over seeds; keep your temper; and never you tell 'em a lie!'

[First published in Fletcher and Kipling, *A School History of England* (1911).]

☒ ☒ ☒

**Danegeld was the tax paid by the Anglo-Saxons (mainly) to
ward off attacks by Viking raiders in the eleventh century. It has
become tied up with the idea of appeasement.**

DANE-GELD

A.D. 980–1016

IT IS ALWAYS A temptation to an armed and agile nation
    To call upon a neighbour and to say:–
'We invaded you last night – we are quite prepared to fight,
    Unless you pay us cash to go away.'

And that is called asking for Dane-geld,
    And the people who ask it explain
That you've only to pay 'em the Dane-geld
    And then you'll get rid of the Dane!

It is always a temptation for a rich and lazy nation,
    To puff and look important and to say:–
'Though we know we should defeat you, we have not the time to
        meet you.
    We will therefore pay you cash to go away.'

And that is called paying the Dane-geld;
    But we've proved it again and again,
That if once you have paid him the Dane-geld
    You never get rid of the Dane.

It is wrong to put temptation in the path of any nation,
    For fear they should succumb and go astray;
So when you are requested to pay up or be molested,
    You will find it better policy to say:–

'We never pay *any*-one Dane-geld,
    No matter how trifling the cost;
For the end of that game is oppression and shame,
    And the nation that pays it is lost!'

[First published in Fletcher and Kipling, *A School History of England* (1911).]

THE FIRST WORLD
WAR AND AFTER

Published a month after the outbreak of the First World War, this is a heartfelt call to arms, reiterating warnings Kipling had made for several years about Germany's war-like intentions.

FOR ALL WE HAVE AND ARE

1914

FOR ALL WE HAVE and are,
For all our children's fate,
Stand up and take the war.
The Hun is at the gate!
Our world has passed away,
In wantonness o'erthrown.
There is nothing left to-day
But steel and fire and stone!
    Though all we knew depart,
    The old Commandments stand:–
    'In courage keep your heart,
    In strength lift up your hand.'

Once more we hear the word
That sickened earth of old:–
'No law except the Sword
Unsheathed and uncontrolled.'
Once more it knits mankind,
Once more the nations go
To meet and break and bind
A crazed and driven foe.

Comfort, content, delight,
The ages' slow-bought gain,
They shrivelled in a night.
Only ourselves remain
To face the naked days
In silent fortitude,
Through perils and dismays
Renewed and re-renewed.
   Though all we made depart,
   The old Commandments stand:–
   'In patience keep your heart,
   In strength lift up your hand.'

No easy hope or lies
Shall bring us to our goal,
But iron sacrifice
Of body, will, and soul.
There is but one task for all –
One life for each to give.
What stands if Freedom fall?
Who dies if England live?

[First published in *The Times*, 2 September 1914, and then collected in *The Years Between* (London: Methuen, 1919).]

This article comes from a series of six which Kipling wrote at the start of the war about the training of Britain's new volunteer army.

THE NEW ARMY IN TRAINING

III
Guns and Supply

Under all and after all the Wheel carries everything.

Proverb

ONE HAD KNOWN THE place for years as a picturesque old house, standing in a peaceful park; had watched the growth of certain young oaks along a new-laid avenue, and applauded the owner's enterprise in turning a stretch of pasture to plough. There are scores of such estates in England which the motorist, through passing so often, comes to look upon almost as his own. In a single day the brackened turf between the oaks and the iron road-fence blossomed into tents, and the drives were all cut up with hoofs and wheels. A little later, one's car sweeping home of warm September nights was stopped by sentries, who asked her name and business; for the owner of that retired house and discreetly wooded park had gone elsewhere in haste, and his estate was taken over by the military.

Later still, one met men and horses arguing with each other for miles about that country-side; or the car would be flung on her brakes by artillery issuing from cross-lanes – clean batteries jingling off to their work on the Downs, and hungry ones coming back to meals. Every day brought the men and the horses and the weights behind them to a better understanding, till in a little while the car could pass a quarter of a mile of them without having to hoot more than once.

'Why are you so virtuous?' she asked of a section encountered at a blind and brambly corner. 'Why do you obtrude your personality less than an average tax-cart?'

'Because,' said a driver, his arm flung up to keep the untrimmed hedge from sweeping his cap off, 'because those are our blessed orders. We don't do it for love.'

No one accuses the Gunner of maudlin affection for anything except his beasts and his weapons. He hasn't the time. He serves at least three jealous gods – his horse and all its saddlery and harness; his gun, whose least detail of efficiency is more important than men's lives; and, when these have been attended to, the never-ending mystery of his art commands him.

It was a wettish, windy day when I visited the so-long-known house and park. Cock pheasants ducked in and out of trim rhododendron clumps, neat gates opened into sacredly preserved vegetable gardens, the many-coloured leaves of specimen trees pasted themselves stickily against sodden tent walls, and there was a mixture of circus smells from the horse-lines and the faint, civilised breath of chrysanthemums in the potting sheds. The main drive was being relaid with a foot of flint; the other approaches were churned and pitted under the gun wheels and heavy supply wagons. Great breadths of what had been well-kept turf between unbrowsed trees were blanks of slippery brown wetness, dotted with picketed horses and field-kitchens. It was a crazy mixture of stark necessity and manicured luxury, all cheek by jowl, in the undiscriminating rain.

SERVICE CONDITIONS

The cook-houses, store-rooms, forges, and work-shops were collections of tilts, poles, rick-cloths, and odd lumber, beavered together as on service. The officers' mess was a thin, soaked marquee. Less than a hundred yards away were dozens of vacant, well-furnished rooms in the big brick house, of which the Staff furtively occupied one corner. There was accommodation for very many men in its stables and out-houses alone; or the whole building might have been gutted and rearranged for barracks twice over in the last three months. Scattered among the tents were rows of half-built tin sheds, the ready-prepared lumber and the corrugated iron lying beside them, waiting to be pieced together like children's toys. But there were no workmen. I was told that they had come that morning, but had knocked off because it was wet.

'I see. And where are the batteries?' I demanded.

'Out at work, of course. They've been out since seven.'

'How shocking! In this dreadful weather, too!'

'They took some bread and cheese with them. They'll be back about dinner-time if you care to wait. Here's one of our field-kitchens.'

Batteries look after their own stomachs, and are not catered for by contractors. The cook-house was a wagon-tilt. The wood, being damp, smoked a good deal. One thought of the wide, adequate kitchen ranges and the concrete passages of the service quarters in the big house just behind. One even dared to think Teutonically of the perfectly good panelling and the thick hard-wood floors that could —

'Service conditions, you see,' said my guide, as the cook inspected the baked meats and the men inside the wagon-tilt grated the carrots and prepared the onions. It was old work to them after all these months – done swiftly, with the clean economy of effort that camp life teaches.

'What are these lads when they're at home?' I inquired.

'Londoners chiefly – all sorts and conditions.'

The cook in shirt sleeves made another investigation, and sniffed judicially. He might have been cooking since the Peninsular. He looked at his watch and across towards the park gates. He was responsible for one hundred and sixty rations, and a battery has the habit of saying quite all that it thinks of its food.

'How often do the batteries go out?' I continued.

''Bout five days a week. You see, we're being worked up a little.'

'And have they got plenty of ground to work over?'

'Oh – yes-s.'

'What's the difficulty this time? Birds?'

'No; but we got orders the other day not to go over a golf-course. That rather knocks the bottom out of tactical schemes.'

Perfect shamelessness, like perfect virtue, is impregnable; and, after all, the lightnings of this war, which have brought out so much resolve and self-sacrifice, must show up equally certain souls and institutions that are irredeemable.

The weather took off a little before noon. The carpenters could have put in a good half-day's work on the sheds, and even if they had been rained upon they had roofs with fires awaiting their return. The batteries had none of these things.

THE GUNNER AT HOME

They came in at last far down the park, heralded by that unmistakable half-grumble, half-grunt of guns on the move. The picketed horses heard it first, and one of them neighed long and loud, which proved that he had abandoned civilian habits. Horses in stables and mews seldom do more than snicker, even when they are halves of separated pairs. But these gentlemen had a corporate life of their own now, and knew what 'pulling together' means.

When a battery comes into camp it 'parks' all six guns at the appointed place, side by side in one mathematically straight line, and the accuracy of the alignment is, like ceremonial drill with the Foot, a fair test of its attainments. The ground was no treat for parking. Specimen trees and draining ditches had to be avoided and circumvented. The gunners, their reins, the guns, the ground, were equally wet, and the slob dropped away like gruel from the brake-shoes. And they were Londoners – clerks, mechanics, shop assistants, and delivery men – anything and everything that you please. But they were all home and at home in their saddles and seats. They said nothing; their officers said little enough to them. They came in across what had once been turf; wheeled with tight traces; halted, unhooked; the wise teams stumped off to their pickets, and, behold, the six guns were left precisely where they should have been left to the fraction of an inch. You could see the wind blowing the last few drops of wet from each leather muzzle-cover at exactly the same angle. It was all old known evolutions, taken unconsciously in the course of their day's work by men well abreast of it.

'Our men have one advantage,' said a voice. 'As Territorials they were introduced to unmade horses once a year at training. So they've never been accustomed to made horses.'

'And what do the horses say about it all?' I asked, remembering what I had seen on the road in the early days.

'They said a good deal at first, but our chaps could make allowances for 'em. They know now.'

Allah never intended the Gunner to talk. His own arm does that for him. The batteries off-saddled in silence, though one noticed on all sides little quiet caresses between man and beast – affectionate nuzzlings and nose-slappings. Surely the Gunner's relation to his horse is more intimate even than the cavalryman's; for a lost horse only turns cavalry into infantry, but trouble in a gun team may mean death all round. And this is the Gunner's war. The young wet officers said so joyously as they passed to and fro picking up scandal about breast-straps and breechings, examining the collars of ammunition-wagon teams, and listening to remarks on shoes. Local blacksmiths, assisted by the battery itself, do the shoeing. There are master smiths and important farriers, who have cheerfully thrown up good wages to help the game, and their horses reward them by keeping fit. A fair proportion of the horses are aged – there was never a Gunner yet satisfied with his team or its rations till he had left the battery – but they do their work as steadfastly and whole-heartedly as the men. I am persuaded the horses like being in society and working out their daily problems of draught and direction. The English, and Londoners particularly, are the kindest and most reasonable of folk with animals. If it were not our business strictly to underrate ourselves for the next few years, one would say that the Territorial batteries had already done wonders. But perhaps it is better to let it all go with the grudging admission wrung out of a wringing wet bombardier, 'Well, it isn't so dam' bad – considering.'

I left them taking their dinner in mess tins to their tents, with a strenuous afternoon's cleaning-up ahead of them. The big park held some thousands of men. I had seen no more than a few hundreds, and had missed the howitzer-batteries after all. A cock pheasant chaperoned me down the drive, complaining loudly that where he was used to walk with his ladies under the beech trees, some unsporting people had built a miniature landscape with tiny villages, churches, and factories, and came there daily to point cannon at it.

'Keep away from that place,' said I, 'or you'll find yourself in a field-kitchen.'

'Not me!' he crowed. 'I'm as sacred as golf-courses.'

MECHANISM AND MECHANICS

There was a little town a couple of miles down the road where one used to lunch in the old days, and had the hotel to oneself. Now there are six ever-changing officers in billet there, and the astonished houses quiver all day to traction engines and high-piled lorries. A unit of the Army Service Corps and some mechanical transport lived near the station, and fed the troops for twenty miles around.

'Are your people easy to find?' I asked of a wandering private, with the hands of a sweep, the head of a Christian among lions, and suicide in his eye.

'Well, the A.S.C. are in the Territorial Drill Hall for one thing; and for another you're likely to hear us! There's some motors come in from Bulford. He snorted and passed on, smelling of petrol. The drill-shed was peace and comfort. The A.S.C. were getting ready there for pay-day and for a concert that evening. Outside in the wind and the occasional rain-spurts, life was different. The Bulford motors and some other crocks sat on a side-road between what had been the local garage and a newly-erected workshop of creaking scaffold-poles and bellying slatting rick-cloths, where a forge glowed and general repairs were being effected. Beneath the motors men lay on their backs and called their friends to pass them spanners, or, for pity's sake, to shove another sack under their mud-wreathed heads.

A corporal, who had been nine years a fitter and seven in a city garage, briefly and briskly outlined the more virulent diseases that develop in Government rolling-stock. (I heard quite a lot about Bulford.) Hollow voices from beneath eviscerated gear-boxes confirmed him. We withdrew to the shelter of the rick-cloth workshop – that corporal; the sergeant who had been a carpenter, with a business of his own, and, incidentally, had served through the Boer War; another sergeant who was a member of the Master Builders' Association; and a private who had also been fitter, chauffeur, and a few other things. The third sergeant, who kept a poultry-farm in Surrey, had some duty elsewhere.

A man at a carpenter's bench was finishing a spoke for a newly-painted cart. He squinted along it.

That's funny,' said the master builder. 'Of course in his own business he'd chuck his job sooner than do wood-work. But it's all funny.'

'What I grudge,' a sergeant struck in, 'is havin' to put mechanics to loading and unloading beef. That's where modified conscription for the beauties that won't roll up 'ld be useful to us. We want hewers of wood, we do. And I'd hew 'em!'

'I want that file.' This was a private in a hurry, come from beneath an unspeakable Bulford. Some one asked him musically if he 'would tell his wife in the morning who he was with to-night.'

'You'll find it in the tool-chest,' said the sergeant. It was his own sacred tool-chest which he had contributed to the common stock.

'And what sort of men have you got in this unit?' I asked.

'Every sort you can think of. There isn't a thing you couldn't have made here if you wanted to. But' – the corporal, who had been a fitter, spoke with fervour – 'you can't expect us to make big-ends, can you? That five-ton Bulford lorry out there in the wet.'

'And she isn't the worst,' said the master builder. 'But it's all part of the game. And so funny when you come to think of it. Me painting carts, and certificated plumbers loading frozen beef!'

'What about the discipline?' I asked.

The corporal turned a fitter's eye on me. 'The mechanism is the discipline,' said he, with most profound truth. 'Jockeyin' a sick car on the road is discipline, too. What about the discipline?' He turned to the sergeant with the carpenter's chest. There was one sergeant of Regulars, with twenty years' service behind him and a knowledge of human nature. He struck in.

'You ought to know. You've just been made corporal,' said that sergeant of Regulars.

'Well, there's so much which everybody knows has got to be done that – that – why, we all turn in and do it,' quoth the corporal. 'I don't have any trouble with my lot.'

'Yes; that's how the case stands,' said the sergeant of Regulars. 'Come and see our stores.' They were beautifully arranged in a shed which felt like a monastery after the windy, clashing world without; and the young private who acted as checker – he came from some railway office – had the thin, keen face of the cleric.

'We're in billets in the town,' said the sergeant who had been a carpenter. 'But I'm a married man. I shouldn't care to have men billeted on us at home, an' I don't want to inconvenience other people. So I've knocked up a bunk for myself on the premises. It's handier to the stores, too.'

'THE HUMOUR OF IT'

We entered what had been the local garage. The mechanical transport were in full possession, tinkering the gizzards of more cars. We discussed chewed-up gears (samples to hand), and the civil population's old-time views of the military. The corporal told a tale of a clergyman in a Midland town who, only a year ago, on the occasion of some manoeuvres, preached a sermon warning his flock to guard their womenfolk against the soldiers.

'And when you think – when you know,' said the corporal, 'what life in those little towns really is!' He whistled.

'See that old landau,' said he, opening the door of an ancient wreck jammed against a wall. 'That's two of our chaps' dressing-room. They don't care to be billeted, so they sleep 'tween the landau and the wall. It's handier for their work, too. Work comes in at all hours. I wish I was cavalry. There's some use in cursing a horse.'

Truly, it's an awful thing to belong to a service where speech brings no alleviation.

'You!' A private with callipers turned from the bench by the window. 'You'd die outside of a garage. But what you said about civilians and soldiers is all out of date now.'

The sergeant of Regulars permitted himself a small, hidden smile. The private with the callipers had been some twelve weeks a soldier.

'I don't say it isn't,' said the corporal, 'I'm saying what it used to be.'

'We-ell,' the private screwed up the callipers, 'didn't you feel a little bit that way yourself – when you were a civilian?'

'I-I don't think I did.' The corporal was taken aback. 'I don't think I ever thought about it.'

'Ah! There you are!' said the private, very drily.

Some one laughed in the shadow of the landau dressing-room. 'Anyhow, we're all in it now, Private Percy,' said a voice.

There must be a good many thousand conversations of this kind being held all over England nowadays. Our breed does not warble much about patriotism or Fatherland, but it has a wonderful sense of justice, even when its own shortcomings are concerned.

We went over to the drill-shed to see the men paid. The first man I ran across there was a sergeant who had served in the Mounted Infantry in the South African picnic that we used to call a war. He had been a private chauffeur for some years – long enough to catch the professional look, but was joyously reverting to service type again. The men lined up, were called out, saluted emphatically at the pay-table, and fell back with their emoluments. They smiled at each other.

'An' it's all so funny,' murmured the master builder in my ear. 'About a quarter – no, less than a quarter of what one 'ud be making on one's own!'

'Fifty bob a week, cottage, and all found, I was. An' only two cars to look after.' said a voice behind. 'An' if I'd been asked – simply asked – to lie down in the mud all the afternoon—!' The speaker looked at his wages with awe. Some one wanted to know, sotto voce, if 'that was union rates,' and the grin spread among the uniformed experts. The joke, you will observe, lay in situations thrown up, businesses abandoned, and pleasant prospects cut short at the nod of duty.

'Thank Heaven!' said one of them at last, 'it's too dark to work on those blessed Bulfords any more to-day. We'll get ready for the concert.'

But it was not too dark, half an hour later, for my car to meet a big lorry storming back in the wind and the wet from the northern camps. She gave me London allowance – half one inch between hub and hub – swung her corner like a Brooklands professional, changed gear for the uphill with a sweet click, and charged away. For aught I knew, she was driven by an ex-'fifty-bob-a-week-a-cottage-and-all-found'-er, who next month might be dodging shells with her and thinking it 'all so funny,' Horse, Foot, even the Guns may sometimes get a little rest, but so long as men eat thrice a day there is no rest for the Army Service Corps. They carry the campaign on their all-sustaining backs.

[First published in the *Daily Telegraph*, 14 December 1914.]

⚔ ⚔ ⚔

Kipling kept up his angry propagandist output, emphasising the barbarity of the Germans who had overrun Belgium in the early weeks of the war, creating waves of refugees (many of whom came to Britain). *King Albert's Book* was published to raise funds for this influx of destitute people.

THE OUTLAWS

1914

THROUGH LEARNED AND LABORIOUS years
   They set themselves to find
Fresh terrors and undreamed-of fears
   To heap upon mankind.

All that they drew from Heaven above
　　Or digged from earth beneath,
They laid into their treasure-trove
　　And arsenals of death:

While, for well-weighed advantage sake,
　　Ruler and ruled alike
Built up the faith they meant to break
　　When the fit hour should strike.

They traded with the careless earth,
　　And good return it gave:
They plotted by their neighbour's hearth
　　The means to make him slave.

When all was ready to their hand
　　They loosed their hidden sword,
And utterly laid waste a land
　　Their oath was pledged to guard.

Coldly they went about to raise
　　To life and make more dread
Abominations of old days,
　　That men believed were dead.

They paid the price to reach their goal
　　Across a world in flame;
But their own hate slew their own soul
　　Before that victory came.

[First published in *King Albert's Book* (London: Daily Telegraph, 1914) on behalf of Belgian refugees.]

✠　✠　✠

Kipling's 18-year-old son John was killed at the Battle of Loos on 27 September 1915, two days after the start of a major Allied offensive along the 90-kilometre front from Loos in the north to Vimy Ridge in the south. Kipling was devastated by the loss of John, who was officially declared missing in action. He devoted a lot of time after the war to grieving and commemorating what had taken place. As part of this process he wrote his two-volume history, *The Irish Guards in the Great War*.

1915 – Loos and the First Autumn

OFFICIALLY, THE FORMATION OF the 2nd Battalion of the Irish Guards dates from the 15th July 1915, when it was announced that His Majesty the King had been 'graciously pleased to approve' of the formation of two additional Battalions of Foot Guards – the 4th Grenadier Guards, and the 2nd Battalion Irish Guards, which was to be made up out of the personnel of the 2nd (Reserve) Battalion. And, officially, on the 18th July that formation took place. But those who knew the world in the old days, and specially the busy part of it that had Warley Barracks for its heart, know that the 2nd Battalion was born in spirit as in substance, long ere the authorities bade it to be. The needs of the war commanded it; the abundance of the reserves then justified it; and, though Warley Barracks had been condemned as unfit for use by the Honourable the East India Company a trifle of fifty odd years ago, this was not the hour to stand on ancient tradition. So the old, crazy barracks overflowed; the officers' damp and sweating dog-kennels were double-crammed; and, by sheer goodwill and stark discipline, the work went forward to the creation. Officers and men alike welcomed it, for it is less pleasing to be absorbed in drafts and driblets by an ever-hungry 1st Battalion in France, than to be set apart for the sacrifice as a veritable battalion on its own responsibility, with its own traditions (they sprang up immediately) and its own jealous esprit-de-corps. A man may join for the sake of 'King and Country' but he goes over the top for the honour of his own platoon, company, and battalion; and, the heart of man being what it is, so soon as the 2nd Battalion opened its eyes, the first thing that it beheld was its 1st Battalion, as an elder brother to measure its stature against in all things. Yet, following the ancient mystery of all armies, there were not two battalions, but one regiment; officers and men interchangeable, and equally devoted to the battalion that they served for the time, though in their deeper minds, and sometimes confessing it, more devoutly attached to one or the other of the two.

By summer of '15 the tide of special reserve officers was towards its flood, and the 2nd Battalion was largely filled by them. They hailed from every quarter of the Empire, and represented almost every profession and state of life in it, from the schoolboy of eighteen to the lawyer of forty odd. They had parted long ago with any delusion as to the war ending that year or the next. The information that came to them by word of mouth was not of the sort dispensed in the Press, and they knew, perhaps a little more than the public, how inadequate were our preparations. One and all they realised that humanly speaking, unless fortune favoured them with permanent disablement they were doomed men; since all who recovered from their wounds were returned to the war and sooner or later despatched. He was lucky in those days who survived whole for three months; and six without hurt was almost unheard of. So the atmosphere of their daily lives, underneath the routine and the carefully organised amusements that the world then offered to its victims, had an unreality, comparable in some degree, to the elaborately articulated conversation and serious argument over utterly trivial matters that springs up among officers in that last hour of waiting under the thunder of the preliminary bombardment before the word is given that hoists all ranks slowly and methodically into a bone-naked landscape.

Lieut. Colonel the Earl of Kerry, M.V.O., D.S.O., who commanded the reserve and whose influence over the men was unbounded, began the work of making the 2nd Battalion, and, later on, Major G.H.C. Madden was recalled from duty in France to be its senior major. Captain the Hon. T.E. Vesey was the first adjutant and, with a tight hand which was appreciated afterwards, showed all that young community how to take care of itself. It was a time for understanding much and overlooking little. 'Or else,' as the sergeants explained, 'ye'll die before ye've killed a Jerry.'

On the 27th July, Major and Brevet-Lieut. Colonel the Hon. L.J.P. Butler took over command, and on 6th August the Battalion with full transport, and packs, paraded as such for its first route-march, of sixteen miles in the flat country, filled with training troops, that lies round Warley. The weather was very hot, nor did that officer who had bethought him to fill his 'full pack' with a full-blown air-cushion, take much reward of his ingenuity when his unlucky fraud betrayed him by bursting almost under the adjutant's eye. Men said that that was their real introduction to the horrors of war.

They were inspected on the 10th August by Major-General Sir Francis Lloyd, commanding the London District who, after the usual compliments on their physique and steadiness, told them they were due for France in a few days. Lord Kitchener came down and addressed them on the 13th of the month, was photographed with a group of all the officers of the 2nd Battalion and Reserve Battalions, and expressed his belief that they would be a credit to the Guards Division then, as we know, being formed in France.

On the 16th they left Brentwood Station, that has seen so many thousands depart; and that evening were packed tightly at Southampton in the *Anglo-Canadian* and the *Viper*. Duly escorted by destroyers, for the seas were troubled by submarines, both ships tied up at Havre in stillness and strange 'foreign' smells at midnight. The city and its outskirts for miles round had long since been turned wholly to the monotonous business of expediting troops and supplies; and the camps that ringed it spread and linked on almost daily. The French were used, now, to our armed Empire at large flooding their streets. Wonder and welcome had passed. No pretty maids met them with wine or garlands, and their route inland to their work was as worn and smooth as the traffic-burnished metals from Brentwood to the sea. But the country and its habits were new to all those new hands, trained in a strict school; and it filled them with joy to behold the casual manner in which a worn and dusty French sentry was relieved while they were marching to their first wonderful camp outside the city.

They entrained for Lumbres on the 18th August and were bidden, next day, to march to billets at Acquin, a little village on a hill-side a few miles from St. Omer, in a fold of the great Sussex-like downs. It is a place both steep and scattered, cramped and hot, and when the air-war was in full swing had its small share of bombs intended for Army Headquarters at St. Omer, and the adjacent aerodromes. The men were billeted in barns forty and fifty at a time which, specially for a new battalion, was rather unhandy, as offering many ups and downs and corners, which afford chances for delays and misunderstandings. But it was to be their first and only experience of comfort for any consecutive time, and of French life a little untouched by war. They most deeply enjoyed the simple kindliness of the village-folk, and the graceless comments of the little sharp-faced French children at the halting attempts of the Irish to talk French; the glimpses of intimate domestic days, when sons and brothers of their hosts, returned on a few days' leave from far-away battlefields in the Argonne or beyond, were shown with pride to the visitors who were helping the villagers to cart their corn – 'precisely as our own sons would have done.' They talked, too, with veterans of '70 met in the fields and at the cafes, who told them in set and rounded phrases that war was serious. And the French men and women upon whom they were billeted liked them well and remembered them long. Said one, years after, with tears in the eyes: 'Monsieur, if you drew a line in the air and asked those children not to cross it, it was as a wall to them. They played, monsieur, like infants, without any thought of harm or unkindness; and then they would all become men again, very serious – all those children of yours.'

So things were gracious and kindly about them in that little village where every one had suffered loss, and was making their resolute, curt, French best of it; and the 2nd Battalion settled down to an eleventh-hour course of instruction in everything that the war of that day might call for – except, it may be, how to avoid their own cavalry on the march.

The historic first meeting between the 1st and 2nd Battalions took place on the 30th August on a march out to St. Pierre, when the units of the different Guards Brigades were drawing in together for combined work preparatory to the Battle of Loos. The veterans of the 1st were personal in their remarks, deriding the bright cap-stars of the 2nd Battalion, and telling them that they would soon know better than to advertise their rank under fire. The 2nd Battalion Diary notes a point that the 1st, doubtless through delicacy, omits – that when the merry gathering under the trees in the field was at an end, after dinner, the 2nd Battalion fell in and marched off the ground 'before the critical eyes of their older comrades, and the 1st followed.' No fault was found, but it was a breathless business, compared, by one who took part, to the performances of rival peacocks. ('There was not any one else, that we considered; but we knew that, if we put a foot wrong in that parade in front of them we'd be in the road to hear tell of it the rest of our lives.') And it was on this great day, too, that the Rev. Father Knapp joined as R.C. Chaplain to the Battalion, and thereafter proved himself as far forward on all fields as any of the rest of his brethren.

LOOS

They began to learn something about service conditions when, on the 1st September, they joined up with their Brigade, the 2nd Guards Brigade, and shared a wet day of advancing, on parallel roads, with three Guards Brigades, for practice at coming up into the line. Otherwise, they dug trenches by day and night, developed, more or less, their own system of laying them out in the dark, and their brigade's idea of storming trenches with the help of bombers who had had very little practice with the live bomb; and kept their ears open for any news about conditions on the front. The 'smoke-helmets' issued on the eve of the Battalion's departure from England were new also. Many of the talc eye-pieces had cracked in transit, and had to be replaced, and the men instructed how to slip them on against time. This was even more important than the 'attack of villages,' which was another part of their curriculum at Avroult, Wismes, Wavrans, Tatinghem, Wisques, Dohem, and the like in that dry autumn weather that was saving itself to break filthily at Loos.

On the 5th September, knowing extremely well what they were intended for, after battalion drill, Lieut. General Haking, commanding the Eleventh Corps, addressed all the Officers of the 2nd Guards Brigade at the 1st Coldstream Mess at Lumbres. The summary is set down in the Diary with no more comment than three exclamation points at the end.

He told them that an attack on the German lines was close at hand; that the Germans had but forty thousand men at the selected point to oppose our two hundred thousand; and that behind their firing-line and supports were only six divisions as a reserve to their whole western front. This may or may not have been true at the time. What follows has a more direct bearing, perhaps, on the course of events, so far as the Battalion was concerned. General Haking said that almost everything depended on the platoon leaders, and 'he instructed them always to push on boldly whenever an opportunity offered, even at the expense of exposing and leaving unguarded their flanks.' Hence, perhaps, the exclamation points. From the civilian point of view the advice seems hardly safe to offer to a battalion of at least average courage a few days before they are to meet singularly well-posted machine-guns, and carefully trained bombers.

Ceremonial drill of the whole of the 2nd Guards Brigade followed the next day, when they were inspected by Major-General the Earl of Cavan, marched past in column of double platoons, returned to line in mass, complimented on their appearance and so forth, after which, in the evening the C.O. of the Battalion with General Feilding (1st Guards Brigade), Captain Viscount Gort (B.M. 1st Guards Brigade), and Colonel Corry commanding the 3rd Grenadier Guards, went off in a car to 'see the country south-east of Béthune.' This was not a sector that improved on acquaintance; and in the days that followed all senior officers looked at and pondered over the unwholesome open scarred ground over which 'the greatest battle in the history of the world,' as General Haking said, was to take place. Meantime, among the drills held at Acquin appear orders, presumably for the first time, that every one was to fire ten rounds 'from his rifle while wearing his smoke-helmet.' The result on the targets of this solitary experiment is not recorded; but it takes some time for a man to get used to sighting through dingy talc eye-pieces. Nor is it likely to be known in this world whether the 'six young officers' who attended riding-school just before the march towards Loos, derived much benefit from their instruction.

They moved on the evening of the 22nd September and marched to Dohem where they picked up their Brigade Headquarters and some other units, and thence, next day, in heavy rain to billets in Linghem. General Haking delivered another speech at the Corps Conference on the 24th, explaining the broad outlines of the 'greatest battle, etc.' which at that moment was opening. He dwelt specially on the part to be played by the Eleventh Corps, as well as the necessity for speed and for the use of reserves. It may have occurred to some of his hearers that they were the reserves, but that speed was out of the question, for the roads were clotted with cavalry, and there did not seem to be any great choice of those 'parallel roads' on which they had been exercised, or any vast crush of motor-buses. When they got away from Linghem on the early morning of the 25th and marched with their brigade to Burbure and Haquin, they enjoyed continuous halts, owing to the cavalry going forward, which meant, for the most part, through them, and the wounded of the battle being brought back – all on the same road. They billeted (this was merely a form) at Haquin 'very wet and tired' about one on the morning of the 26th, having been on their feet standing, marching, or variously shifted about, for twenty odd hours. The men's breakfasts were issued at half-past four that same dawn 'as there was a possibility of an early move.'

No orders, however, came, the world around them being busied with the shifting phases of the opening of Loos, which had begun with an advance at some spots along the line, and at others was hung up among wire that our two or three hours' bombardment did not seem to have wholly removed. The 2nd Guards Brigade, then, waited on at Haquin till shortly after noon, and moved via Nœux-les-Mines, Sailly-Labourse, Noyelles, and Vermelles, large portions of which were then standing and identifiable, to trenches in front of Le Rutoire. Here the German lines had been driven back a little, and Captains Alexander and Hubbard commanding the two leading companies of the Battalion were sent on to look at them in daylight. The results of the Captains' adventure, when it is recalled that one set of trenches, at the best of times, looks remarkably like another, and that this was far from being a good time, were surprisingly satisfactory. 'There was no one to tell them exactly which trenches were to be taken over, but, from instructions given on the map, and in consultation with the 1st Scots Guards who had to occupy ground on their right, they arranged which set of them to inhabit. Owing to congestion of roads, and having to go across much broken country, etc., it was nearly midnight before the Battalion got into the selected spot – an old line of captured German trenches in front of Lone Tree.' This, as is well known to all regimental historians, was a mark of the German guns almost to the inch, and, unfortunately, formed one of our dressing-stations. At a moderate estimate the Battalion had now been on foot and livelily awake for forty-eight hours; the larger part of that time without any food. It remained for them merely to go into the fight, which they did at half-past two on the morning of the 27th September when they received 'verbal instructions to push forward to another line of captured German trenches, some five hundred yards, relieving any troops that might happen to be there.' It was nearly broad daylight by the time that this disposition was completed, and they were much impressed with the permanence and solidity of the German works in which they found themselves, and remarked jestingly one to another, that 'Jerry must have built them with the idea of staying there for ever.' As a matter of fact, 'Jerry' did stay within half a mile of that very line for the next three years and six weeks, less one day. They had their first hint of his intentions when patrols pushed out from Nos. 2 and 3 Companies in the forenoon, reported that they were unable to get even a hundred yards ahead, on account

of rifle-fire. Men said, long afterwards, that this was probably
machine-gun fire out of the Bois Hugo; which thoroughly swept all
open communications, for the enemy here as elsewhere had given
ground a little without losing his head, and was hitting back as
methodically as ever.

The attack of their Brigade developed during the course of the
day. The four C.O.s of the Battalions met their Brigadier at the
1st Grenadier Guards Headquarters. He took them to a point just
north of Loos, whence they could see Chalk-Pit Wood, and the
battered bulk of the colliery head and workings known as Puits 14
bis, together with what few small buildings still stood thereabouts,
and told them that he proposed to attack as follows: At half-past
two a heavy bombardment lasting for one hour and a half would
be delivered on that sector. At four the Second Irish Guards would
advance upon Chalk-Pit Wood and would establish themselves
on the north-east and south-east faces of it, supported by the 1st
Coldstream. The 1st Scots Guards were to advance echeloned to
the right rear of the Irish, and to attack Puits 14 bis moving round
the south side of Chalk-Pit Wood, covered by heavy fire from the
Irish out of the Wood itself. For this purpose, four machine-guns
of the Brigade Machine-gun Company were to accompany the
latter battalion. The 3rd Grenadiers were to support the 1st Scots
in their attack on the Puits. Chalk-Pit Wood at that time existed as
a somewhat dishevelled line of smallish trees and brush running
from north to south along the edge of some irregular chalk
workings which terminated at their north end, in a deepish circular
quarry. It was not easy to arrive at its precise shape and size, for
the thing, like so much of the war-landscape of France, was seen
but once by the men vitally concerned in its features, and thereafter
changed outline almost weekly, as gun-fire smote and levelled it
from different angles.

The orders for the Battalion, after the conference and the short
view of the ground, were that No. 3 Company (Captain Wynter)
was to advance from their trenches when the bombardment
stopped, to the southern end of Chalk-Pit Wood, get through and
dig itself in in the tough chalk on the farther side. No. 2 Company
(Captain Bird), on the left of No. 3, would make for the centre of the
wood, dig in too, on the far side, and thus prolong No. 3's line up to
and including the Chalk-Pit – that is to say, that the two companies
would hold the whole face of the Wood.

Nos. 1 and 4 Companies were to follow and back up Nos. 3 and 2 respectively. At four o'clock the two leading companies deployed and advanced, 'keeping their direction and formation perfectly.' That much could be seen from what remained of Vermelles water-tower, where some of the officers of the 1st Battalion were watching, regardless of occasional enemy shell. They advanced quickly, and pushed through to the far edge of the Wood with very few casualties, and those, as far as could be made out, from rifle or machine-gun fire. (Shell-fire had caught them while getting out of their trenches, but, notwithstanding, their losses had not been heavy till then.) The rear companies pushed up to thicken the line, as the fire increased from the front, and while digging in beyond the Wood, 2nd Lieutenant Pakenham-Law was fatally wounded in the head. Digging was not easy work, and seeing that the left of the two first companies did not seem to have extended as far as the Chalk-Pit, at the north of the Wood, the C.O. ordered the last two platoons of No. 4 Company which were just coming up, to bear off to the left and get hold of the place. In the meantime, the 1st Scots Guards, following orders, had come partly round and partly through the right flank of the Irish, and attacked Puits 14 bis, which was reasonably stocked with machine-guns, but which they captured for the moment. Their rush took with them 'some few Irish Guardsmen,' with 2nd Lieutenants W.F.J. Clifford and J. Kipling of No. 2 Company who went forward not less willingly because Captain Cuthbert commanding the Scots Guards party had been adjutant to the Reserve Battalion at Warley ere the 2nd Battalion was formed, and they all knew him. Together, this rush reached a line beyond the Puits, well under machine-gun fire (out of the Bois Hugo across the Lens–La Bassee road). Here 2nd Lieutenant Clifford was shot and wounded or killed – the body was found later – and 2nd Lieutenant Kipling was wounded and missing. The Scots Guards also lost Captain Cuthbert, wounded or killed, and the combined Irish and Scots Guards party fell back from the Puits and retired 'into and through Chalk-Pit Wood in some confusion.' The C.O. and Adjutant, Colonel Butler and Captain Vesey went forward through the Wood to clear up matters, but, soon after they had entered it the Adjutant was badly wounded and had to be carried off. Almost at the same moment, 'the men from the Puits came streaming back through the Wood, followed by a great part of the line which had been digging in on the farther side of it.'

Evidently, one and a half hour's bombardment, against a country-side packed with machine-guns, was not enough to placate it. The Battalion had been swept from all quarters, and shelled at the same time, at the end of two hard days and sleepless nights, as a first experience of war, and had lost seven of their officers in forty minutes. They were reformed somewhat to the rear along the Loos–Hulluch road. ('Jerry did himself well at Loos upon us innocents. We went into it, knowing no more than our own dead what was coming, and Jerry fair lifted us out of it with machine-guns. That was all there was to it *that* day.') The watchers on the Vermelles water-tower saw no more than a slow forward wave obscured by Chalk-Pit Wood; the spreading of a few scattered figures, always, it seemed, moving leisurely; and then a return, with no apparent haste in it, behind the wood once more. They had a fair idea, though, of what had happened, and guessed what was to follow. The re-formed line would go up again exactly to where it had come from. While this was being arranged, and when a couple of companies of the 1st Coldstream had turned up in a hollow on the edge of the Loos–Hulluch road, to support the Battalion, a runner came back with a message from Captain Alexander saying that he and some men were still in their scratch-trenches on the far side of Chalk-Pit Wood, and he would be greatly obliged if they would kindly send some more men up, and with speed. The actual language was somewhat crisper, and was supplemented, so the tale runs, by remarks from the runner addressed to the community at large. The demand was met at once, and the rest of the line was despatched to the near side of the Wood in support. The two companies of the Coldstream came up on the left of the Irish Guards, and seized and settled down in the Chalk-Pit itself. They all had a night's energetic digging ahead of them, with but their own entrenching tools to help, and support-trenches had to be made behind the Wood in case the enemy should be moved to counter-attack. To meet that chance, as there was a gap between the supporting Coldstream Companies and the First Guards Brigade on the left, the C.O. of the 2nd Battalion collected some hundred and fifty men of various regiments, during the dusk, and stuffed them into an old German communication-trench as a defence. No counter-attack developed, but it was a joyless night that they spent among the uptorn trees and lumps of unworkable chalk. Their show had failed with all the others along the line, and 'the greatest battle in the history of the world' was frankly stuck. The most they could do was to hang on and wait developments. They were shelled throughout the next day, heavily but inaccurately, when 2nd Lieutenant Sassoon was wounded by a rifle bullet. In the evening they watched the 1st Coldstream make an unsuccessful attack on Puits 14 bis, for the place was a well-planned machine-gun nest – the first of many that they were fated to lose their strength against through the years to come. That night closed in rain, and they were left to the mercy of Providence. No one could get to them, and they could get at nobody; but they could and did dig deeper into the chalk, to keep warm, and to ensure against the morrow (29th September) when the enemy guns found their range and pitched the stuff fairly into the trenches 'burying many men and blowing a few to pieces.' Yet, according to the count, which surely seems inaccurate, they only lost twenty dead in the course of the long day. The 3rd Guards Brigade on their right, sent in word that the Germans were massing for attack in the Bois Hugo in front of their line. 'All ranks were warned,' which, in such a situation, meant no more than that the experienced among them, of whom there were a few, waited for the cessation of shell-fire, and the inexperienced, of whom there were many, waited for what would come next. ('And the first time that he is under *that* sort of fire, a man stops his thinking. He's all full of wonder, sweat, and great curses.') No attack, however, came, and the Gunners claimed that their fire on Bois Hugo had broken it up. Then the Brigade on their left cheered them with instructions that Chalk-Pit Wood must be 'held at all costs,' and that they would not be relieved for another two days; also, that 'certain modifications of the Brigade line would take place.' It turned out later that these arrangements did not affect the battalions. They were taken out of the line 'wet, dirty, and exhausted' on the night of the 30th September when, after a heavy day's shelling, the Norfolks relieved them, and they got into billets behind Sailly-Lebourse. They had been under continuous strain since the 25th of the month, and from the 27th to the 30th in a punishing action which had cost them, as far as could be made out, 324 casualties, including 101 missing. Of these last, the Diary records that 'the majority of them were found to have been admitted to some field ambulance, wounded. The number of known dead is set down officially as not more than 25, which must be below the mark. Of their officers, 2nd Lieutenant Pakenham-Law had died of wounds; 2nd Lieutenants Clifford

and Kipling were missing, Captain and Adjutant the Hon. T.E.
Vesey, Captain Wynter, Lieutenant Stevens, and 2nd Lieutenants
Sassoon and Grayson were wounded, the last being blown up by a
shell. It was a fair average for the day of a debut, and taught them
somewhat for their future guidance. Their commanding officer
told them so at Adjutant's Parade, after they had been rested and
cleaned on the 2nd October at Verquigneul; but it does not seem
to have occurred to any one to suggest that direct infantry attacks,
after ninety-minute bombardments, on works begotten out of a
generation of thought and prevision, scientifically built up by
immense labour and applied science, and developed against all
contingencies through nine months, are not likely to find a fortunate
issue. So, while the Press was explaining to a puzzled public what
a far-reaching success had been achieved, the 'greatest battle in the
history of the world' simmered down to picking up the pieces on
both sides of the line, and a return to autumnal trench-work, until
more and heavier guns could be designed and manufactured in
England. Meantime, men died.

THE HOHENZOLLERN AND TRENCH WORK

The Battalion, a little rested, and strengthened by four officers from
the 1st Irish Guards (Lieutenant and temporary Captain FitzGerald,
Lieutenants Rankin and Montgomery, and 2nd Lieutenant Langrishe)
as well as a draft of a hundred men under Lieutenant Hamilton, was
introduced to the trenches on the 3rd October, when they moved to
Vermelles and hid themselves in the ruins and cellars of as much
as the enemy had allowed to remain of it. It was an unpleasant
experience. The following comment covers it, and the many others
of the same sort that followed: 'We was big men for the most part,
and this creeping and crawling in and out of what's left of houses,
was not our ways of living. Maybe some of the little fellows in the
Line would have found it easier. And there's a smell to that kind o'
billet worse than graves – a smell off the house-plaster where it lies,
and the wall-paper peelin' off the walls, and what's in the sand-bags
that we build acrost the passages an' the sculleries, ye'll understand,
and the water on the floors stinkin' and rottin'. Ye hear it drip like
dhrums through ceilings in the night. And ye go in an' out of them
dark, stinkin' places always stoopin' an' steppin' on bits o' things.
Dead houses put the wind up a man worse than trenches.'

Next day they were turned down into the multitude of trenches, established or in the making, which lay between Vermelles and the great Hohenzollern redoubt that swept every line of approach with its sudden fires. They were led out (5th October) at dusk across a muddy field beside a dead town, and entered that endless communication-trench called Central Boyau, whose length was reckoned by hours. It led them to the line held by the East Yorks Regiment and two companies of the K.O.Y.L.I. they were relieving. Men forget much, but no man of any battalion ever forgets his first introduction to the stable, deadly fire-line, as distinguished from the casual field-trench. An hour or so before they moved off, a 5.9 burst in a ruined cottage where all the Battalion Staff was sitting, and might well have destroyed the sergeant-major, drill-sergeants and signallers, etc. The only casualty, however, was one pioneer killed, while the officers of the Battalion Staff in the next mound of ruins escaped unhurt.

Then began the slow and repeatedly checked sidle in the dusk, of single men up Central Boyau, which was also a thoroughfare for other units falling, tripping, and cursing among festoons of stray telephone wires. From Vermelles to their trenches was a mile and a quarter. They began at seven at night and completed the relief at six in the morning. Not much shelling greeted them, but the darkness was 'tickled up,' as one man put it, with bullets from all angles, and while No. 3 Company was settling in to reserve-trenches just at the point of grey dawn, 2nd Lieutenant Hine showed himself by getting up on to the parapet, and was shot through the head at once, probably by a sniper. Over and above the boy's natural fearlessness, by which he had already distinguished himself at Loos (for he had helped Captain Alexander to hold the men in Chalk-Pit Wood after the failure of Coldstream attack on Puits 14 bis), he was utterly convinced he would not be killed in the war. Others of his companions had presentiments of their own death more than once, and yet survived to the end with nothing worse than a wound or gassing. It may be worth noting, as far as this sort of information goes, that a man who felt that he was 'for it' on the eve of an engagement was seldom found to be wrong. Occasionally, too, it would come over a man in the trenches that that day or night would be his last. Indeed the very hour would sometimes forespeak itself as with an audible voice, and he, chosen, would go forward to the destined spot – so men have said who saw it – already divorced from this world.

But at the beginning, before nerves wore down, there was hope and interest for every one. The enemy had probably learned of the fresh material before them, for they filled the day of the 6th October with alternate whizz-bangs and large-size H.E. howitzers; the crack and gravel-like smash of the small stuff alternating with the grunt, vomit, and stamp of the Jack Johnsons. Every one was hit by the flying dirt, and well-nigh choked by the stench, and some officers visiting the front line had their first experience of crawling in cold blood across bits of broken trench, where the debris of corpses was so mingled with the untidy dirt that one could not be sure till later what hand or foot had met. It struck some of the young officers as curious that they were not more impressed. Others were frankly sick; while others found that the sights lifted from them the dread fear of being afraid which waits at every generous man's shoulder. But they all owned, according to their separate temperaments, that they were quite sufficiently frightened for working purposes, and so – went on with their work.

Between the 5th and the 7th October the Battalion lost one officer (2nd Lieutenant Hine) and six other ranks killed and twenty-one wounded. Their trenches were moderately good, and had been regularly used, and they discovered dug-outs here and there, which enabled some of them to doze lying down instead of propped against the side of a trench full of moving men. This was great luxury to them, though their revolvers punched holes in their hips and their boots drew like blisters. The more imaginative wrote home that the life was something like camping out. The truthful merely said that they were having an interesting time, and gave their families peace. There was no need to explain how their servants brought them up their meals, dodging, balancing, and ducking along a trench as the fire caught it, or how, even while the hungry youngsters waited and watched, both food and servant would be wiped out, together with a stretch of the parapet under which they had decided to eat.

Just where the Battalion lay, our front line was two hundred yards from the enemy – too far for hand-bombing, but deadly for artillery and machine-gun work. Our artillery was declared to be more numerous and powerful than the German, which generally showered our supports and reserves with shrapnel, while machine-guns kept down the heads of the front line with small-arm fire. Orders had been issued at that moment that recesses should be built, at twenty-five-yard intervals in our fire-trench parapets, for mounting gas-cylinders, and the Battalion worked at this new fatigue under the direction of an Engineer Officer, Lieutenant Ritchie. The recesses meant nothing in particular, but gave people a pleasant feeling that there was abundance of gas somewhere in the background. They were regularly shelled, but, mankind being infinitely adaptable, had come in the few days of this new life to look on it as almost normal, and to alleviate it with small shifts and contrivances. 'I think,' says one of the beginners, 'that in those days we were as self-centred as a suburban villa-residence. The fact of not being able to put your head up without having a shot through it kept us from worrying about our neighbours.' Their first experience of external trouble in their underground world began on the afternoon of the 8th October, when loud bombing and shelling broke out two battalions down the line to the right, and some one from the 3rd Grenadiers came charging round the traverses asking for all available bombers, because the Germans had got into their line and were making rather a hash of things. Bombers were accordingly sent, though their experience with the live bomb was limited, and the two companies on the right got to work on sandbags to bulkhead their right flank in case of a break through. No one really thought that they would be attacked, possibly for the reason that such a thing had not happened to them personally before. 'You see, we had lost count of time – even of the days of the week. Every day seemed as long as a year, and I suppose we considered ourselves like aged men – prisoners of Chillon, you know. We didn't think anything could happen.' On that occasion they were correct. The riot died down and they fell back into normal night routine, every second man in the fire-trench on sentry, every fifth man in support seventy or eighty yards behind, and relief every hour; one officer sitting, between rounds, on one particular spot of the fire-step (so that every one knew where to find him), discussing life, death, Very lights, and politics with his C.S.M. and at intervals peering over the parapet; another officer pervading the support-trench where bayonet charges are supposed to be supplied from, and where the men grumble that they are always set to make fancy improvements. Meantime, the dim dark on every hand is marked with distant pin-pricks and dots, or nearer blurs or blasts of fire, that reveal the torn edges of the shell-holes like wave-crests of a petrified ocean. Yet, after a few nights, the men in the front line said their chief difficulty was to avoid dozing off 'because there was nothing to do.'

They lost three killed and nineteen wounded from all causes between the 7th and 8th October, but completed the recesses for the gas-cylinders, and cleaned out an indescribably old trench, needed for future operations, of its stale corpses mixed with bomb-boxes. While this delicate job was in progress, the enemy started shelling that section with high explosives and shrapnel. They had to shift twenty boxes of bombs under, first, a particular and next a general bombardment, which was connected with a German attack a little farther down the line. Their relief came that same day, on the 12th October, after their first full week in the trenches. It was not a cheerful affair. Three battalions were involved in the chaos, as far as the 2nd Irish Guards was concerned. What befell the rest of their Brigade may be left to the imagination. A reconnoitring party of the 1st Monmouths – four officers and eight other ranks – turned up at a quarter-past five to look over the Irish Guards' trenches before their own men came. They were sitting just outside Battalion Headquarters when a 5.9 killed one of the officers and three of the other ranks, wounded the three other officers, and buried the whole party. The Diary, rightly regardful of the interests of the Battalion, observes: 'Another lucky escape for our Battalion H.Q. Staff. For this was the spot in the trench normally occupied by the senior drill-sergeant and all the orderlies.' Even so, the Monmouths were the only relieving unit that had any idea where they were or what they were to take over. The others, the 4th and 5th Leicesters, lost themselves on the way and wandered blasphemous among trenches. 'The consequent confusion was deplorable.' The Battalion were chaperoning themselves and others from half-past ten to a quarter-past four in the morning. Then began the mile and a half of nightmare-like crawl up the seven-foot-deep communication-trench, whose sides took strange Egyptian-desert-like colours in the dawn-light, and whose bends and windings bewildered all sense of direction. They shuffled in file behind each other like migrating caterpillars, silently except for the grunt and jerk of a tired man slipping in mud, and whispers along the echoing cut bidding them always 'close up.' They were all out, in every way, at five o'clock. The relief had begun at eight. After this, they marched three or four hours to billets at Vaudricourt and Drouvin, within sound but out of reach of the guns, where they dropped and slept and shaved and washed, and their officers were grateful to pig down, six together, on the floor of a loft, and none troubled them till four in the afternoon when they were ordered to parade 'clean.'

Only two nights were allowed for rest and refit, during which time a draft of fifty men under Lieutenant Kinahan joined, and the Battalion bombers were 'organised' (they had not thrown very well lately) and made up to eight per platoon. That was on the 14th October. Next morning the Brigadier called up the C.O.s of all four battalions and instructed them that every bomber was, as far as possible, to be given the chance of throwing a live bomb before going into the trenches again. He added that 'again' meant next morning. On the morning of the 15th October, then, each one of those one hundred and twenty-eight organised bombers did, at practice, throw one live bomb. Says the Diary, without even a note of exclamation, 'With the knowledge, experience, and confidence thus gained, they had to face trained German bombers a few days later.' They might have had to face them that same evening when they took over some Brigade Reserve trenches, directly behind those of their first tour, from the 7th and 8th Sherwood Foresters; but they were merely shelled as they settled in, and the bombing fell farther down the line. Their new trenches were dirty and badly knocked about, but, by some obscure forethought or other, well provided with small and fairly safe dug-outs which gave cover to almost all. Though they were heavily shelled their first two days, and many direct hits fell on the parapet itself, and many men were buried, only two were killed outright and thirty-two wounded. The sensation of being pinned, even when one has one's head above ground, by a weight of pressing earth, added to natural speculation as to whether the next shell may complete the burial, is a horror that returns to a man in his dreams, and takes the heart out of some even more than dysentery. ('There's something in being held tight that makes you lose hold of yourself. I've seen men screamin' and kickin' like wired hares, and them no more than caught by one leg or two. 'Tis against Nature for a man to be buried with his breath in him.')

[First published in *The Irish Guards in the Great War*, Volume 2 (London: Macmillan, 1923).]

In August 1915, just as his son John was departing to join the Irish Guards, Kipling was recruited by the War Propaganda Bureau to travel to Paris and to the front in Alsace to report on conditions there.

TRENCHES ON A MOUNTAIN SIDE

VERY EARLY IN THE morning I met Alan Breck, with a half-healed bullet-scrape across the bridge of his nose, and an Alpine cap over one ear. His people a few hundred years ago had been Scotch. He bore a Scotch name, and still recognized the head of his clan, but his French occasionally ran into German words, for he was an Alsatian on one side.

'This,' he explained, 'is the very best country in the world to fight in. It's picturesque and full of cover. I'm a gunner. I've been here for months. It's lovely.'

It might have been the hills under Mussoorie, and what our cars expected to do in it I could not understand. But the demon-driver who had been a road-racer took the 70 h.p. Mercedes and threaded the narrow valleys, as well as occasional half-Swiss villages full of Alpine troops, at a restrained thirty miles an hour. He shot up a new-made road, more like Mussoorie than ever, and did not fall down the hillside even once. An ammunition-mule of a mountain-battery met him at a tight corner, and began to climb a tree.

'See! There isn't another place in France where that could happen,' said Alan. 'I tell you, this is a magnificent country.'

The mule was hauled down by his tail before he had reached the lower branches, and went on through the woods, his ammunition-boxes jinking on his back, for all the world as though he were rejoining his battery at Jutogh. One expected to meet the little Hill people bent under their loads under the forest gloom. The light, the colour, the smell of wood smoke, pine-needles, wet earth, and warm mule were all Himalayan. Only the Mercedes was violently and loudly a stranger.

'Halt!' said Alan at last, when she had done everything except imitate the mule.

'The road continues,' said the demon-driver seductively.

'Yes, but they will hear you if you go on. Stop and wait. We've a mountain-battery to look at.'

They were not at work for the moment, and the Commandant, a grim and forceful man, showed me some details of their construction. When we left them in their bower – it looked like a Hill priest's wayside shrine – we heard them singing through the steep-descending pines. They, too, like the 75s, seem to have no pet name in the service.

It was a poisonously blind country. The woods blocked all sense of direction above and around. The ground was at any angle you please, and all sounds were split up and muddled by the tree-trunks, which acted as silencers. High above us the respectable, all-concealing forest had turned into sparse, ghastly blue sticks of timber – an assembly of leper-trees round a bald mountain top. 'That's where we're going,' said Alan. 'Isn't it an adorable country?'

TRENCHES

A machine-gun loosed a few shots in the fumbling style of her kind when they feel for an opening. A couple of rifle-shots answered. They might have been half a mile away or a hundred yards below. An adorable country! We climbed up till we found once again a complete tea-garden of little sunk houses, almost invisible in the brown-pink recesses of the thick forest. Here the trenches began, and with them for the next few hours life in two dimensions – length and breadth. You could have eaten your dinner almost anywhere off the swept dry ground, for the steep slopes favoured draining, there was no lack of timber, and there was unlimited labour. It had made neat double-length dug-outs where the wounded could be laid in during their passage down the mountain side; well-tended occasional latrines properly limed; dug-outs for sleeping and eating; overhead protections and tool-sheds where needed, and, as one came nearer the working face, very clever cellars against trench-sweepers. Men passed on their business; a squad with a captured machine-gun which they tested in a sheltered dip; armourers at their benches busy with sick rifles; fatigue-parties for straw, rations, and ammunition; long processions of single blue figures turned sideways between the brown sunless walls. One understood after a while the nightmare that lays hold of trench-stale men, when the dreamer wanders for ever in those blind mazes till, after centuries of agonizing flight, he finds himself stumbling out again into the white blaze and horror of the mined front – he who thought he had almost reached home!

IN THE FRONT LINE

There were no trees above us now. Their trunks lay along the edge of the trench, built in with stones, where necessary, or sometimes overhanging it in ragged splinters or bushy tops. Bits of cloth, not French, showed, too, in the uneven lines of debris at the trench lip, and some thoughtful soul had marked an unexploded Boche trench-sweeper as 'not to be touched.' It was a young lawyer from Paris who pointed that out to me.

We met the Colonel at the head of an indescribable pit of ruin, full of sunshine, whose steps ran down a very steep hillside under the lee of an almost vertically plunging parapet. To the left of that parapet the whole hillside was one gruel of smashed trees, split stones, and powdered soil. It might have been a rag-picker's dump-heap on a colossal scale.

Alan looked at it critically. I think he had helped to make it not long before.

'We're on the top of the hill now, and the Boches are below us,' said he. 'We gave them a very fair sickener lately.'

'This,' said the Colonel, 'is the front line.'

There were overhead guards against hand-bombs which disposed me to believe him, but what convinced me most was a corporal urging us in whispers not to talk so loud. The men were at dinner, and a good smell of food filled the trench. This was the first smell I had encountered in my long travels uphill – a mixed, entirely wholesome flavour of stew, leather, earth, and rifle-oil.

FRONT-LINE PROFESSIONALS

A proportion of men were standing to arms while others ate; but dinner-time is slack time, even among animals, and it was close on noon.

'The Boches got *their* soup a few days ago,' some one whispered. I thought of the pulverized hillside, and hoped it had been hot enough.

We edged along the still trench, where the soldiers stared, with justified contempt, I thought, upon the civilian who scuttled through their life for a few emotional minutes in order to make words out of their blood. Somehow it reminded me of coming in late to a play and incommoding a long line of packed stalls. The whispered dialogue was much the same: 'Pardon!' 'I beg your pardon, monsieur.' 'To the right, monsieur.' 'If monsieur will lower his head.' 'One sees best from here, monsieur,' and so on. It was their day- and night-long business, carried through without display or heat, or doubt or indecision. Those who worked, worked; those off duty, not five feet behind them in the dug-outs, were deep in their papers, or their meals or their letters; while death stood ready at every minute to drop down into the narrow cut from out of the narrow strip of unconcerned sky. And for the better part of a week one had skirted hundreds of miles of such a frieze!

The loopholes not in use were plugged rather like old-fashioned hives. Said the Colonel, removing a plug: 'Here are the Boches. Look, and you'll see their sandbags.' Through the jumble of riven trees and stones one saw what might have been a bit of green sacking. 'They're about seven metres distant just here,' the Colonel went on. That was true, too. We entered a little fortalice with a cannon in it, in an embrasure which at that moment struck me as unnecessarily vast, even though it was partly closed by a frail packing-case lid. The Colonel sat him down in front of it, and explained the theory of this sort of redoubt. 'By the way,' he said to the gunner at last, 'can't you find something better than *that*?' He twitched the lid aside. 'I think it's too light. Get a log of wood or something.'

HANDY TRENCH-SWEEPERS

I loved that Colonel! He knew his men and he knew the Boches – had them marked down like birds. When he said they were beside dead trees or behind boulders, sure enough there they were! But, as I have said, the dinner-hour is always slack, and even when we came to a place where a section of trench had been bashed open by trench-sweepers, and it was recommended to duck and hurry, nothing much happened. The uncanny thing was the absence of movement in the Boche trenches. Sometimes one imagined that one smelt strange tobacco, or heard a rifle-bolt working after a shot. Otherwise they were as still as pig at noonday.

We held on through the maze, past trench-sweepers of a handy light pattern, with their screw-tailed charge all ready; and a grave or so; and when I came on men who merely stood within easy reach of their rifles, I knew I was in the second line. When they lay frankly at ease in their dug-outs, I knew it was the third. A shot-gun would have sprinkled all three.

'No flat plains,' said Alan. 'No hunting for gun positions – the hills are full of them – and the trenches close together and commanding each other. You see what a beautiful country it is.'

The Colonel confirmed this, but from another point of view. War was his business, as the still woods could testify – but his hobby was his trenches. He had tapped the mountain streams and dug out a laundry where a man could wash his shirt and go up and be killed in it, all in a morning; had drained the trenches till a muddy stretch in them was an offence; and at the bottom of the hill (it looked like a hydropathic establishment on the stage) he had created baths where half a battalion at a time could wash. He never told me how all that country had been fought over as fiercely as Ypres in the West; nor what blood had gone down the valleys before his trenches pushed over the scalped mountain top. No. He sketched out new endeavours in earth and stones and trees for the comfort of his men on that populous mountain.

And there came a priest, who was a sub-lieutenant, out of a wood of snuff-brown shadows and half-veiled trunks. Would it please me to look at a chapel? It was all open to the hillside, most tenderly and devoutly done in rustic work with reedings of peeled branches and panels of moss and thatch – St. Hubert's own shrine. I saw the hunters who passed before it, going to the chase on the far side of the mountain where their game lay.

A BOMBARDED TOWN

Alan carried me off to tea the same evening in a town where he seemed to know everybody. He had spent the afternoon on another mountain top, inspecting gun positions; whereby he had been shelled a little – *marmite* is the slang for it. There had been no serious *marmitage*, and he had spotted a Boche position which was *marmitable*.

'And we may get shelled now,' he added, hopefully. 'They shell this town whenever they think of it. Perhaps they'll shell us at tea.'

It was a quaintly beautiful little place, with its mixture of French and German ideas; its old bridge and gentle-minded river, between the cultivated hills. The sand-bagged cellar doors, the ruined houses, and the holes in the pavement looked as unreal as the violences of a cinema against that soft and simple setting. The people were abroad in the streets, and the little children were playing. A big shell gives notice enough for one to get to shelter, if the shelter is near enough. That appears to be as much as any one expects in the world where one is shelled, and that world has settled down to it. People's lips are a little firmer, the modelling of the brows is a little more pronounced, and, maybe, there is a change in the expression of the eyes; but nothing that a casual afternoon caller need particularly notice.

CASES FOR HOSPITAL

The house where we took tea was the 'big house' of the place, old and massive, a treasure house of ancient furniture. It had everything that the moderate heart of man could desire – gardens, garages, outbuildings, and the air of peace that goes with beauty in age. It stood over a high cellarage, and opposite the cellar door was a brand-new blindage of earth packed between timbers. The cellar was a hospital, with its beds and stores, and under the electric light the orderly waited ready for the cases to be carried down out of the streets.

'Yes, they are all civil cases,' said he.

They come without much warning – a woman gashed by falling timber; a child with its temple crushed by a flying stone; an urgent amputation case, and so on. One never knows. Bombardment, the Boche text-books say, 'is designed to terrify the civil population so that they may put pressure on their politicians to conclude peace.' In real life, men are very rarely soothed by the sight of their women being tortured.

We took tea in the hall upstairs, with a propriety and an interchange of compliments that suited the little occasion. There was no attempt to disguise the existence of a bombardment, but it was not allowed to overweigh talk of lighter matters. I know one guest who sat through it as near as might be inarticulate with wonder. But he was English, and when Alan asked him whether he had enjoyed himself, he said: 'Oh, yes. Thank you very much.'

'Nice people, aren't they?' Alan went on.

'Oh, very nice. And – and such good tea.'

He managed to convey a few of his sentiments to Alan after dinner.

'But what else could the people have done?' said he. 'They are French.'

[First published in the *Daily Telegraph* and the *New York Sun*, 6–17 September 1915, and then collected in *France at War* (London: Macmillan, 1915).]

✠ ✠ ✠

Kipling followed his trip to the front in France with a similar propaganda exercise visting and reporting on the exploits of the Royal Navy in the Channel off Dover and on the east coast out of Harwich.

OUT WITH THE FLEET

The Oldest Navy

IT WAS A BRUTAL age, ministered to by hard-fisted men, and we had put it a hundred decent years behind us when – it all comes back again! To-day there are no prisons for the crews of merchantmen, but they can go to the bottom by mine and torpedo even more quickly than their ancestors were run into Le Havre. The submarine takes the place of the privateer; the Line, as in the old wars, is occupied, bombarding and blockading, elsewhere, but the sea-borne traffic must continue, and that is being looked after by the lineal descendants of the crews of the long extinct cutters and sloops and gun-brigs. The hour struck, and they reappeared, to the tune of fifty thousand odd men in more than two thousand ships, of which I have seen a few hundred. Words of command may have changed a little, the tools are certainly more complex, but the spirit of the new crews who come to the old job is utterly unchanged. It is the same fierce, hard-living, heavy-handed, very cunning service out of which the Navy as we know it to-day was born. It is called indifferently the Trawler and Auxiliary Fleet. It is chiefly composed of fishermen, but it takes in every one who may have maritime tastes – from retired admirals to the son of the sea-cook. It exists for the benefit of the traffic and the annoyance of the enemy. Its doings are recorded by flags stuck into charts;

its casualties are buried in obscure corners of the newspapers. The Grand Fleet knows it slightly; the restless light cruisers who chaperon it from the background are more intimate; the destroyers working off unlighted coasts over unmarked shoals come, as you might say, in direct contact with it; the submarine alternately praises and – since one periscope is very like another – curses its activities; but the steady procession of traffic in home waters, liner and tramp, six every sixty minutes, blesses it altogether.

Since this most Christian war includes laying mines in the fairways of traffic, and since these mines may be laid at any time by German submarines especially built for the work, or by neutral ships, all fairways must be swept continuously day and night. When a nest of mines is reported, traffic must be hung up or deviated till it is cleared out. When traffic comes up Channel it must be examined for contraband and other things; and the examining tugs lie out in a blaze of lights to remind ships of this. Months ago, when the war was young, the tugs did not know what to look for specially. Now they do. All this mine-searching and reporting and sweeping, *plus* the direction and examination of the traffic, *plus* the laying of our own ever-shifting mine-fields, is part of the Trawler Fleet's work, because the Navy-as-we-knew-it is busy elsewhere. And there is always the enemy submarine with a price on her head, whom the Trawler Fleet hunts and traps with zeal and joy. Add to this, that there are boats, fishing for real fish, to be protected in their work at sea or chased off dangerous areas where, because they are strictly forbidden to go, they naturally repair, and you will begin to get some idea of what the Trawler and Auxiliary Fleet does.

[First published in the *Daily Telegraph* in the UK and in the *New York American* and other Hearst newspapers, 20 November–2 December 1915, and then collected in *The Fringes of the Fleet* (London: Macmillan, 1915).]

Mines had first been used at sea by the Russians in the Crimean War. Kipling's reference to the Foreland indicates that this poem came about from a trip to Dover. South and North Foreland are respectively 5 and 20 miles north of Dover, and, because of sandbanks, 'awkward water to sweep'.

MINE SWEEPERS

1914–18

DAWN OFF THE FORELAND – the young flood making
    Jumbled and short and steep –
Black in the hollows and bright where it's breaking –
    Awkward water to sweep.
        'Mines reported in the fairway,
        Warn all traffic and detain.
'Sent up *Unity, Claribel, Assyrian, Stormcock,* and *Golden Gain.'*

Noon off the Foreland – the first ebb making
    Lumpy and strong in the bight.
Boom after boom, and the golf-hut shaking
    And the jackdaws wild with fright!
        'Mines located in the fairway,
        Boats now working up the chain,
'Sweepers – *Unity, Claribel, Assyrian, Stormcock,* and *Golden Gain.'*

Dusk off the Foreland – the last light going
    And the traffic crowding through,
And five damned trawlers with their syreens blowing
    Heading the whole review!
        'Sweep completed in the fairway.
        No more mines remain.
'Sent back *Unity, Claribel, Assyrian, Stormcock,* and *Golden Gain.'*

[First published with 'The Auxiliary Fleet', no. 2 of 'The Fringes of the Fleet', *Daily Telegraph,* 23 November 1915. Collected in *The Fringes of the Fleet.*]

✠ ✠ ✠

Another slightly later propaganda foray took Kipling to Rome and to northern Italy, where Britain's Italian allies were confronting the Austrians. He had been invited there by an old friend, the British ambassador to Rome, Sir Rennell Rodd, who was concerned that the British did not know enough about what was happening on this Alpine/Dolomite front.

THE TRENTINO FRONT

IT DOES NOT NEED an expert to distinguish the notes of the several Italian fronts. One picks them up a long way behind the lines, from the troops in rest or the traffic on the road. Even behind Browning's lovely Asolo where, you will remember, Pippa passed, seventy-six years since, announcing that 'All's right with the world,' one felt the tightening in the air.

The officer, too, explained frankly above his map:

'See where our frontier west of the Dolomites dips south in this V-like spearhead. That's the Trentino. Garibaldi's volunteers were in full possession of it in our War of Independence. Prussia was our ally then against Austria, but Prussia made peace when it suited her – I'm talking of 1864 – and we had to accept the frontier that she and Austria laid down. The Italian frontier is a bad one everywhere – Prussia and Austria took care of that – but the Trentino section is specially bad.'

Mist wrapped the plateau we were climbing. The mountains had changed into rounded, almost barrel-shaped heights, steep above dry valleys. The roads were many and new, but the lorries held their pace; the usual old man and young boy were there to see to that. Scotch moors, red uplands, scarred with trenches and punched with shell-holes, a confusion of hills without colour and, in the mist, almost without shape, rose and dropped behind us. They hid the troops in their folds – always awaiting troops – and the trenches multiplied themselves high and low on their sides.

We descended a mountain smashed into rubbish from head to heel, but still preserving the outline, like wrinkles on a forehead, of trenches that had followed its contours. A narrow, shallow ditch (it might have been a water-main) ran vertically up the hill, cutting the faded trenches at right angles.

'That was where our men stood before the Austrians were driven back in their last push – the Asiago push, don't you call it? It took the Austrians ten days to work half-way down from the top of the mountain. Our men drove that trench straight up the hill, as you see. Then they climbed, and the Austrians broke. It's not as bad as it looks, because, in this sort of work, if the enemy uphill misses his footing, he rolls down among your men, but if you stumble, you only slip back among your friends.'

'What did it cost you?' I whispered.

'A good deal. And on that mountain across the gorge – but the mist won't let you see it – our men fought for a week – mostly without water. The Austrians were the first people to lay out a line of twelve-inch shell-holes on a mountain's side to serve as trenches. It's almost a regulation trick on all the fronts now, but it's annoying.'

He told tales of the long, bitter fight when the Austrians thought, till General Cadorna showed them otherwise, they had the plains to the south at their mercy. I should not care to be an Austrian with the Boche behind me and the exercitus Romanus in front.

It was the quietest of fronts and the least ostentatious of armies. It lived in great towns among forests where we found snow again in dirty, hollow-flanked drifts, that were giving up all the rubbish and refuse that winter had hidden. Labour battalions dealt with the stuff, and there were no smells. Other gangs mended shell-holes with speed; the lorries do not like being checked.

Another township, founded among stones, stood empty except for the cooks and a bored road-mender or two. The population was up the hill digging and blasting; or in wooded park-like hollows of lowland. Battalions slipped like shadows through the mists between the pines. When we reached the edge of everything, there was, as usual, nothing whatever, except uptorn breadths of grass and an 'unhealthy' house – the battered core of what had once been human – with rain-water dripping through the starred ceilings. The view from it included the sight of the Austrian trenches on pale slopes and the noise of Austrian guns – not lazy ones this time, but eager, querulous, almost questioning.

There was no reply from our side. 'If they want to find out anything, they can come and look,' said the officer.

One speculated how much the men behind those guns would have given for a seat in the car through the next few hours that took us along yet another veiled line of arms. But perhaps by now the Austrians have learned.

The mist thickened around us, and the far shoulders of mountains, and the suddenly-seen masses of men who loomed out of it and were gone. We headed upwards till the mists met the clouds, by a steeper road than any we had used before. It ended in a rock gallery where immense guns, set to a certain point when a certain hour should come, waited in the dark.

'Mind how you walk! It's rather a sharp turn there.'

The gallery came out on a naked space, and a vertical drop of hundreds of feet of striated rock tufted with heath in bloom. At the wall-foot the actual mountain, hardly less steep, began, and, far below that again, flared outward till it became more reasonable slopes, descending in shoulders and knolls to the immense and ancient plains four thousand feet below.

The mists obscured the northern views, but to the southward one traced the courses of broad rivers, the thin shadows of aqueducts, and the piled outlines of city after city whose single past was worth more than the future of all the barbarians clamouring behind the ranges that were pointed out to us through the observatory windows. The officer finished his tales of year-long battles and bombardments among them.

'And that nick in the skyline to the right of that smooth crest under the clouds is a mine we sprung,' said he.

The observation shutter behind its fringe of heather-bells closed softly. They do everything without noise in this hard and silent land.

[First published in the *Daily Telegraph* and the *New York Tribune*, 6, 9, 13,16 and 20 June 1917, and then collected in *The War in the Mountains* (New York: Doubleday, Page and Co., 1917).]

Often erroneously thought to be about the death of Kipling's son, John (who was never called Jack), this poem almost certainly refers to Jack Cornwell, a gallant 16-year-old sailor who was killed at the Battle of Jutland on 2 June 1916 and who was posthumously awarded a Victoria Cross.

MY BOY JACK

'HAVE YOU NEWS OF my boy Jack?'
Not this tide.
'When d'you think that he'll come back?'
Not with this wind blowing, and this tide.
'Has anyone else had word of him?'
Not this tide.
For what is sunk will hardly swim,
Not with this wind blowing and this tide.
'Oh, dear, what comfort can I find?'
None this tide,
Nor any tide,
Except he did not shame his kind –
Not even with that wind blowing, and that tide.
Then hold your head up all the more,
This tide,
And every tide;
Because he was the son you bore,
And gave to that wind blowing and that tide!

[First published in *The Times*, *Daily Telegraph* and the *New York Times*, 19 October 1916.]

Although the Irish Guards were institutionally formed under Lord Roberts during the Boer War, Kipling here takes their fighting tradition back to the (mainly Jacobite) Irish Brigades known as the 'Wild Geese', who fought with the French against the British from Louis XIV's time and very nearly broke up the attacks of the Coldstream Guards at Fontenoy in 1745.

THE IRISH GUARDS

1918

WE'RE NOT SO OLD in the Army List,
But we're not so young at our trade,
For we had the honour at Fontenoy
Of meeting the Guards' Brigade.
'Twas Lally, Dillon, Bulkeley, Clare,
And Lee that led us then,
And after a hundred and seventy years
We're fighting for France again!

Old Days! The wild geese are flighting,
Head to the storm as they faced it before!
For where there are Irish there's bound to be fighting,
And when there's no fighting, it's Ireland no more!
Ireland no more!

The fashion's all for khaki now,
But once through France we went
Full-dressed in scarlet Army cloth,
The English-left at Ghent.
They're fighting on our side to-day
But, before they changed their clothes,
The half of Europe knew our fame,
As all of Ireland knows!

Old Days! The wild geese are flying,
Head to the storm as they faced it before!
For where there are Irish there's memory undying,
And when we forget, it is Ireland no more!
Ireland no more!

From Barry Wood to Gouzeaucourt,
From Boyne to Pilkem Ridge,
The ancient days come back no more
Than water under the bridge.
But the bridge it stands and the water runs
As red as yesterday,
And the Irish move to the sound of the guns
Like salmon to the sea.

Old Days! The wild geese are ranging,
Head to the storm as they faced it before!
For where there are Irish their hearts are unchanging,
And when they are changed, it is Ireland no more!
Ireland no more!

We're not so old in the Army List,
But we're not so new in the ring,
For we carried our packs with Marshal Saxe
When Louis was our King.
But Douglas Haig's our Marshal now
And we're King George's men,
And after one hundred and seventy years
We're fighting for France again!
Ah, France! And did we stand by you,
When life was made splendid with gifts and rewards?
Ah, France! And will we deny you
In the hour of your agony, Mother of Swords?

Old Days! The wild geese are flying,
Head to the storm as they faced it before!
For where there are Irish there's loving and fighting
And when we stop either, it's Ireland no more!
Ireland no more!

[First published in *The Years Between* (1919).]

This is one of Kipling's most poignant war poems, reflecting the emotions of a British soldier who finds himself finally called upon to fight at the front. It is redolent with Biblical imagery, suggesting the inevitability of the soldier's death in the cause of some greater good.

GETHSEMANE

The Garden Called Gethsemane

IN PICARDY IT WAS,
   And there the people came to see
The English soldiers pass,
   We used to pass – we used to pass
Or halt, as it might be,
   And ship our masks in case of gas
Beyond Gethsemane.
   The Garden called Gethsemane,
It held a pretty lass,
   But all the time she talked to me
I prayed my cup might pass.

The officer sat on the chair,
   The men lay on the grass,
And all the time we halted there
   I prayed my cup might pass.
It didn't pass – it didn't pass –
   It didn't pass from me.
I drank it when we met the gas
   Beyond Gethsemane.

[First published in *The Years Between* (1919).]

Here Kipling shows his anger at the incompetence of the army generals in fighting the Turks in the Middle East. This poem refers in particular to the incident when British troops under General Sir Charles Townsend were forced to surrender after being besieged in the town of Kut in Iraq in April 1916.

MESOPOTAMIA

THEY SHALL NOT RETURN to us, the resolute, the young
The eager and whole-hearted whom we gave:
But the men who left them thriftily to die in their own dung,
Shall they come with years and honour to the grave?
They shall not return to us, the strong men coldly slain
In sight of help denied from day to day:
But the men who edged their agonies and chid them in their pain,
Are they too strong and wise to put away?
Our dead shall not return to us while Day and Night divide –
Never while the bars of sunset hold.
But the idle-minded overlings who quibbled while they died,
Shall they thrust for high employments as of old?
Shall we only threaten and be angry for an hour?
When the storm is ended shall we find
How softly but how swiftly they have sidled back to power
By the favour and contrivance of their kind?
Even while they soothe us, while they promise large amends,
Even while they make a show of fear,
Do they call upon their debtors, and take council with their
       friends,
To confirm and re-establish each career?
Their lives cannot repay us – their death could not undo –
The shame that they have laid upon our race.
But the slothfulness that wasted and the arrogance that slew,
Shall we leave it unabated in its place?

[First published in the *Morning Post*, 11 July 1917.]

Drawing on his recollections of life in the African bush, Kipling here compares to hyaenas those people (mainly politicians) who malign the dead.

THE HYAENAS

AFTER THE BURIAL-PARTIES LEAVE
    And the baffled kites have fled;
The wise hyænas come out at eve
    To take account of our dead.
How he died and why he died
    Troubles them not a whit.
They snout the bushes and stones aside
    And dig till they come to it.
They are only resolute they shall eat
    That they and their mates may thrive,
And they know that the dead are safer meat
    Than the weakest thing alive.
(For a goat may butt, and a worm may sting,
    And a child will sometimes stand;
But a poor dead soldier of the King
    Can never lift a hand.)
They whoop and halloo and scatter the dirt
    Until their tushes white
Take good hold in the army shirt,
    And tug the corpse to light,
And the pitiful face is shewn again
    For an instant ere they close;
But it is not discovered to living men –
    Only to God and to those
Who, being soulless, are free from shame,
    Whatever meat they may find.
Nor do they defile the dead man's name –
    That is reserved for his kind.

[First published in *The Years Between* (1919).]

Writing at the end of the war in October 1918, shortly before the
Armistice in November, Kipling insisted that Germany, which
had now been defeated, should not be allowed the easy option of
a negotiated peace, but should be made to pay for its war crimes.

JUSTICE

October, 1918

ACROSS A WORLD WHERE all men grieve
    And grieving strive the more,
The great days range like tides and leave
    Our dead on every shore.
Heavy the load we undergo,
    And our own hands prepare,
If we have parley with the foe,
    The load our sons must bear.

Before we loose the word
    That bids new worlds to birth,
Needs must we loosen first the sword
    Of Justice upon earth;
Or else all else is vain
    Since life on earth began,
And the spent world sinks back again
    Hopeless of God and Man.

A People and their King
    Through ancient sin grown strong,
Because they feared no reckoning
    Would set no bound to wrong;
But now their hour is past,
    And we who bore it find
Evil Incarnate held at last
    To answer to mankind.

For agony and spoil
    Of nations beat to dust,
For poisoned air and tortured soil

And cold, commanded lust,
And every secret woe
  The shuddering waters saw –
Willed and fulfilled by high and low –
  Let them relearn the Law:

That when the dooms are read,
  Not high nor low shall say:–
'My haughty or my humble head
  Has saved me in this day.'
That, till the end of time,
  Their remnant shall recall
Their fathers' old, confederate crime
  Availed them not at all:

That neither schools nor priests,
  Nor Kings may build again
A people with the heart of beasts
  Made wise concerning men.
Whereby our dead shall sleep
  In honour, unbetrayed,
And we in faith and honour keep
  That peace for which they paid.

[First published in *The Times*, 24 October 1918, and then collected in *The Years Between* (1919).]

Kipling based these pithy epitaphs about those who had lost their lives during the war on an Ancient Greek text, *The Greek Anthology*, in which some of the short verses date back to the sixth century BC. Kipling stressed that his epitaphs were works of the imagination, and not to be confused with the inscriptions he wrote for the Imperial War Graves Commission.

EPITAPHS OF THE WAR

1914–18

'EQUALITY OF SACRIFICE'

A. 'I was a Have.' B. 'I was a "Have-not."'
(*Together*) 'What hast thou given which I gave not?'

A SERVANT

We were together since the War began.
He was my servant – and the better man.

A SON

My son was killed while laughing at some jest. I would I knew
What it was, and it might serve me in a time when jests are few.

AN ONLY SON

I have slain none except my Mother. She
(Blessing her slayer) died of grief for me.

EX-CLERK

Pity not! The Army gave
Freedom to a timid slave:
In which Freedom did he find
Strength of body, will, and mind:
By which strength he came to prove
Mirth, Companionship, and Love:

For which Love to Death he went:
In which Death he lies content.

THE WONDER

Body and Spirit I surrendered whole
To harsh Instructors – and received a soul ...
If mortal man could change me through and through
From all I was – what may The God not do?

HINDU SEPOY IN FRANCE

This man in his own country prayed we know not to what Powers.
We pray Them to reward him for his bravery in ours.

THE COWARD

I could not look on Death, which being known,
Men led me to him, blindfold and alone.

SHOCK

My name, my speech, my self I had forgot.
My wife and children came – I knew them not.
I died. My Mother followed. At her call
And on her bosom I remembered all.

A GRAVE NEAR CAIRO

Gods of the Nile, should this stout fellow here
Get out – get out! He knows not shame nor fear.

PELICANS IN THE WILDERNESS

(A Grave Near Halfa)
The blown sand heaps on me, that none may learn
    Where I am laid for whom my children grieve ...
O wings that beat at dawning, ye return
    Out of the desert to your young at eve!

TWO CANADIAN MEMORIALS

I

We giving all gained all.
    Neither lament us nor praise.
Only in all things recall,
    It is Fear, not Death that slays.

II

From little towns in a far land we came,
    To save our honour and a world aflame.
By little towns in a far land we sleep;
    And trust that world we won for you to keep!

THE FAVOUR

Death favoured me from the first, well knowing I could not endure
    To wait on him day by day. He quitted my betters and came
Whistling over the fields, and, when he had made all sure,
    'Thy line is at end,' he said, 'but at least I have saved its name.'

THE BEGINNER

On the first hour of my first day
    In the front trench I fell.
(Children in boxes at a play
    Stand up to watch it well.)

R.A.F. (AGED EIGHTEEN)

Laughing through clouds, his milk-teeth still unshed,
Cities and men he smote from overhead.
His deaths delivered, he returned to play
Childlike, with childish things now put away.

THE REFINED MAN

I was of delicate mind. I stepped aside for my needs,
    Disdaining the common office. I was seen from afar and killed ...

How is this matter for mirth? Let each man be judged by his deeds.
I have paid my price to live with myself on the terms that I willed.

NATIVE WATER-CARRIER (M.E.F.)

Prometheus brought down fire to men,
    This brought up water.
The Gods are jealous – now, as then,
    Giving no quarter.

BOMBED IN LONDON

On land and sea I strove with anxious care
To escape conscription. It was in the air!

THE SLEEPY SENTINEL

Faithless the watch that I kept: now I have none to keep.
I was slain because I slept: now I am slain I sleep.
Let no man reproach me again, whatever watch is unkept –
I sleep because I am slain. They slew me because I slept.

BATTERIES OUT OF AMMUNITION

If any mourn us in the workshop, say
We died because the shift kept holiday.

COMMON FORM

If any question why we died,
Tell them, because our fathers lied.

A DEAD STATESMAN

I could not dig: I dared not rob:
Therefore I lied to please the mob.
Now all my lies are proved untrue
And I must face the men I slew.
What tale shall serve me here among
Mine angry and defrauded young?

THE REBEL

If I had clamoured at Thy Gate
    For gift of Life on Earth,
And, thrusting through the souls that wait,
    Flung headlong into birth –
Even then, even then, for gin and snare
    About my pathway spread,
Lord, I had mocked Thy thoughtful care
    Before I joined the Dead!
But now? ... I was beneath Thy Hand
    Ere yet the Planets came.
And now – though Planets pass, I stand
    The witness to Thy shame!

THE OBEDIENT

Daily, though no ears attended,
    Did my prayers arise.
Daily, though no fire descended,
    Did I sacrifice.
Though my darkness did not lift,
    Though I faced no lighter odds,
Though the Gods bestowed no gift,
      None the less,
      None the less, I served the Gods!

A DRIFTER OFF TARENTUM

He from the wind-bitten North with ship and companions
    descended,
  Searching for eggs of death spawned by invisible hulls.
Many he found and drew forth. Of a sudden the fishery ended
  In flame and a clamorous breath known to the eye-pecking
    gulls.

DESTROYER IN COLLISION

For Fog and Fate no charm is found
    To lighten or amend.

I, hurrying to my bride, was drowned –
   Cut down by my best friend.

CONVOY ESCORT

I was a shepherd to fools
   Causelessly bold or afraid.
They would not abide by my rules.
   Yet they escaped. For I stayed.

UNKNOWN FEMALE CORPSE

Headless, lacking foot and hand,
Horrible I come to land.
I beseech all women's sons
Know I was a mother once.

RAPED AND REVENGED

One used and butchered me: another spied
Me broken – for which thing an hundred died.
So it was learned among the heathen hosts
How much a freeborn woman's favour costs.

SALONIKAN GRAVE

I have watched a thousand days
Push out and crawl into night
Slowly as tortoises.
Now I, too, follow these.
It is fever, and not the fight –
Time, not battle, – that slays.

THE BRIDEGROOM

Call me not false, beloved,
   If, from thy scarce-known breast
So little time removed,
   In other arms I rest.

> For this more ancient bride,
>   Whom coldly I embrace,
> Was constant at my side
>   Before I saw thy face.
>
> Our marriage, often set –
>   By miracle delayed –
> At last is consummate,
>   And cannot be unmade.
>
> Live, then, whom Life shall cure,
>   Almost, of Memory,
> And leave us to endure
>   Its immortality.

V.A.D. (MEDITERRANEAN)

Ah, would swift ships had never been, for then we ne'er had found,
These harsh Aegean rocks between, this little virgin drowned,
Whom neither spouse nor child shall mourn, but men she nursed
  through pain
And – certain keels for whose return the heathen look in vain.

ACTORS
ON A MEMORIAL TABLET IN HOLY TRINITY CHURCH,
STRATFORD-ON-AVON

> We counterfeited once for your disport
>   Men's joy and sorrow: but our day has passed.
> We pray you pardon all where we fell short –
>   Seeing we were your servants to this last.

JOURNALISTS
ON A PANEL IN THE HALL OF THE INSTITUTE OF JOURNALISTS

> We have served our day.

[First published in *The Years Between* (1919).]

REFLECTIONS ON
THE MILITARY LIFE

Kipling was interested in the emotional experience of comradeship during war. In this story a soldier recalls his mystification at
the strange language he had found bandied around at the front.
He learned this was based on a shared enthusiasm for the works
of Jane Austen, an author Kipling revered – and thus the title,
'The Janeites', coined by his friend George Saintsbury, denoting
avid fans of Austen.

THE JANEITES

IN THE LODGE OF Instruction attached to 'Faith and Works No. 5837
E.C.,' which has already been described, Saturday afternoon was
appointed for the weekly clean-up, when all visiting Brethren were
welcome to help under the direction of the Lodge Officer of the day:
their reward was light refreshment and the meeting of companions.

This particular afternoon – in the autumn of '20 – Brother Burges,
P.M., was on duty and, finding a strong shift present, took advantage
of it to strip and dust all hangings and curtains, to go over every
inch of the Pavement – which was stone, not floorcloth – by hand;
and to polish the Columns, Jewels, Working outfit and organ. I was
given to clean some Officers' Jewels – beautiful bits of old Georgian
silver-work humanised by generations of elbow-grease – and

retired to the organ-loft; for the floor was like the quarterdeck of a battleship on the eve of a ball. Half-a-dozen brethren had already made the Pavement as glassy as the aisle of Greenwich Chapel; the brazen chapiters winked like pure gold at the flashing Marks on the Chairs; and a morose one-legged brother was attending to the Emblems of Mortality with, I think, rouge.

'They ought,' he volunteered to Brother Burges as we passed, 'to be betwixt the colour of ripe apricots an' a half-smoked meerschaum. That's how we kept 'em in my Mother-Lodge – a treat to look at.'

'I've never seen spit-and-polish to touch this,' I said.

'Wait till you see the organ,' Brother Burges replied. 'You could shave in it when they've done. Brother Anthony's in charge up there – the taxi-owner you met here last month. I don't think you've come across Brother Humberstall, have you?'

'I don't remember—' I began.

'You wouldn't have forgotten him if you had. He's a hairdresser now, somewhere at the back of Ebury Street. 'Was Garrison Artillery. 'Blown up twice.'

'Does he show it?' I asked at the foot of the organ-loft stairs.

'No-o. Not much more than Lazarus did, I expect.' Brother Burges fled off to set some one else to a job.

Brother Anthony, small, dark, and humpbacked, was hissing groom-fashion while he treated the rich acacia-wood panels of the Lodge organ with some sacred, secret composition of his own. Under his guidance Humberstall, an enormous, flat-faced man, carrying the shoulders, ribs, and loins of the old Mark '14 Royal Garrison Artillery, and the eyes of a bewildered retriever, rubbed the stuff in. I sat down to my task on the organ-bench, whose purple velvet cushion was being vacuum-cleaned on the floor below.

'Now,' said Anthony, after five minutes' vigorous work on the part of Humberstall. '*Now* we're gettin' somethin' worth lookin' at! Take it easy, an' go on with what you was tellin' me about that Macklin man.'

'I-I 'adn't anything against 'im,' said Humberstall, 'excep' he'd been a toff by birth; but that never showed till he was bosko absoluto. Mere bein' drunk on'y made a common 'ound of 'im. But when bosko, it all came out. Otherwise, he showed me my duties as mess-waiter very well on the 'ole.'

'Yes, yes. But what in 'ell made you go *back* to your Circus? The Board gave you down-an'-out fair enough, you said, after the dump went up at Eatables?'

'Board or no Board, *I* 'adn't the nerve to stay at 'ome – not with Mother chuckin' 'erself round all three rooms like a rabbit every time the Gothas tried to get Victoria; an' sister writin' me aunts four pages about it next day. Not for *me*, thank you! till the war was over. So I slid out with a draft – they wasn't particular in '17, so long as the tally was correct – and I joined up again with our Circus somewhere at the back of Lar Pug Noy, I think it was.' Humberstall paused for some seconds and his brow wrinkled. 'Then I-I went sick, or somethin' or other, they told me; but I know *when* I reported for duty, our Battery Sergeant-Major says that I wasn't expected back, an'-an', one thing leadin' to another – to cut a long story short – I went up before our Major-Major – I shall forget my own name next – Major—'

'Never mind,' Anthony interrupted. 'Go on! It'll come back in talk!'

''Alf a mo'. 'Twas on the tip o' my tongue then.'

Humberstall dropped the polishing-cloth and knitted his brows again in most profound thought. Anthony turned to me and suddenly launched into a sprightly tale of his taxi's collision with a Marble Arch refuge on a greasy day after a three-yard skid.

''Much damage?' I asked.

'Oh no! Ev'ry bolt an' screw an' nut on the chassis strained; *but* nothing carried away, you understand me, an' not a scratch on the body. You'd never 'ave guessed a thing wrong till you took 'er in hand. It was a *wop* too: 'ead-on – like this!' And he slapped his tactful little forehead to show what a knock it had been.

'Did your Major dish you up much?' he went on over his shoulder to Humberstall, who came out of his abstraction with a slow heave.

'We-ell! He told me I wasn't expected back either; an' he said 'e couldn't 'ang up the 'ole Circus till I'd rejoined; an' he said that my ten-inch Skoda which I'd been Number Three of, before the dump went up at Eatables, had 'er full crowd. But, 'e said, as soon as a casualty occurred he'd remember me. "Meantime," says he, "I particularly want you for actin' mess-waiter."

'"Beggin' your pardon, sir," I says perfectly respectful; "but I didn't exactly come back for *that*, sir."

'"Beggin' *your* pardon, 'Umberstall," says 'e, "but I 'appen to command the Circus! Now, you're a sharp-witted man," he says; "an' what we've suffered from fool-waiters in Mess 'as been somethin' cruel. You'll take on, from now – under instruction to Macklin 'ere." So this man, Macklin, that I was tellin' you about, showed me my duties ... 'Ammick! I've got it! 'Ammick was our Major, an' Mosse was Captain!' Humberstall celebrated his recapture of the name by labouring at the organ-panel on his knee.

'Look out! You'll smash it,' Anthony protested.

'Sorry! Mother's often told me I didn't know my strength. Now, here's a curious thing. This Major of ours – it's all comin' back to me – was a high-up divorce-court lawyer; an' Mosse, our Captain, was Number One o' Mosse's Private Detective Agency. You've heard of it? Wives watched while you wait, an' so on. Well, these two 'ad been registerin' together, so to speak, in the Civil line for years on end, but hadn't ever met till the War. Consequently, at Mess their talk was mostly about famous cases they'd been mixed up in. 'Ammick told the Law-courts' end o' the business, an' all what had been left out of the pleadin's; an' Mosse 'ad the actual facts concernin' the errin' parties – in hotels an' so on. I've heard better talk in our Mess than ever before or since. It comes o' the Gunners bein' a scientific corps.'

'That be damned!' said Anthony. 'If anythin' 'appens to 'em they've got it all down in a book. There's no book when your lorry dies on you in the 'Oly Land. *That's* brains.'

'Well, *then*,' Humberstall continued, 'come on this Secret Society business that I started tellin' you about. When those two – 'Ammick an' Mosse – 'ad finished about their matrimonial relations – and, mind you, they weren't radishes – they seldom or ever repeated – they'd begin, as often as not, on this Secret Society woman I was tellin' you of – this Jane. She was the only woman I ever 'eard 'em say a good word for. 'Cordin' to them Jane was a none-such. *I* didn't know then she was a Society. 'Fact is, I only 'ung out 'arf an ear in their direction at first, on account of bein' under instruction for mess-duty to this Macklin man. What drew *my* attention to her was a new Lieutenant joinin' up. We called 'im "Gander" on account of his profeel, which was the identical bird. 'E'd been a nactuary – workin' out 'ow long civilians 'ad to live. Neither 'Ammick nor Mosse wasted words on 'im at Mess. They went on talking as usual, an' in due time, as usual, they got back to Jane. Gander cocks one of his big chilblainy ears an' cracks his cold finger joints. "By God! Jane?" says 'e. "Yes, Jane," says 'Ammick pretty short an' senior. "Praise 'Eaven!" says Gander. "It was 'Bubbly' where I've come from down the line." (Some damn revue or other, I expect.) Well, neither 'Ammick nor Mosse was easy-mouthed, or for that matter mealy-mouthed; but no sooner 'ad Gander passed that remark than they both shook 'ands with the young squirt across the table an' called for the port back again. It *was* a password, all right! Then they went at it about Jane – all three, regardless of rank. That made me listen. Presently, I 'eard 'Ammick say—'

"Arf a mo',' Anthony cut in. 'But what was *you* doin' in Mess?'

'Me an' Macklin was refixin' the sand-bag screens to the dug-out passage in case o' gas. We never knew when we'd cop it in the 'Eavies, don't you see? But we knew we 'ad been looked for for some time, an' it might come any minute. But, as I was sayin', 'Ammick says what a pity 'twas Jane 'ad died barren. "I deny that," says Mosse. "I maintain she was fruitful in the 'ighest sense o' the word." An' Mosse knew about such things, too. "I'm inclined to agree with 'Ammick," says young Gander. "Any'ow, she's left no direct an' lawful prog'ny." I remember every word they said, on account o' what 'appened subsequently. I 'adn't noticed Macklin much, or I'd ha' seen he was bosko absoluto. Then 'e cut in, leanin' over a packin'-case with a face on 'im like a dead mackerel in the dark. "Pa-hardon me, gents," Macklin says, "but this is a matter on which I *do* 'appen to be moderately well-informed. She *did* leave lawful issue in the shape o' one son; an' 'is name was 'Enery James."

'"By what sire? Prove it," says Gander, before 'is senior officers could get in a word.

'"I will," says Macklin, surgin' on 'is two thumbs. *An'*, mark you, none of 'em spoke! I forget whom he said was the sire of this 'Enery James-man; but 'e delivered 'em a lecture on this Jane-woman for more than a quarter of an hour. I know the exact time, because my old Skoda was on duty at ten-minute intervals reachin' after some Jerry formin'-up area; and her blast always put out the dug-out candles. I relit 'em once, an' again at the end. In conclusion, this Macklin fell flat forward on 'is face, which was how 'e generally wound up 'is notion of a perfect day. Bosko absoluto!

'"Take 'im away," says 'Ammick to me. "E's sufferin' from shell-shock."

'To cut a long story short, *that* was what first put the notion into my 'ead. Wouldn't it you? Even 'ad Macklin been a 'ighup Mason—'

'Wasn't 'e, then?' said Anthony, a little puzzled.

''E'd never gone beyond the Blue Degrees, 'e told me. Any'ow, 'e'd lectured 'is superior officers up an' down; 'e'd as good as called 'em fools most o' the time, in 'is toff's voice. I 'eard 'im an' I saw 'im. An' all he got was – me told off to put 'im to bed! And all on account o' Jane! Would *you* have let a thing like that get past you? Nor me, either! Next mornin', when his stummick was settled, I was at him full-cry to find out 'ow it was worked. Toff or no toff, 'e knew his end of a bargain. First, 'e wasn't takin' any. He said I wasn't fit to be initiated into the Society of the Janeites. That only meant five bob more – fifteen up to date.

'"Make it one Bradbury," 'e says. "It's dirt-cheap. You saw me 'old the Circus in the 'ollow of me 'and?"

'No denyin' it. I 'ad. So, for one pound, he communicated me the Password of the First Degree, which was *Tilniz an' trap-doors*.

'"I know what a trap-door is," I says to 'im, "but what in 'ell's *Tilniz*?"

'"You obey orders," 'e says, "an' next time I ask you what you're thinkin' about you'll answer, '*Tilniz an' trap-doors*,' in a smart and soldierly manner. I'll spring that question at me own time. All you've got to do is to be distinck."

'We settled all this while we was skinnin' spuds for dinner at the back o' the rear-truck under our camouflage-screens. Gawd, 'ow that glue-paint did stink! Otherwise, 'twasn't so bad, with the sun comin' through our pantomime-leaves, an' the wind marcelling the grasses in the cutting. Well, one thing leading to another, nothin' further 'appened in this direction till the afternoon. We 'ad a high standard o' livin' in Mess – an' in the Group, for that matter. I was takin' away Mosse's lunch – dinner 'e would never call it – an' Mosse was fillin' 'is cigarette-case previous to the afternoon's duty. Macklin, in the passage, comin' in as if 'e didn't know Mosse was there, slings 'is question at me, an' I give the countersign in a low but quite distinck voice, makin' as if I 'adn't seen Mosse. Mosse looked at me through and through, with his cigarette-case in his 'and. Then 'e jerks out 'arf a dozen – best Turkish – on the table an' exits. I pinched 'em an' divvied with Macklin.

'"You see 'ow it works," says Macklin. "Could you 'ave invested a Bradbury to better advantage?"

'"So far, no," I says. "Otherwise, though, if they start provin' an' tryin' me, I'm a dead bird. There must be a lot more to this Janeite game."

'"'Eaps an' 'eaps," he says. "But to show you the sort of 'eart I 'ave, I'll communicate you all the 'Igher Degrees among the Janeites, includin' the Charges, for another Bradbury; but you'll 'ave to work, Dobbin."'

'"Pretty free with your Bradburys, wasn't you?" Anthony grunted disapprovingly.

'What odds? *Ac*-tually, Gander told us, we couldn't expect to av'rage more than six weeks longer apiece, an', any'ow, *I* never regretted it. But make no mistake – the preparation was somethin' cruel. In the first place, I come under Macklin for direct instruction *re* Jane.'

'Oh! Jane *was* real, then?' Anthony glanced for an instant at me as he put the question. 'I couldn't quite make that out.'

'Real!' Humberstall's voice rose almost to a treble. 'Jane? Why, she was a little old maid 'oo'd written 'alf a dozen books about a hundred years ago. 'Twasn't as if there was anythin' *to* 'em, either. *I* know. I had to read 'em. They weren't adventurous, nor smutty, nor what you'd call even interestin' – all about girls o' seventeen (they begun young then, I tell you), not certain 'oom they'd like to marry; an' their dances an' card-parties an' picnics, and their young blokes goin' off to London on 'orseback for 'air-cuts an' shaves. It took a full day in those days, if you went to a proper barber. They wore wigs, too, when they was chemists or clergymen. All that interested me on account o' me profession, an' cuttin' the men's 'air every fortnight. Macklin used to chip me about bein' an 'air-dresser. 'E *could* pass remarks, too!'

Humberstall recited with relish a fragment of what must have been a superb commination service, ending with, 'You lazy-minded, lousyheaded, long-trousered, perfumed perookier.'

'An' you took it?' Anthony's quick eyes ran over the man.

'Yes. I was after my money's worth; an' Macklin, havin' put 'is 'and to the plough, wasn't one to withdraw it. Otherwise, if I'd pushed 'im, I'd ha' slew 'im. Our Battery Sergeant Major nearly did. For Macklin had a wonderful way o' passing remarks on a man's civil life; an' he put it about that our B.S.M. had run a dope an' dolly-shop with a Chinese woman, the wrong end o' Southwark

Bridge. Nothin' you could lay 'old of, o' course; but—' Humberstall let us draw our own conclusions.

'That reminds me,' said Anthony, smacking his lips. 'I 'ad a bit of a fracas with a fare in the Fulham Road last month. He called me a paras-tit-ic Forder. I informed 'im I was owner-driver, an' 'e could see for 'imself the cab was quite clean. That didn't suit 'im. 'E said it was crawlin'.'

'What happened?' I asked.

'One o' them blue-bellied Bolshies of postwar Police (neglectin' point-duty, as usual) asked us to flirt a little quieter. My joker chucked some Arabic at 'im. That was when we signed the Armistice. 'E'd been a Yeoman – a perishin' Gloucestershire Yeoman – that I'd helped gather in the orange crop with at Jaffa, in the 'Oly Land!'

'And after that?' I continued.

'It 'ud be 'ard to say. I know 'e lived at Hendon or Cricklewood. I drove 'im there. We must 'ave talked Zionism or somethin', because at seven next mornin' him an' me was tryin' to get petrol out of a milkshop at St. Albans. They 'adn't any. In lots o' ways this war has been a public noosance, as one might say, but there's no denyin' it 'elps you slip through life easier. The dairyman's son 'ad done time on Jordan with camels. So he stood us rum an' milk.'

'Just like 'avin' the Password, eh?' was Humberstall's comment.

'That's right! Ours was *Imshee kelb*. Not so 'ard to remember as your Jane stuff.'

'Jane wasn't so very 'ard – not the way Macklin used to put 'er,' Humberstall resumed. 'I 'ad only six books to remember. I learned the names by 'eart as Macklin placed 'em. There was one called *Persuasion*, first; an' the rest in a bunch, except another about some Abbey or other – last by three lengths. But, as I was sayin', what beat me was there was nothin' *to* 'em nor *in* 'em. Nothin' at all, believe me.'

'You seem good an' full of 'em, any'ow,' said Anthony.

'I mean that 'er characters was no *use*! They was only just like people you run across any day. One of 'em was a curate – the Reverend Collins – always on the make an' lookin' to marry money. Well, when I was a Boy Scout, 'im or 'is twin brother was our troop-leader. An' there was an upstandin' 'ard-mouthed Duchess or a Baronet's wife that didn't give a curse for any one 'oo wouldn't do what she told 'em to; the Lady – Lady Catherine (I'll get it in a minute) De Bugg. Before Ma bought the 'airdressin' business in

London I used to know of an 'olesale grocer's wife near Leicester (I'm Leicestershire myself) that might 'ave been 'er duplicate. And – oh yes – there was a Miss Bates; just an old maid runnin' about like a hen with 'er 'ead cut off, an' her tongue loose at both ends. I've got an aunt like 'er. Good as gold – but, *you* know.'

'Lord, yes!' said Anthony, with feeling. 'An' did you find out what *Tilniz* meant? I'm always huntin' after the meanin' of things mesel.'

'Yes, 'e was a swine of a Major-General, retired, and on the make. They're all on the make, in a quiet way, in Jane. 'E was so much of a gentleman by 'is own estimation that 'e was always be'avin' like a hound. *You* know the sort. 'Turned a girl out of 'is own 'ouse because she 'adn't any money – *after*, mark you, encouragin' 'er to set 'er cap at his son, because 'e thought she had.'

'But that 'appens all the time,' said Anthony. 'Why, me own mother—'

'That's right. So would mine. But this Tilney was a man, an' some'ow Jane put it down all so naked it made you ashamed. I told Macklin that, an' he said I was shapin' to be a good Janeite. 'Twasn't *his* fault if I wasn't. 'Nother thing, too; 'avin' been at the Bath Mineral Waters 'Ospital in 'Sixteen, with trench-feet, was a great advantage to me, because I knew the names o' the streets where Jane 'ad lived. There was one of 'em – Laura, I think, or some other girl's name – which Macklin said was 'oly ground. "If you'd been initiated *then*," he says, "you'd ha' felt your flat feet tingle every time you walked over those sacred pavin'-stones."

'"My feet tingled right enough," I said, "but not on account of Jane. Nothin' remarkable about that," I says.

'"'Eaven lend me patience!" he says, combin' 'is 'air with 'is little hands. "Every dam' thing about Jane is remarkable to a pukka Janeite! It was there," he says, "that Miss What's-her-Name" (he had the name; I've forgotten it) "made up 'er engagement again, after nine years, with Captain T'other Bloke." An' he dished me out a page an' a half of one of the books to learn by 'eart – *Persuasion*, I think it was.'

"You quick at gettin' things off by 'eart?' Anthony demanded.

'Not as a rule. I was then, though, or else Macklin knew 'ow to deliver the Charges properly. 'E said 'e'd been some sort o' schoolmaster once, and he'd make my mind resume work or break 'imself. That was just before the Battery Sergeant-Major 'ad it in for him on account o' what he'd been sayin' about the Chinese wife an' the dollyshop.'

'What did Macklin really say?' Anthony and I asked together. Humberstall gave us a fragment. It was hardly the stuff to let loose on a pious post-war world without revision.

'And what had your B.S.M. been in civil life?' I asked at the end.

''Ead-embalmer to an 'olesale undertaker in the Midlands,' said Humberstall; 'but, o' course, *when* he thought 'e saw his chance he naturally took it. He came along one mornin' lickin' 'is lips. "You don't get past me this time," 'e says to Macklin. "You're for it, Professor."

'"'Ow so, me gallant Major," says Macklin; "an' what for?"

'"For writin' obese words on the breech o' the ten-inch," says the B.S.M. She was our old Skoda that I've been tellin' you about. We called 'er "Bloody Eliza." She 'ad a badly wore obturator an' blew through a fair treat. I knew by Macklin's face the B.S.M. 'ad dropped it somewhere, but all he vow'saifed was, "Very good, Major. We will consider it in Common Room." The B.S.M. couldn't ever stand Macklin's toff's way o' puttin' things; so he goes off rumblin' like 'ell's bells in an 'urricane, as the Marines say. Macklin put it to me at once, what had I been doin'? Some'ow he could read me like a book.

'Well, all I'd done – an' I told 'im *he* was responsible for it – was to chalk the guns. 'Ammick never minded what the men wrote up on 'em. 'E said it gave 'em an interest in their job. You'd see all sorts of remarks chalked on the sideplates or the gear-casin's.'

'What sort of remarks?' said Anthony keenly.

'Oh! 'Ow Bloody Eliza, or Spittin' Jim – that was our old Mark Five Nine-point-two – felt that mornin', an' such things. But it 'ad come over me – more to please Macklin than anythin' else – that it was time we Janeites 'ad a look in. So, as I was tellin' you, I'd taken an' rechristened all three of 'em, on my own, early that mornin'. Spittin' Jim I 'ad chalked "The Reverend Collins" – that Curate I was tellin' you about; an' our cut-down Navy Twelve, "General Tilney," because it was worse wore in the groovin' than anything I'd ever seen. The Skoda (an' that was where I dropped it) I 'ad chalked up "The Lady Catherine De Bugg." I made a clean breast of it all to Macklin. He reached up an' patted me on the shoulder. "You done nobly," he says. "You're bringin' forth abundant fruit, like a good Janeite. But I'm afraid your spellin' has misled our worthy B.S.M.

That's what it is," 'e says, slappin' 'is little leg. "'Ow might you 'ave spelt De Bourgh for example?"

'I told 'im. 'Twasn't right; an' 'e nips off to the Skoda to make it so. When 'e comes back, 'e says that the Gander 'ad been before 'im an' corrected the error. But we two come up before the Major, just the same, that afternoon after lunch; 'Ammick in the chair, so to speak, Mosse in another, an' the B.S.M. chargin' Macklin with writin' obese words on His Majesty's property, on active service. When it transpired that me an' not Macklin was the offendin' party, the B.S.M. turned 'is hand in and sulked like a baby. 'E as good as told 'Ammick 'e couldn't hope to preserve discipline unless examples was made – meanin', o' course, Macklin.'

'Yes, I've heard all that,' said Anthony, with a contemptuous grunt. 'The worst of it is, a lot of it's true.'

"Ammick took 'im up sharp about Military Law, which he said was even more fair than the civilian article.'

'My Gawd!' This came from Anthony's scornful midmost bosom.

'"Accordin' to the unwritten law of the 'Eavies," says 'Ammick, "there's no objection to the men chalkin' the guns, if decency is preserved. On the other 'and," says he, "we 'aven't yet settled the precise status of individuals entitled so to do. I 'old that the privilege is confined to combatants only."

'"With the permission of the Court," says Mosse, who was another born lawyer, "I'd like to be allowed to join issue on that point. Prisoner's position is very delicate an' doubtful, an' he has no legal representative."

'"Very good," says 'Ammick. "Macklin bein' acquitted—"

'"With submission, me lud," says Mosse. "I hope to prove 'e was accessory before the fact."

'"*As* you please," says 'Ammick. "But in that case, 'oo the 'ell's goin' to get the port I'm tryin' to stand the Court?"

'"I submit," says Mosse, "prisoner, bein' under direct observation o' the Court, could be temporarily enlarged for that duty."

'So Macklin went an' got it, an' the B.S.M. had 'is glass with the rest. Then they argued whether mess servants an' non-combatants was entitled to chalk the guns ('Ammick *versus* Mosse). After a bit, 'Ammick as C.O. give 'imself best, an' me an' Macklin was severely admonished for trespassin' on combatants' rights, an' the B.S.M. was warned that if we repeated the offence 'e could deal with us summ'rily. He 'ad some glasses o' port an' went out quite 'appy. Then my turn come, while Macklin was gettin' them their tea; an' one thing leadin' to another, 'Ammick put me through all the Janeite Degrees, you might say. 'Never 'ad such a doin' in my life.'

'Yes, but what did you tell 'em?' said Anthony. 'I can't ever *think* my lies quick enough when I'm for it.'

'No need to lie. I told 'em that the backside view o' the Skoda, when she was run up, put Lady De Bugg into my 'ead. They gave me right there, but they said I was wrong about General Tilney. 'Cordin' to them, our Navy twelve-inch ought to 'ave been christened Miss Bates. I said the same idea 'ad crossed my mind, till I'd seen the General's groovin'. Then I felt it had to be the General or nothin'. But they give me full marks for the Reverend Collins – our Nine-point-two.'

'An' you fed 'em *that* sort o' talk?' Anthony's fox-coloured eyebrows climbed almost into his hair.

'While I was assistin' Macklin to get tea – yes. Seem' it was an examination, I wanted to do 'im credit as a Janeite.'

'An'-an' what did they say?'

'They said it was 'ighly creditable to us both. I don't drink, so they give me about a hundred fags.'

'Gawd! What a Circus you must 'ave been,' was Anthony's gasping comment.

'It *was* a 'appy little Group. I wouldn't 'a changed with any other.'

Humberstall sighed heavily as he helped Anthony slide back the organ-panel. We all admired it in silence, while Anthony repocketed his secret polishing mixture, which lived in a tin tobacco-box. I had neglected my work for listening to Humberstall. Anthony reached out quietly and took over a Secretary's Jewel and a rag. Humberstall studied his reflection in the glossy wood.

'Almost,' he said critically, holding his head to one side.

'Not with an Army. You could with a Safety, though,' said Anthony. And, indeed, as Brother Burges had foretold, one might have shaved in it with comfort.

'Did you ever run across any of 'em afterwards, any time?' Anthony asked presently.

'Not so many of 'em left to run after, now. With the 'Eavies it's mostly neck or nothin'. We copped it. In the neck. In due time.'

'Well, *you* come out of it all right.' Anthony spoke both stoutly and soothingly; but Humberstall would not be comforted.

'That's right; but I almost wish I 'adn't,' he sighed. 'I was 'appier there than ever before or since. Jerry's March push in 'Eighteen did us in; an' yet, 'ow could we 'ave expected it? 'Ow *could* we 'ave expected it? We'd been sent back for rest an' runnin'-repairs, back pretty near our base; an' our old loco' that used to shift us about o' nights, she'd gone down the line for repairs. But for 'Ammick we wouldn't even 'ave 'ad our camouflage-screens up. He told our Brigadier that, whatever 'e might be in the Gunnery line, as a leadin' Divorce lawyer he never threw away a point in argument. So 'e 'ad us all screened in over in a cuttin' on a little spur-line near a wood; an' 'e saw to the screens 'imself. The leaves weren't more than comin' out then, an' the sun used to make our glue-paint stink. Just like actin' in a theatre, it was! But 'appy. *But* 'appy! I expect if we'd been caterpillars, like the new big six-inch hows, they'd ha' remembered us. But we was the old La Bassée '15 Mark o' Heavies that ran on rails – not much more good than scrap-iron that late in the war. An', believe me, gents – or Brethren, as I should say – we copped it cruel. Look 'ere! It was in the afternoon, an' I was watchin' Gander instructin' a class in new sights at Lady Catherine. All of a sudden I 'eard our screens rip overhead, an' a runner on a motor-bike come sailin', sailin' through the air – like that bloke that used to bicycle off Brighton Pier – and landed one awful wop almost atop o' the class. "'Old 'ard," says Gander. "That's no way to report. What's the fuss?" "Your screens 'ave broke my back, for one thing," says the bloke on the ground; "an' for another, the 'ole front's gone." "Nonsense," says Gander. 'E 'adn't more than passed the remark when the man was vi'lently sick an' conked out. 'E 'ad plenty papers on 'im from Brigadiers and C.O.s reporting 'emselves cut off an' askin' for orders. 'E was right both ways – his back an' our front. The 'ole Somme front washed out as clean as kiss-me-'and!' His huge hand smashed down open on his knee.

'We 'eard about it at the time in the 'Oly Land. Was it reelly as quick as all that?' said Anthony.

'Quicker! Look 'ere! The motor-bike dropped in on us about four pip-emma. After that, we tried to get orders o' some kind or other, but nothin' came through excep' that all available transport was in use and not likely to be released. *That* didn't 'elp us any. About nine o'clock comes along a young Brass 'At in brown gloves. We was quite a surprise to 'im. 'E said they were evacuating the area and we'd better shift. "Where to?" says 'Ammick, rather short.

'"Oh, somewhere Amiens way," he says. "Not that I'd guarantee Amiens for any length o' time; but Amiens might do to begin with." I'm giving you the very words. Then 'e goes off swingin' 'is brown gloves, and 'Ammick sends for Gander and orders 'im to march the men through Amiens to Dieppe; book thence to New'aven, take up positions be'ind Seaford, an' carry on the war. Gander said 'e'd see 'im damned first. 'Ammick says 'e'd see 'im courtmartialled after. Gander says what 'e meant to say was that the men 'ud see all an' sundry damned before they went into Arniens with their gunsights wrapped up in their puttees. 'Ammick says 'e 'adn't said a word about puttees, an' carryin' off the gunsights was purely optional. "Well, anyhow," says Gander, "puttees *or* drawers, they ain't goin' to shift a step unless you lead the procession."

'"Mutinous 'ounds," says 'Ammick. "But we live in a democratic age. D'you suppose they'd object to kindly diggin' 'emselves in a bit?" "Not at all," says Gander. "The B.S.M.'s kept 'em at it like terriers for the last three hours." "That bein' so," says 'Ammick, "Macklin'll now fetch us small glasses o' port." Then Mosse comes in – he could smell port a mile off – an' he submits we'd only add to the congestion in Amiens if we took our crowd there, whereas, if we lay doggo where we was, Jerry might miss us, though he didn't seem to be missin' much that evenin'.

'The 'ole country was pretty noisy, an' our dumps we'd lit ourselves flarin' heavens-high as far as you could see. Lyin' doggo was our best chance. I believe we might ha' pulled it off, if we'd been left alone, but along towards midnight – there was some small stuff swishin' about, but nothin' particular – a nice little bald-headed old gentleman in uniform pushes into the dug-out wipin' his glasses an' sayin' 'e was thinkin' o' formin' a defensive flank on our left with 'is battalion which 'ad just come up. 'Ammick says 'e wouldn't form much if 'e was 'im. "Oh, don't say *that*," says the old gentleman, very shocked. "One must support the Guns, mustn't one?"

"Ammick says we was refittin' an' about as effective, just then, as a public lav'tory. "Go into Amiens," he says, "an' defend 'em there." "Oh no," says the old gentleman, "me an' my laddies *must* make a defensive flank for you," an' he flips out of the dug-out like a performin' bullfinch, chirruppin' for his "laddies." Gawd in 'Eaven knows what sort o' push they was – little boys mostly – but they 'ung on to 'is coat-tails like a Sunday-school treat, an' we 'eard 'em muckin' about in the open for a bit. Then a pretty tight barrage was slapped down for ten minutes, an' 'Ammick thought the laddies had copped it already. "It'll be our turn next," says Mosse. "There's been a covey o' Gothas messin' about for the last 'alf-hour – lookin' for the Railway Shops, I expect. They're just as likely to take us." "Arisin' out o' that," says 'Ammick, "one of 'em sounds pretty low down now. We're for it, me learned colleagues!" "Jesus!" says Gander, "I believe you're right, sir." And that was the last word I 'eard on the matter.'

'Did they cop you then?' said Anthony.

'They did. I expect Mosse was right, an' they took us for the Railway Shops. When I come to, I was lyin' outside the cuttin', which was pretty well filled up. The Reverend Collins was all right; but Lady Catherine and the General was past prayin' for. I lay there, takin' it in, till I felt cold an' I looked at meself. Otherwise, I 'adn't much on excep' me boots. So I got up an' walked about to keep warm. Then I saw somethin' like a mushroom in the moonlight. It was the nice old gentleman's bald 'ead. I patted it. 'Im and 'is laddies 'ad copped it right enough. Some battalion run out in a 'urry from England, I suppose. They 'adn't even begun to dig in – pore little perishers! I dressed myself off 'em there, an' topped off with a British warm. Then I went back to the cuttin' an' some one says to me: "Dig, you ox, dig! Gander's under." So I 'elped shift things till I threw up blood an' bile mixed. Then I dropped, an' they brought Gander out – dead – an' laid 'im next me. 'Ammick 'ad gone too – fair tore in 'alf, the B.S.M. said; but the funny thing was he talked quite a lot before 'e died, an' nothin' to 'im below 'is stummick, they told me. Mosse we never found. 'E'd been standing by Lady Catherine. She'd up-ended an' gone back on 'em, with 'alf the cuttin' atop of 'er, by the look of things.'

'And what come to Macklin?' said Anthony.

'Dunno … 'E was with 'Ammick. I expect I must ha' been blown clear of all by the first bomb; for I was the on'y Janeite left. We lost about half our crowd, either under, or after we'd got 'em out. The B.S.M. went off 'is rocker when mornin' came, an' he ran about from one to another sayin': "That was a good push! That was a great crowd! Did ye ever know any push to touch 'em?" An' then 'e'd cry. So what was left of us made off for ourselves, an' I came across a lorry, pretty full, but they took me in.'

'Ah!' said Anthony with pride. '"They all take a taxi when it's rainin'".' 'Ever 'eard that song?'

'They went a long way back. Then I walked a bit, an' there was a hospital-train fillin' up, an' one of the Sisters – a grey-headed one – ran at me wavin' 'er red 'ands an' sayin' there wasn't room for a louse in it. I was past carin'. But she went on talkin' and talkin' about the war, an' her pa in Ladbroke Grove, an' 'ow strange for 'er at 'er time of life to be doin' this work with a lot o' men, an' next war, 'ow the nurses 'ud 'ave to wear khaki breeches on account o' the mud, like the Land Girls; an' that reminded 'er, she'd boil me an egg if she could lay 'ands on one, for she'd run a chicken-farm once. You never 'eard anythin' like it – outside o' Jane. It set me off laughin' again. Then a woman with a nose an' teeth on 'er, marched up. "What's all this?" she says. "What do you want?" "Nothing," I says, "only make Miss Bates, there, stop talkin' or I'll die." "Miss Bates?" she says. "What in 'Eaven's name makes you call 'er that?" "Because she is," I says. "D'you know what you're sayin'?" she says, an' slings her bony arm round me to get me off the ground. "'Course I do," I says, "an' if you knew Jane you'd know too." "That's enough," says she. "You're comin' on this train if I have to kill a Brigadier for you," an' she an' an ord'ly fair hove me into the train, on to a stretcher close to the cookers. That beef-tea went down well! Then she shook 'ands with me an' said I'd hit off Sister Molyneux in one, an' then she pinched me an extra blanket. It was 'er own 'ospital pretty much. I expect she was the Lady Catherine de Bourgh of the area. Well, an' so, to cut a long story short, nothing further transpired.'

"'Adn't you 'ad enough by then?' asked Anthony.

'I expect so. Otherwise, if the old Circus 'ad been carryin' on, I might 'ave 'ad another turn with 'em before Armistice. Our B.S.M. was right. There never was a 'appier push. 'Ammick an' Mosse an' Gander an' the B.S.M. an' that pore little Macklin man makin' an' passin' an' raisin' me an' gettin' me on to the 'ospital train after 'e was dead, all for a couple of Bradburys. I lie awake nights still, reviewing matters. There never was a push to touch ours – never!'

Anthony handed me back the Secretary's Jewel resplendent.

'Ah,' said he. 'No denyin' that Jane business was more useful to you than the Roman Eagles or the Star an' Garter. 'Pity there wasn't any of you Janeites in the 'Oly Land. I never come across 'em.'

'Well, as pore Macklin said, it's a very select Society, an' you've got to be a Janeite in your 'eart, or you won't have any success. An' yet he made *me* a Janeite! I read all her six books now for pleasure 'tween times in the shop; an' it brings it all back – down to the smell of the glue-paint on the screens. You take it from me, Brethren, there's no one to touch Jane when you're in a tight place. Gawd bless 'er, whoever she was.'

Worshipful Brother Burges, from the floor of the Lodge, called us all from Labour to Refreshment. Humberstall hove himself up – so very a cart-horse of a man one almost expected to hear the harness creak on his back – and descended the steps.

He said he could not stay for tea because he had promised his mother to come home for it, and she would most probably be waiting for him now at the Lodge door.

'One or other of 'em always comes for 'im. He's apt to miss 'is gears sometimes,' Anthony explained to me, as we followed.

'Goes on a bust, d'you mean?'

''Im! He's no more touched liquor than 'e 'as women since 'e was born. No, 'e's liable to a sort o' quiet fits, like. They came on after the dump blew up at Eatables. But for them, 'e'd ha' been Battery Sergeant-Major.'

'Oh!' I said. 'I couldn't make out why he took on as mess-waiter when he got back to his guns. That explains things a bit.'

''Is sister told me the dump goin' up knocked all 'is Gunnery instruction clean out of 'im. The only thing 'e stuck to was to get back to 'is old crowd. Gawd knows 'ow 'e worked it, but 'e did. He fair deserted out of England to 'em, she says; an' when they saw the state 'e was in, they 'adn't the 'eart to send 'im back or into 'ospital. They kep' 'im for a mascot, as you might say. That's *all* dead-true. 'Is sister told me so. But I can't guarantee that Janeite business, excep' 'e never told a lie since 'e was six. 'Is sister told me so. What do *you* think?'

'He isn't likely to have made it up out of his own head,' I replied.

'But people don't get so crazy-fond o' books as all that, do they? 'E's made 'is sister try to read 'em. She'd do anythin' to please him. But, as I keep tellin' 'er, so'd 'is mother. D'you 'appen to know anything about Jane?'

'I believe Jane was a bit of a match-maker in a quiet way when she was alive, and I know all her books are full of match-making,' I said. '*You'd* better look out.'

'Oh, *that's* as good as settled,' Anthony replied, blushing.

[First published in *Debits and Credits* (London: Macmillan, 1926).]

⊠ ⊠ ⊠

This talk was given at the opening of a new rifle range at Winchester College on 11 December 1915. The range was built in memory of a former pupil, George Cecil, who had lost his life at Villers-Cotterêts at the very start of the First World War in September 1914. Cecil was the son of Kipling's friends, Lord Edward and Lady Violet Cecil (she was later Lady Milner). The talk was particularly emotional for Kipling as he had recently learned that his son John had gone missing in action at Loos.

THE WAR AND THE SCHOOLS

O foreign-tongued woodlands, we confide to you a child of that generation for whom their fathers prepared such distant graves.
Winchester College, December 1915

I HAVE BEEN HONOURED by a request that I should help to dedicate this rifle range to the memory of an old Wykehamist – George Cecil, Ensign of Grenadiers, killed in action. Cecil was not very long before your time, as once time was reckoned, but since each month now equals a year he dates, so far as you are concerned, to the beginning of history. He was one of that original army in France which was sacrificed almost to a man, in order that England might gain time to create those armies which, till then, she had not thought necessary. He was killed just before the long retreat from Mons came to an end – killed leading his platoon in the woods round Villers Cotterets fifteen months ago.

He did no more and no less than thousands have done since, and many thousands are preparing themselves to do; for it would be difficult to find a household in England to-day free from the fact or the fear of a similar loss.

Yet in one respect he differed from some of his fellows. He was devoted by instinct to the profession of arms, and had made it his consuming interest and study, not through any child's delight in its glitter, but because he absolutely believed in the imminence of that very war in which he fell. It was curious in a world full of wise grown men, who would not or could not understand, to listen to his unshaken conviction on this matter; and to watch the extraordinarily thorough way in which he set about fitting himself to meet it. Both at Sandhurst and during his short time in the Service, he toiled, as I know, at the details of his profession with the passion of a boy, and studied the wider aspects of it with the judgement of a man. I remember a couple of years ago the boy, for he was little more then, saying to me across an atlas: 'We shall be sent to prolong the French left – *here*! We shall not have enough men to do it, and we shall be cut up. But with any luck I ought to be in it.' His fortune allowed him to fight with the best for the best. He is among the first of that vast company of young dead who live without change in the hearts of those who love them.

I speak now to such of you as propose to follow him. Being who you are, you realise what your Foundation has taught its scholars from the beginning – that as Freedom is indispensable, so is Liberty impossible, to a gentleman. This is knowledge which will serve you when you go out into a world whose every landmark has been violently removed, and every distinction save one – an aristocracy of blood – emptied of all significance. Thanks to the unwisdom of your forefathers, the rescue of a wrecked civilisation has been laid upon you and those very little senior to you. Were I addressing men of my own age, I should say that this task was a heavy one. But I speak to youth which can accomplish everything, precisely because it accepts no past, obeys no present, and fears no future. For that reason, I do not doubt your future, nor as much of our future as is in your keeping. It is for your generation to make well sure that those who have defied God and man shall learn to walk humbly before both as long as fear can endure.

The making of the new world that will rise out of these present judgements will fall to your generation also – not only to those in the field, but to those who, for any reason, are afraid that they can never take part in the great work. They need have no fear. After the brute issue of the war shall have been decided on the fronts, all men, all capacities, all attainments, will be called upon to the uttermost to establish civilisation. For then the work will begin of reconstructing, not only England and the Empire, but the whole world – on a scale which outruns imagination. Every aspect of life as we have known life hitherto will have disappeared. National boundaries and national sympathies, powers, responsibilities, and habits of thought will have shifted and been transformed. Our neighbours of yesterday will be our blood-brethren of that to-morrow, bound to us, as we throughout the Empire are bound to each other, by the most far-reaching and intimate ties of common loss and common devotion, and labouring side by side to bring order out of the appalling chaos that humanity has drawn upon itself.

Let no one, whatever his physical disabilities, or however meanly he may think of himself, let no one dream for a moment he will not be needed, and urgently needed, in the new order of things. His duty is to prepare himself now. This is harder for him than for the combatant officer, since an officer's work is continually tested against actual warfare. The men of the second line – the civil reserve that will take over when the sword is sheathed – have no such check, nor have they the officer's spur of visible responsibility. Their turn comes later. Till it comes they must work on honour, that they may be ready to uphold the honour of civilisation. They have not long to wait. In a few years some of you must be working with our Allies at the administration of what may be left of Central Europe, where you will have to invent new systems to meet new conditions almost as swiftly as, during the war, new weapons were invented to meet new forms of attack. I say in a few years, because the youngest captain I know is twenty-one; the youngest I have heard of is nineteen. And so it will be on the civil side. The war has given the youth of all our world a step in age – additional seniority of three years. You may say – though your relatives are more likely to think it – that your youth has been taken from you. I prefer to put it, that your manhood has been thrust on you early – at the sword's point. Fit yourself for it then, not according to the measure of your years, but to the measure of our world's great need.

You have seen and realised the very things which young Cecil felt would befall. As far as his short life allowed he ordered himself so that he might not be overwhelmed by them when they were upon him. He died – as many of you too will die – but he died knowing the issue for which he died. It is well to die for one's country. But that is not enough. It is also necessary that, so long as he lives, a man should give to his country, as George Cecil gave, a mind and soul neither ignorant nor inadequate.

[First published in The Wykehamist, December 1915 and collected in A Book of Words (London: Macmillan, 1928).]

✠ ✠ ✠

In another talk, Kipling imparts aspects of his curiously mystical view of soldiering to a group of officer cadets in Bushey, Hertfordshire.

THE MAGIC SQUARE

Certain it is men have fallen upon each other from the first. This is a business which the Gods lay upon the Young; leaving the Old to weary with words the unreturning phalanx.
Household Brigade Officers' Cadet Corps, Bushey, 1917

MY LECTURE THIS MORNING deals with the origin, development, and moral significance of Drill among mankind from the earliest ages.

What put the idea of drill into man's head at the beginning of things? As Shakespeare so beautifully observes, 'What made man first drill upon the Square, with Sergeants running round and round?'

And when I say man, I do not mean any sort of man that we are acquainted with, or of which we have any record. The man I ask you to imagine is a prehistoric person with a vocabulary of a few score words, who had not long given up living in trees and who moved in little family groups of small associated tribes, in or on the edge of immense primeval forests, much as gorillas and chimpanzees do to-day in the tropical African forests. I'm going to call him George Robey. He was a creature who still fought with his teeth and nails like the animals: but he could break off a branch, trim it, and use it as a club or a lance; he could throw stones with accuracy; scrape out holes in the ground; plait or weave branches together; swim; and climb trees. Besides this, he possessed what you and I would call a reasoning mind. He knew what he was doing, he could remember what he had done, and he could estimate the consequences of what he might do. With this equipment and an omnivorous appetite, he had to make his living or die. War wasn't man's business in the beginning. No animal makes a business of war except for food. Man's business in those days was food. He *had* to hunt, and he *had* to understand the tactics of hunting.

That is why tactics, in my opinion, were developed before drill. An eminent tactician once told me that all tactics boiled down either to some sort of frontal feint with a flank diversion, or some sort of ambush into which the enemy could be pushed or drawn. We may be sure that George Robey found out very early in the day that if some of the family – the younger members for choice – capered and shouted in front of any large eatable animal, the rest of the group had a chance to run in on the beast's flank and kill it. That's elementary. When wolves are hunting a single buffalo, or moose, or elk, that shows fight, they employ just these tactics; and I believe they also send scouts upwind to drive the buck down to the main pack. Those were George Robey's simple but sound tactics. Frontal feint with flank attack, or a retirement or a push towards ground where the quarry could be made helpless. Result, if successful, a good meal; if not, hunger.

Now, how could he get his men on to the hunting grounds without making too much noise, which would scare the game; and without leaving too conspicuous a trail, which might bring some dangerous wild beast after them? The simplest – the only – way of walking through thick jungle, as our troops knew in the Cameroons campaign, is in single file – down the bush-paths, if there are any. Where there are no paths, or where the ground is boggy or covered with fallen trees, each man has to step in the track of the next ahead. If he doesn't, he steps on the next man's heels, where he may throw him off his balance, and – what is more important – make a noise. So, whether he likes it or not, a man in single file has to keep step. The penalty for not keeping step when keeping step was first invented, was, in all probability, a severe reprimand on the head with a club.

'And thus, my beloved 'earers', as Mr. Jorrocks says in his sporting lectures – thus did George Robey's company learn to keep step, which is the first essential of all drill.

And, after all, what does drill come to? This – the step, which includes keeping step – the line, by which I mean any sort of line, close or extended – the wheel, which includes a line changing direction – and, most important of all, because it is the foundation that makes every move possible, forming fours. There you have it all, gentlemen – the four sides of the Magic Square. The Step and keeping step – the Line, close or extended – Wheeling and changing direction – and Forming Fours. S.W.L.F. So We Learned Fighting.

Single line ahead – single file – is the weakest of all formations. By the way, a man in the German East Africa campaign told me that one of his columns, which was about a mile and a half long, moving in single file through heavy bush, was charged and scattered eleven times in one day by rhinoceroses. At the end of that time he was a little fed-up with big game. This will give you some idea of what the wretched George Robey had to put up with when he took his company through the forest in single file; for I believe the rhino of George's day, so far as we can judge from its fossil remains, stood about seven feet at the shoulder. There was only one advantage in single file. George's human enemies were as helpless to attack him as his own lot would have been to attack them. On open ground or in the big natural glades and parks inside forests, single line ceased to have any advantage. George might want to beat over a clearing in the woods for small game, or it might be necessary to drive some big animal that had been marked down by scouts towards some place where another detachment of the tribe was waiting for it. Those things would depend on the nature of the ground; but, one way or another, George had to get his whole string of men into some sort of line abreast before he could beat for game. Listening to instructors on the Square, I have often wondered whether George Robey, with his limited vocabulary, didn't blow up with suppressed indignation. But it is more likely that he bit the nearest man on the ear.

Consider for a moment what that early drill involved! Obviously, the whole line had to draw clear of the woods and halt. Then it had to extend till it had stretched all across the clearing they were going to beat. It had to keep touch, because if it didn't the game would bolt back through the gaps when the drive began. Next, at a given signal, the line had to rise and rush forward to start the small game – or, if it was big game, to make just enough noise to keep the beast moving towards the desired ambush. To appreciate the magnitude of the problem involved, gentlemen, you have only to go out in a five-acre field with half a dozen friends and try to catch an old and cunning horse who doesn't want to be caught. Then you'll understand what the first drill-instructor had to contend with. There must have been some reprimands delivered, in the morning of the world, that beat anything at Caterham, where, I have heard, 'they tame lions'.

Under these circumstances, what did George Robey do? He did what any thinking being would have done after he had missed his meat-ration three times running. Remember, his reasoning mind made him realise that if this silly catch-as-catch-can business went on the tribe would get no food. So he said to the younger men: 'We will practise the motions of hunting game several times over before we hunt game in earnest. Report to me outside the caves at sunrise to-morrow.' That was the first, cold, grey dawn of Drill in the world!

It must have been a slow process, but – what a thing to have seen being born! Remember, the tribe had already been forced to learn how to keep step and form some sort of line to beat with. Imagine George Robey when it first dawned on him that if all his men brought down their right or left foot at the same time, they could make noise enough to scare off a marauding wild beast or a human enemy without fighting! Imagine the first time he taught fifty or even twenty men to do it every time he shouted: 'Stamp!' An animal often stamps when it is angry or wishes to frighten somebody; but no herd of animals ever stamp simultaneously and move forward one pace at each stamp. That was the first exhibition of organised 'frightfulness' that the world ever saw.

Let us go a step further. George Robey has managed, by bites and blows and howls, to get a few individuals to stand in line; at first, shoulder to shoulder; next, with a sufficient interval between each to allow one to handle his club without hitting his neighbour. He has also taught the line to stamp with its feet at each step when he tells 'em to. He can do a lot with this formation. If the individuals in the line turn right or left, the line becomes a single file again that can make its way through the forest like a snake. If it advances as a line, it thoroughly beats out all the ground in front of it, and can extend and envelop either flank of the enemy, like the old cow's-horn formation of the Zulu *Impi*. If any animal breaks through the first line during the beat, there is nothing easier than to put a second line or a third behind it, at whatever distance may be advisable. And when both lines, or all lines, stamp their feet at once the noise is twice as impressive. Consequently, on account of these wonderful inventions, George Robey's tribe gets plenty to eat, and is less worried by wild beasts or enemies.

But I don't think human enemies entered largely into man's calculations at first. By what one can make out from the manners and customs of the gorillas and the larger apes of to-day, there could not have been much actual fighting; and what there was, was rarely to the death, unless, of course, it was two males fighting for a female. I take it that it was a long while before there was organised war of man against man in the world. I fancy the earliest forms of drill were evolved originally more on account of man's necessities as a hunter than from his needs as a warrior. Keeping in step and beating over ground in line are hunting dodges. Now for the wheel, or change of direction, and the marking time that goes with it.

Some years ago I saw a line of beaters in one of the Native States in India beating a big jungle to drive game up to the shooting-stand, where the Raja and his guests sat with rifles. They had put up a lot of buck and small game, and a panther or two, which they wished to head off down one particular rocky ravine. About fifty of them were acting as stops, lying hidden among rocks and bushes out on one flank of the drive. As the game began to come through, and showed signs of scattering over the open plain, the men rose, formed line, and wheeled inward, shouting and waving, till all the game turned left into the ravine. These men ran at a quick stooping shuffle, but they kept their line perfectly. What struck me most when the first man – the pivot man – of the wheel, and the others, came into their places on the new alignment parallel with the side of the ravine, was the way they danced and capered with excitement. But they always came down in the same place! It was like a lunatic asylum marking time. As I watched – and I can see those wild, little black legs now – it occurred to me that marking-time, as practised in the civilised armies of the world, must be just the last, last remnant of that wild dance of excited hunters, coming into position when a drive halts, ready to lead off on either foot as soon as the drive goes forward again. I have a theory, based on what I have read about primitive dances and children's games, and some of the figures in square dances like quadrilles and lancers, that George Robey may have originally taught his line of men to wheel on parade by making them hold hands. However he came by the notion, it was a splendid idea, and it completed three sides of the Magic Square – the Step – the Line – the Wheel or incline.

But if you ask me how George Robey conceived the idea of forming fours, I tell you frankly I am up a tree. I argue that it must have been quite a late development. Here are my reasons. First, the world wasn't fitted for route-marching in fours in those days. Fours require something wider than a bush-track. Single file would be the natural formation till tracks were developed or men lived in open country. Secondly, column of fours isn't directly a hunting formation like the line or the wheel. It's only a means to an end. Thirdly, it was a long, long time before primitive man learned to count. And the odds are that it was another long time before he counted further than his own fingers and toes, as primitive tribes do to-day. The Esquimaux word for twenty-one is about seven syllables long, and literally translated it means 'one finger on the other man's hand'. The word for fifty-three is *inuppinga-jugson-arkanek-pingasut*, which means 'on the third man, on the first foot, three'. This would make numbering off a platoon last as long as the War.

So the nature of the ground, the nature of the formation, and the difficulty of counting have delayed the epoch-making discovery of forming fours. It has been lost and rediscovered many times since; but the more one looks at the evolution, the more one is impressed by its astounding simplicity and cunning. Here are two lines of men, one behind the other. Somebody utters a magic howl, or yelp, or bark – the sound of words of command hasn't altered much since the beginning – and, behold, the lines become a compact and supple column, capable of moving in any direction, and capable, if anyone says the magic word, of becoming two lines once more! Look at it from primitive man's point of view, and you'll see what a miracle it must have been the first time it was shown to the tribe. But how – how – how – did George Robey get the idea; and, having got it, how did he push, and pull, and haul his men into fours? My own theories on the subject would be too fantastic, probably, for your acceptance. I merely suggest that forming fours was originally not a hunting formation at all, but a portion of ceremonial drill which later was employed, when going to battle or the hunt, on account of its many conveniences.

I have used the words 'ceremonial drill'.

Side by side with this practical drill, or rehearsal for the business of hunting and war, there developed the rudiments of what, later on, became ceremonial drill. Why? Here is my reason. The natural instinct of a man, after he has done anything worth talking about, is to talk about it; and George Robey was extremely natural. When he had finished a successful day's hunting or had cleverly knocked an enemy on the head, he went home and told his wife and the children all about it. Like all persons with a limited vocabulary, he had to act most of his story and piece it out, precisely as children do, with innumerable repetitions of the same word. His tale wouldn't grow less in the telling. Tales don't. His actual fight was probably a crude affair; but he would act it at home before the family with stately leaps and bounds to represent the death-scuffle, and with elaborate wavings of his club and thrustings with his lance to show how he did his man in. At the end of his story there would certainly be a solemn walk round the fire to let the females admire him and the young bloods be impressed with him. It's too long a subject to go into to-night; but you can take it that when a male animal has accomplished a kill of any kind, he generally indulges in a sort of triumphal demonstration – a tense, highly braced walk or promenade round and above the carcass, especially if there is a female of his species near by. At the very first, when George Robey was only the hairy, low-browed head of a family, he would declaim and prance alone. Later, as the families grew into groups and tribes, the other men who had assisted at the hunt or the battle would have their say, and their shout, and their walk-round, in the open spaces before the caves. It may be that the idea of forming fours was first originated at those processional walk-rounds where there was open space to manœuvre and safety in which to correct errors. You can imagine how, as these men danced and leaped, they would all sing like children: 'This is the way we kill a bison. This is how we stand up to a tiger. This is how we tackle men.' The drama would be accepted as the real thing by the women and the juniors, till at last the bison, or the tiger, or the man-killing charade would become a religious ceremonial – a thing to be acted, said, or sung before going up to battle or chase, with invocations to great hunters in the past, and so on. It would end by being a magic ritual, sure to bring good luck if it was properly performed. And so far as that ritual, with its dances, and chants, and stampings, and marches round, gave the men cohesion and confidence, it would go far towards success in the field. That principle holds good to this day.

I was at Edinburgh Castle a few weeks ago, watching a squad marching in slow time, and doing it rather badly. The instructor told 'em so. Then he said: 'You're lazy! You're lazy! Point that toe! There's not a *fut* among ye!'

It is hard work trying to get recruits to reproduce in cold blood, on a cold morning, in cold boots, something of the wonderful grace and poise and arrested motion of the bare-footed, perfectly balanced, perfectly healthy primitive man rejoicing over his kill.

The nearest thing I ever saw to the genuine article must have been sham-fight among Kaffirs in a compound at the Kimberley Diamond-fields. It finished with a walk-round in slow time, and I remember that every Kaffir's foot shot out as straight as the forefoot of a trotting horse. You could almost hear the hip and knee and ankle joint click as the toe was pointed. Now, it's a far cry from a Kaffir compound to a Guard Mount at Buckingham Palace; but if you stand three-quarters on to the Colours as they come out of the gate with the Guard, you'll catch just a far-off shadow of what the march in slow time originally sprung from, and what it meant.

Very good! Now, I've sketched roughly the earliest developments of certain evolutions of the earliest men that later developed into field and ceremonial drill. I have given the outlines of the Magic Square – the Step, the Line, the Wheel, and the Forming Fours, which is the foundation of the whole mystery of drill. These things, according to my theory, were first discovered in the very dawn of human consciousness on earth.

Pass on a few thousand, or hundred thousand years, and we reach the beginnings of some sort of civilisation. By this time man has begun to specialise in his work. Everybody doesn't hunt; everybody doesn't fight; everybody doesn't prepare his own food or make his own weapons for himself. Experience has shown mankind that it is more convenient to tell off certain men for these duties.

Here we come to a curious fact in human nature.

As soon as any man is detailed for a particular job – that is to say, a duty that he has to perform for somebody else's sake – he gets, whether he likes it or not, the beginnings of an ideal of conduct. He may loathe the job; but that reasoning mind that I've mentioned makes him uncomfortable in himself if he neglects the job. The worst of it is that any being who knows what he is doing, remembers what he has done, and can estimate the probable consequence of what he is going to do, knows also what he *ought* to do. That's the beginning of Conscience. I grant you it's an infernal nuisance; but it's true. As a compensation, all men have a tendency to glorify and make much of their own special duty, no matter how humble they or the job may be.

But the primitive warrior was far from humble. He was a man set apart by his strength, skill, or courage, for work on which the very existence of his tribe depended. As such, he was entitled to extra or more varied rations in order that he might do that work properly.

Primitive tribes at the present day have long lists of certain foods and special portions of game which are forbidden to be eaten by the women, or by the men before they come to manhood. The fighting men of the tribe are freed from any restrictions on this head, and the best cuts and joints are reserved for them – like the Captain's Wing. Three years ago, scientific men called these restrictions the outcome of savage superstition. Now, we have food-regulations of our own, and, you will observe, the rationing of the Army and Navy is the most important matter of all, because the safety of the tribe depends upon it.

Besides these advantages, the primitive fighting man had behind him an enormous mass of tradition and ritual, and song and dance and ceremony handed down through generation to generation from prehistoric days, which dealt with everything that he did in the performance of his duties or in the preparation for his duties. The crude drills and hunting rehearsals of George Robey's time had developed into complicated sacred dances of fabulous antiquity. Every detail connected with war had its special rite or incantation. The warrior himself, his clothes, the paints he used for personal decoration, his weapons, his form of attack, his particular fashion of marking or mutilating his enemy after death, his war-cry, the charms that protected him in battle – were all matters of the deepest importance on which the best brains of mankind had spent centuries and centuries of thought, with the object – conscious or unconscious – of creating and improving the *morale* of the individual set apart to fight for the tribe. To-day, these rituals have faded out of the memory of civilised mankind altogether. But, in spite of time and change, one can still trace in our modern days shadows here and there of customs and ceremonial dating from the birth of time – customs which still persist among us because, mark you, they concern the individual and collective *morale* of the warrior – the man set apart to fight for the safety of the tribe.

I give you three instances.

I. It is an offence to draw one's sword in Mess, just as it is a gross liberty to examine or handle any man's sword without first asking his permission.

Why?

Because the Sword is, above all weapons, the most ancient and most holy. Why? Because it was the terrible weapon with the cutting edge and the thrusting point which first superseded the stick and the club among mankind, and gave the tribes that had it power over the tribes that had not. The old fairy-tales of magic swords that cut off people's heads of themselves run back to that dim and distant date when some sword-using tribe broke in upon and scuppered some tribe of club-using primitives. Through thousands and thousands of years the Sword – the manufactured weapon which cannot be extemporised out of a branch, like the club; nor out of a branch and a strip of leather or sinew like the bow – this expensive hand-made Sword has been personal to its owner, slung to his body by day, ready to his hand by night, a thing prayed over and worshipped – the visible shrine, so to speak, of the personal honour of the man who wielded it – the weapon set apart for the man who is set apart for the business of war.

II. It is an offence to mention a woman's name in Mess. Why? Because the warrior's work being war, and the one thing furthest from war being woman, it follows that at no time since fighting began was the warrior encouraged to think of women while preparing for, or engaged in, his job. Because, when the warrior went to war, he was forbidden – as he is forbidden to-day among savages – to have anything to do with women for a certain length of time before starting. The idea of women, and therefore, the name of any woman, was considered distracting, weakening, to a warrior, and for that reason was absolutely forbidden – tabu – to him not only in the field, but also in his ceremonial gatherings with his equals – the men set apart for the business of war.

III. It is extraordinarily difficult to prevent ragging in the Army. Why? Because as soon as men were set apart for the work of fighting, it was necessary for them to find out the character, powers of endurance, and resistance to pain of the young men who from time to time joined them. For that reason, there grew up all the world over, a system of formally initiating young men into the tribe by a series of tests, varying in severity, which ranged – as they do among primitive tribes to-day – from mere flogging to being hung, head down, over smoke, burning on various parts of the body, or being swung from the ground by hooks inserted through their muscles. There were also other tests – spiritual as well as physical. You can see a trace of them in the mediaeval idea of the candidate for knighthood watching his arms before the altar of a church, generally full of tombs, from sunset to sunrise. Men reasoned logically enough: 'If a man can't stand our peacetime tests, he'll fail us in war. Let's see what he *can* stand.' Nowadays, young men argue – or, rather, they don't argue, they feel: 'So-and-so looks rather an ass; or is rather a beast; or carries too much side. Let's rag him.' Then they turn his room inside out, or rub harness-paste into his hair, or sit him in a bath, or make him dance the fox-trot, as the case may be. If he loses his temper he falls in their opinion. If he keeps it, and pays back the rag with interest later on, they say he is a good sort. I'm not defending ragging – I've known cases where everyone who took part in it ought to have been R.T.U. I'm only giving you the primitive reason for the performance which to-day has been watered down into a 'rag'. It rose out of a test that was of vital importance to the men who were set apart for the business of war.

I have tried to make clear that even from the earliest ages, the warrior has been a man set apart for a definite purpose, and surrounded by a definite ritual from which, as you know, he is not permitted to escape. The reason for this is very simple. I will summarise it.

The earliest drill was born of the tactics, first of hunting, then of war. The notion of hunting and fighting in accordance with some preconceived plan – that is to say, an ideal of conduct – was developed and taught in the ceremonial drills and dances before and after hunting and fighting. Then came the period of specialisation, when certain men fought for the tribe – in other words, offered themselves as sacrifices for the tribe. They hoped, of course, to sacrifice the enemy; but if they failed in that, their own bodies, their own lives, would be the sacrifice.

People who think a great deal and know very little will tell you that mankind, as a rule, don't take kindly to the idea of sacrificing themselves unless there is an advantage to be gained from it. But it is worth noting that there is hardly any people in the world so degraded that it cannot appreciate the idea of sacrifice in others, and there are few races or tribes in the world whose legends of their origin or whose religion does not include the story of some tremendous sacrifice made by a hero or demi-god for their sakes. Most of the stories describe at length how the hero or demi-god prepared himself for the sacrifice.

Now, if you think for a moment, you will see that there were only two people in the tribe who were permanently and officially concerned in the theory and practice of sacrifice. They were the

Priest, who was also the doctor or the medicine man; and the fighting-man. The Priest knew the charms and spells that would protect the warrior from hurt in battle, as well as the herbs and dressings that would cure him if he were hurt. Most important of all, he knew how the warrior would stand with the Gods of the tribe after his death. If he had died well, the Gods would be pleased. If he had died badly, the Gods would be angry. In other words, whatever ideals of conduct existed in the tribe, the Priest upheld them. The Priest sacrificed fruits, animals, or human beings to the spirits of the great hunters and fighters of old. And because savages are not infidels, he sacrificed also to the unknown gods, who are above all the demi-gods. But the warrior, remember, stood ready to sacrifice himself. He more than any other needed preparation and setting apart for his task.

If one compares the ritual and the code of conduct required of the Priest with that required of the warrior, one is struck by the curious likeness between them, even at the present time.

The good Priest is required to offer up prayer several times a day, wherever he may be. This is to remind him that he is in a service. Twice a day in peace-time the Soldier has to appear on parade; and the more desolate and God-forsaken his station or post is, the more strict and formal ought the parade to be – for the good of his soul!

Most religions demand that the Priest shall be clean and purified by actual or ceremonial washing before he can take part in any service or sacrifice. I needn't tell you what happens to the Soldier who appears on parade in a condition which is technically called 'dirty'.

The textbooks say that cleanliness and neatness of clothing make for 'smartness'. They don't inform us what 'smartness' signified originally. It meant the absolute cleanliness and purity, so far as was possible, of the man who might himself be the sacrifice for his tribe.

Again, the good Priest is responsible not only for the proper use but for the proper care and keeping of the linen, the vestments, the vessels, the images, and the lights employed in the ritual of his religion. Every one of them must be dealt with, handled, and put away in a certain prescribed manner with certain prescribed motions, that the priest may not at any time be led to treat them as common things. Has anyone here ever had to attend kit-inspection? Well, the earliest kit-inspection began when the earliest hunter or warrior laid out his poor little weapons, his charms, and his food-pouch on the ground in front of him, counted them, and prayed over them, for they were all he had to take him through life. I've never heard of any man praying at kit-inspection since – unless he prayed that the inspecting officer might be struck blind.

Once more, at any hour of the day or night, the good Priest must leave whatever he is doing, so long as it is not the service of his God, and go to any member of his flock who needs him, on the death-bed, or the sick-bed, in trouble of mind, family quarrel, misfortune, or weariness of spirit. So I have seen an Officer put down his drink untasted – the first in twelve hours – and go off to see that his men were properly settled in their billets and lacked nothing that his help or his authority could supply them.

Lastly, however often the Priest enters, leaves, or crosses the holy building of his faith, he must pay due acknowledgement and reverence to the altar or the shrine there. This is that he may not forget, however busy he is, the Spirit Whom he serves. I watched an old Priest in Italy once tidying up an empty church. He knelt and crossed himself before the altar twenty-three times in half an hour as he pottered about. When the war was young, I walked once with a private soldier in London, and he told me what drove him nearly crazy was what he called the 'incessant, foolish, unnecessary, snobbish' saluting. I told the young 'un what I am telling you now – that the Salute was the most important and ancient piece of symbolism invented for the deepest of spiritual reasons, many, many thousand years ago. Originally, it must have been the right hand of the armed man raised high to testify to a companion that he was there. 'Behold me! I am the sacrifice.' In the course of years the violent gesture has been softened down – except among children at school when they want to show that they know the answer to a question. The hand has been dropped to the level of the forehead; but you will observe that the palm of the hand is turned outwards. That is the sign of giving, not of keeping back. If the Salute were, or ever had been a sign of servility, the palm of the hand would have been turned to the inside and slightly hollowed, and the head also would have been bent forward; because that attitude is the immemorial instinctive sign of abasement, which is fear, among all the races of mankind. As it is, the gesture of the Salute is no more than the armed man indicating himself as one of the brotherhood of the sacrifice, and, curiously enough, the higher-spirited the regiment, the keener its tradition and its instinct of service, the more tense and emphatic is the motion of the indicating right hand.

Now, gentlemen, I have tried to give you the rough outline of how Drill was born; how it developed through untold ages; and a little of what it signifies. Many of my ideas will strike you as absurd and fantastic; but, if you think them over, you will see that they are at bottom only an expansion or explanation of the first few paragraphs of Infantry training. Things are said to change in the world. To a certain extent, they do; but the changes are largely confined to making wheels turn faster and throwing weights farther than our ancestors did. The one thing that does not change, as far as we know it, is human nature. What the earliest man faced at the beginning, we have to face now. There were wonders and terrors of death, darkness, fire and lightning, frost, blood, and destruction, all about him. He faced them with such weapons as were within his knowledge, and he supplemented his weapons with what skill and craft life taught him. But behind all was his indomitable soul, the spirit of man that knows what it ought to do, even though it loathes doing it, without which he would have fallen back to be a beast among beasts again.

And, in the meantime, what has happened to the Magic Square I began to talk about? I've neglected it for a little. Before we dismiss, let's run over its outlines again on the blackboard, and make them clearer. Here, as I said, is the Line; here is the Step and the Wheel; and here, at the bottom, the foundation of all, is Forming Fours. You see? Do you notice any other change?

There isn't one, really, because, as I have said, man changes little; but it seems to me that the Magic Square has developed quite simply and naturally into the Altar of Sacrifice. Look! The letters are just the same: S.W.L.F. But the altar is based on Faith, by which we live; it is supported by Wisdom and Strength; and it is crowned by Sacrifice, which is the highest form of Love. So you see: Faith, Wisdom, Strength, and Love – make the Altar of Sacrifice for the Man set apart to save his Tribe.

[First published in *A Book of Words* (1928).]

✠ ✠ ✠

These verses were composed for the Shrine of Remembrance for the First World War dead at St Kilda Road, Melbourne, Australia. Unveiled on 11 November 1934, this memorial was originally commissioned by the state of Victoria, and later adopted by the whole Australian nation. Kipling's ode was cast in bronze and a copy placed in the shrine.

ODE: MELBOURNE SHRINE OF REMEMBRANCE

1934

So LONG AS MEMORY, valour, and faith endure,
   Let these stones witness, through the years to come,
How once there was a people fenced secure
   Behind great waters girdling a far home.

Their own and their land's youth ran side by side
   Heedless and headlong as their unyoked seas –
Lavish o'er all, and set in stubborn pride
   Of judgment, nurtured by accepted peace.

Thus, suddenly, war took them – seas and skies
   Joined with the earth for slaughter. In a breath
They, scoffing at all talk of sacrifice,
   Gave themselves without idle words to death.

Thronging as cities throng to watch a game
   Or their own herds move southward with the year,
Secretly, swiftly, from their ports they came,
So that before half earth had heard their name
   Half earth had learned to speak of them with fear;

Because of certain men who strove to reach,
   Through the red surf, the crest no man might hold,
And gave their name for ever to a beach
   Which shall outlive Troy's tale when Time is old;

Because of horsemen, gathered apart and hid –
   Merciless riders whom Megiddo sent forth

When the outflanking hour struck, and bid
    Them close and bar the drove-roads to the north;

And those who, when men feared the last March flood
    Of Western war had risen beyond recall,
Stormed through the night from Amiens and made good,
    At their glad cost, the breach that perilled all.

Then they returned to their desired land –
The kindly cities and plains where they were bred –
    Having revealed their nation in earth's sight
So long as sacrifice and honour stand,
And their own sun at the hushed hour shall light
    The shrine of these their dead!

[First published in *The Times* and other papers, 12 November 1934.]

FURTHER READING

Allen, Charles, *Kipling Sahib: India and the Making of Rudyard Kipling* (London: Little, Brown, 2007).

Lycett, Andrew, *Rudyard Kipling* (London: Weidenfeld & Nicolson, 1999).

Pinney, Thomas (ed.), *Kipling's India: Uncollected Sketches 1884–88* (London: Macmillan, 1986).

—— (ed.), *The Poems of Rudlard Kipling* (Cambridge: Cambridge University Press, 2013).

Richards, David Alun, *Rudyard Kipling: A Bibliography* (New Castle, DE: Oak Knoll Press, and London: British Library, 2010).

Rutherford, Andrew (ed.), *The Early Verse of Rudyard Kipling 1879–1889* (Oxford: Oxford University Press, 1986).